# EQUITATION:
## Learning and Teaching

## by Jean Froissard
### Ecuyer - Professeur, F.F.S.E.

*Translated by*
*Lily Powell Froissard*

**Published by**
Melvin Powers
**WILSHIRE BOOK COMPANY**
12015 Sherman Road
No. Hollywood, California 91605
*Telephone: (213) 875-1711*

*To my son*
*DAVID*

*Printed by*
HAL LEIGHTON PRINTING COMPANY
P.O. Box 3952
North Hollywood, California 91605
Telephone: (213) 983-1105

Printed in the United States of America

ISBN 0-87980-188-3

# Acknowledgments

My particular gratitude goes to Hofrat Col. Alois Podhajsky for the pictures of the Spanische Reitschule, for the honor he bestowed on me by permitting his portrait to grace the gateway to so modest a work, and most of all for his moral support during the writing.

I salute the Cavalry School of Saumur and thank with a very special feeling its Equerry-in-Chief, Col. de Saint-André, for selecting and contributing the splendid examples of haute-école.

I thank those who helped me gather the illustrations, specifically the late Lt. Col. W. E. Lyon for his lovely little Huntress, and Mrs. Stella A. Walker and Mr. Dorian Williams for introducing us; Mr. A. Mackey-Smith, Editor of *The Chronicle of the Horse,* who contributed the picture of the Cleveland Bay Stallion; Mr. Gaston Cavin of L'Annèe Hippique who gave me the beautiful cover painting of the magazine's 1963 issue; Mr. I. P. Earle of the U. S. Department of Agriculture for his personal interest and assistance; Mr. J. Gendry of the French National Studs for the complete series of French breeds; the School of Veterinary Science of Alfort, France, for permission to reproduce its hippological plates; Dr. Reisner of the House of Bruckmann, Munich, for having found "Le Manège du Roi."

Special recognition goes to Mrs. Vivian A. Hibbs and Mrs. Nada Saporiti of the Metropolitan Museum of Art for their patient and intelligent tracking down of the same elusive engravings and for their help in making possible the partial reproduction in this volume of the royal pupil from the pages of the immortal Pluvinel.

And then there is my wife and alter ego without whom this book would not have been written.

**Hofrat Colonel Alois Podhajsky, on Nero, 1935. (Courtesy Col. Podhajsky)**

# Foreword to the American Edition

I dedicate this book to David and, through him, to all my American pupils; particularly to Jeanne Harvey, Ruth and Hazel Buys, Kendra Newland, Beverly Jones, Cynthia Loftus, Rebecca Anderson, Brenda Carlson, Michael Smyser and Joel Buchwald.

I have given most of them their first leg up. Some have turned into young adults by now which, in equestrian terms, means that they must soon bid farewell to junior events. Someday I shall see them in international competition—in New York, Paris, Rome—for America has become part of the equestrian scene and is holding her own, as she does in everything new she undertakes.

Jeanne, the Buys Twins and all the others will then find it easy to communicate with foreign teams; for their first words of horsemanship were spoken in France, either in French, or in an intentionally hybrid English which strove to get as close as possible to the highly shaded technical language employed in Europe, the cradle of equitation.

They are lucky; for I have seen too many Americans lose themselves in a maze of misunderstandings when talking shop with foreign horsemen, and this for lack of a precise equestrian vocabulary in common with the rest of the world. The absense of a "fixed" technical language, a formidable obstacle to giving precise explanations, even among Americans, is a challenge I am taking up in this book by suggesting ways of "fixing" American equestrian expression along universally established lines.

A horse, a rider—their reactions, the things they can do and that can happen to them are the same, regardless of nationality; despite its finely shaded complexity, the subject is never abstract. There is no reason why a little semantic effort could not find common expressions, the way science, art and crafts of all nations have standardized their language; not excluding psychiatry which deals with the most elusive and fluctuating subject of them all.

I am not quibbling over the grammatical oddity of Americans departing at a canter, at the canter or, simply and unaccountably, departing canter or the canter, cantering off or breaking into a canter or the canter, starting or striking off into a canter or the canter; and this, near fore leading, on the near fore or lead, or simply at the left canter—all this variety, while "the canter on the false lead" and its identical twin, "the false canter," stand all alone and must do for the false canter and countercanter, a term few know and fewer use, so there is no telling from a horseman's speech whether he means a success in training or a disobedience of the horse.

I have no quarrel with it, really, but I do protest most strenuously when in the two most authoritative encyclopedias I find no listing for "Equitation" (not even a modest "Equitation, see HORSEMANSHIP"), while both articles,

**Bronze statuette from a turn-of-the-century clock. (Photo Josserand)**

under the heading "Horsemanship," use the word "equitation," in the generally accepted sense—as a synonym for horsemanship—leaving the average rider out in the cold who only knows it in the totally contrived sense of a beginners' event. And I do get quite miffed when, elsewhere, the French word *rassembler,* for which a perfectly good and current equivalent (collection) exists, is listed as an assimilated term of equestrian English, meaning . . . *champing the bit!*

If this sounds like the griping of an "equestrian codger," let me make a case for adherence to universal terminology by reminding you that in our international contacts we are all under the technical authority of the F.E.I. (Fédération Equestre Internationale) where the determining version of any document is the French by which, wherever there is doubt, we must abide.

Those who do not have the slightest intention or faintest hope of drinking the stirrup cup in cosmopolitan company, though not concerned with what the gentlemen of the Federation might have to say, will find learning to ride easier once we rid ourselves of the habit here of calling three different things by the same name, there the same thing by three different names.

The word, Equitation, which I have not changed in the title of this edition, makes my point; it does not refer to a low-level horse show event. Here, then, follows a list of technical terms as the world at large uses them.

JEAN FROISSARD

San Juan

**The Falconer.** Departure for the Heron Hunt, by **Johann Heinrich Tischbein the Elder, 1722-1789. (Castle Fasanerie, Fulda. Retzlaff Archive)**

L'Amazone dans l'Allée Cavalière au Bois de Boulogne, **by Renoir. (Kunstmuseum, Hamburg)**

# Glossary

### 1. POSITION

is by common definition essentially static; and yet the horseman's problem is to remain joined to the movement of his horse. Thus as a technical term, position rather indicates a succession of positions adapted to the movement of the horse.

Since one and the same position taken by the rider may aid one of the horse's movements while counteracting another, it should be a generally supple attitude (*see* EQUITATION, Position), comprising multiple variations which permit, aid, or prevent, the movements of the horse. These variations may be imperceptible or modify the rider's attitude remarkably, as happens most conspicuously in his successive gestures over the jump.

### 2. SEAT

is the horseman's basic quality which permits him to stay on his mount whatever its reactions. The essential characteristic of the seat should be suppleness.

Mark here the difference between seat and pliancy; *i.e.,* the difference between staying " on one's horse" and "with one's horse."

### 3. FIXITY

is the absence of any needless or involuntary movement. Not to be confused with immobility which signifies absence of all movement.

### 4. PLIANCY

is the result of the rider's seat and fixity which permits him to "go with the horse" in all circumstances.

## 5. Ease

is the image presented by effortless and relaxed action resulting from the rider's mastery and skill.

## 6. Equestrian Tact

enables the rider to use his aids with good measure and timing .

## 7. Impulsion

is the horse's constant desire to move forward. A distinction must be made between natural impulsion, chiefly a psychological trait of the well-bred horse (capable of being modified and channeled by the horseman), and immediate and momentary artificial impulsion created by the horseman's rational use of his aids, as well as spontaneous yet acquired impulsion, inculcated through training where natural impulsion is lacking and which, though of less value than the natural kind, can partially compensate for it.

This is not to be confused with speed, which is the rate at which the horse travels. Impulsion and speed are in the horse as steam pressure and speed in the locomotive which, without rolling fast, may be under strong pressure and vice versa. A colt on a meadow, going into the passage by itself, moves much less swiftly than its cantering neighbor, and yet may have far more impulsion. The most perfect expression of impulsion is the piaffe (a stylized trot on the spot).

## 8. A taut horse

results from combined psychological and physical factors springing from *channeled impulsion.* In this state, the back transmits the impulsive forces of the hindquarters integrally to the forehand, where the reins gather them up. Without losing suppleness of neck, the horse maintains a free and trusting contact with the bit.

## 9. Engagement

of the hind legs is a consequence of the lowering of the haunches through the bending of the hocks, which causes a more advanced position of the hind legs under the body.

## 10. Relaxing at the Jaw

is characterized by the mobilization of the jaw which opens very slightly, just enough to let the bids ride up and then drop back into place with an unmistakable clicking noise. It is the horseman's proof that his horse's mouth is relaxed and thus able to yield easily to the action of the bit.

### 11. Flexions, Lateral and Direct*

Lateral flexions are poll-suppling exercises, making the head pivot to left and right according to a vertical axis passing through the poll and without participation of the neck.

Direct flexions are poll-suppling exercises, demanded after the neck has been raised, for the purpose of drawing the face toward the vertical.

Both flexions aim at suppling the poll region, so as to enable the horse to maintain the head carriage without difficulty.

### 12. To Place**

is to require the horse to take a certain position of the head. It means drawing the head, which must pivot around a verticle passing through the poll, without participation of the neck, in the direction to be followed. A slight crease, just sufficient to show the rider on horseback the orb of the eye on the side of placing, while the other is hidden.

Its natural application occurs when the horse follows a curved line; it is required in the half-pass and, to a slightly lesser degree, in the work at the canter.

### 13. Head Carriage

is an attitude taken by the head at the rider's demand and made possible by an inflexion at the poll (occipital-atlas and atlas-axis joints). The face must approach the vertical, never go beyond it. It must be caused by the advance of the body toward the head, never vice versa.

Do not confuse this with self-carriage, which is the natural way the horse carries his head.

### 14. Horse in Hand

is a state where the horse is ready to obey his rider's indications spontaneously and eagerly. It is characterized by a relaxing at the jaw in the correct position of head carriage.

### 15. Collection

is a state in which engagement of the hind legs and head carriage coincide.

*Flexions are movements, while head carriage and the placing of the head are POSITIONS, wherefore the vague catch-all, Flexion at the Poll, is totally inadequate.

**The horse is said to have his head *flexed* to the left or right, usually in the direction of the movement, a position *resulting* from flexion, but not "flexion."

### 16. LIGHTNESS

is "perfect obedience of the horse to the slightest indications of his rider's hand and heel." (General L'Hotte)

### 17. BALANCE

"Natural balance lies in a rational distribution of the body weight and the load between forehand and hindquarters, as well as in a great mobility of the center of gravity, whereby the ridden or harnessed horse's action is easy, his display of strength unstrained, his paces fluent, thus posing no difficulty in training." (Jacoulet et Chomel, *Traité d'Hippologie.*)

### 18. OVERBENT

A horse is overbent when he draws his neck in downward and backward, his face behind the perpendicular.

### 19. BACKWARD FLOW OF ENERGIES

is a consequence of different false positions taken by the horse, usually due to an awkward action on his rider's part and translating itself by his inability or lack of desire to move forward.

### 20. BEHIND THE BIT

is the state brought about when the horse drops the bit by coiling his neck or retracting his head toward his chest in order to evade the action of the bit, and thereby his rider's will, maintaining his center of gravity too far to the rear.

### 21. BEHIND THE LEGS

is the state in which the rider's legs are impotent to prompt a free forward movement, either because he has placed his horse in a false position which affects the hindquarters, or because the horse himself, seeking to evade the action of the legs, refuses to release his impulsive forces.

### *Index of Glossary of Technical Terms*

General L'Hotte, Chief Equerry and later Commanding General of the Cavalry School of Saumur, on Laruns. (Photo Blanchaud)

# Preface

Das Pferd ist dein Spiegel. Es schmeichelt dir nie. Es spiegelt dein Temperament. Es spiegelt auch seine Schwankungen.

Ärgere dich nie über dein Pferd; du könntest dich ebensowohl über deinen Spiegel ärgern.

—RUDOLPH BINDING

These pages are addressed to all young horsemen, but in particular to the young instructor who finds himself entrusted with beginning riders and with horses which may not always be ideally suited to the riding school. The scant progress made despite his efforts tends to discourage him; at a loss to understand what is expected, his pupils give up or settle into a somewhat dubious kind of horsemanship; and caught between their tense hands and his generously applied lunging whip, his horses fall into a state of restiveness, if not incurable, at least sufficiently advanced to make them inoperable for any but an expert teacher. Since such ills are more easily prevented than cured, I will try to help beginning teachers and their pupils toward fuller harmony and understanding in their work. It will spare both of them the merest trace of discouragement and, incidentally, redound to the benefit of the horse.

I remember my beginnings as pupil and instructor and the difficulties I encountered. Heaven had failed to shower me with brilliant gifts, and perseverance had to teach me what I know. A great riding master guided and stimulated this personal work. Aside from the technique he taught me, he knew how to kindle an enthusiasm not unlike his own and, without robbing me of my personality, he left on me his indelible mark.

Do not forget that he who wishes to receive must know how to give, not only of his heart but of his mind. So set yourself a goal and choose the means to reach it—neither of which being as easy as at first glance it would seem—then arm yourself with all the patience you can muster. Study. Even the beginning teacher needs a thorough knowledge of classical equitation: "in equitation one must know a great deal in order to teach well the very rudiments." (General L'Hotte, *Questions Equestres.*)

What, essentially, is equitation? A pastime, you will be told, or a sport, or an art when carried to the limit of its possibilities. In any case, its practice calls for close cooperation between horse and rider. It is more difficult to practice a sport as part of a team, be it only a twosome, than alone; the more so where your partner is an animal whose intelligence and reflexes differ from yours and who does not understand your language. On the other hand, he is endowed with a sure instict, an excellent memory and great physical strength. Horse and rider must be educated for this partnership, taught a mutually comprehensible language, new to both.

For the horse this educational period means dressage. Starting at zero, you must resort to common sense—so knowingly and aptly called, horse sense—the only kind the horse can understand and respond to. Horsemanship is primarily a question of common sense; to be applied with accuracy, it must be based on constant observation of the horse, at rest, at work under the saddle and, above all, at liberty, when the horseman has a chance to study his partner's behavior at leisure.

One postulate to bear in mind and that can never be emphasized too much with the beginner is that the horse is affected by movements of the rider which totally escape human perception. A skillful horseman can fool everyone except his horse; so why act out a comedy for him which his instinct unfailingly detects? Let your gestures be sober. Aside from presenting the unpleasant sight of senselessly and wildly moving arms, you may make an awkward gesture for which there is no apologizing to the horse. You cannot explain to him that it was a gaucherie on your part, best promptly forgotten. It may take months of patient work to erase this unfortunate movement from his recollection which, like human memory, rather more easily retains bad lessons than it does good.

Although you have been justly taught and have yourself experienced that horsemanship requires great energy, physical as well as moral, ban from it any trace of brutality. Do not ever let an angry gesture carry you away. Aside from being ineffective as to immediate results, it would in a few seconds undo work accomplished over a long period of time and defer the goal you are pursuing; not to mention the sad spectacle of an intelligent creature descending to a level below that of his animal partner. Such movements of wrath only turn against you in that they are admissions of weakness, impotence and incompetence. Spare yourself this disgrace.

Not that you are to accept resistance arms dangling and legs paralyzed; yet punishment must be commensurate with fault and must in no way compromise the rider's calm and self-control. A few moments after punishment, horse and rider should have forgotten all and give us the impression that everything is back to normal. But neither should you take refuge behind this tenet from timidity; for gentleness must not turn into spinelessness. Your horse would quickly find you out and get the upper hand. What is needed is the moral energy to dominate yourself and thereby dominate your horse. Punishment and reward must be meted out instantly after the reaction which has called for it.

What causes irate gestures on the rider's part? The horse's refusal to carry out whatever has been asked of him. However, many a refusal and the anger that ensues are consequences of the rider's inability to graduate his demands, his ignorance of what is possible and what is not. Thus if he does away with the root of the evil, he will cease to incite his horse to disobedience. If nonetheless the required movement is refused, he will have to call upon his stamina, his patience and his reasoning.

You will find among horses characters as infinitely varied as among men. It is up to the horseman to understand the individual he is associating with and to act accordingly to gain his confidence. At first, at any rate, it is for the rider to try to understand his horse, not for the horse to understand his rider. The issue is the rider's winning of the horse and not vice versa.

Once more, as was the case in teaching, you should know how to set yourself a goal and how to find the means to reach it. These means should spring from common sense and logic and be applied with method in brief but lively, varied working sessions, so as to banish any trace of boredom or fatigue. Never begin a session by teaching your horse a new maneuver. "Converse" with him first in the simple language of the movements he knows, and then approach the difficulty with hardly a thought, without any particular concentration. Focusing on a difficulty would make you tense, and your tenseness, however slight, would not go unnoticed by a horse understandably bewildered by your being different from what you were the moment before. Intense concentration should, on the other hand, focus on the overall work. Before mounting you should know the aim of today's lesson, the means you intend to employ. Once in the saddle, you will act much like an automaton, except for choice of timing in showing your horse, when you feel him to be ready, a certain new jump or a certain new movement.

It should be said and understood once and for all that you must yield as soon as your horse yields; for what counts for the rider is that his horse understand his demand and perform the required movement, no matter how much, at least in the beginning, its execution leaves to be desired. In fact, the expression "perform" should be replaced by "give"; because a rider wresting a movement from his horse resembles a dancer forced well-nigh to carry his partner because he is imposing unfamiliar figures on her. With her best will, their movements, meant above all to express the grace and lightness of perfect entente, will be constrained and stiff.

A simple movement, requested with discreet aids and "gaily given," without the slightest blundering or hestitation, is of far more artistic value than a difficult one wrested from a horse who renders it halfheartedly and without grace. All your life you must tirelessly strive for closer communion with your horses till they obey your slightest signals. Their ever increasing refinement is but a measure of your own. De La Guérinière said, *"à main galante, bouche galante"*—an affable mouth to an affable hand. Toward the end of his life, Baucher advocated use of the snaffle alone because it allowed him, said he, to feel the slightest contraction of his horse's mouth which, with a double bridle, he would never have suspected.

Even in competitive jumping, where quick obedience at greater speeds than those of the manège counts most, riders seek this same discreet and precise language in communicating with their horses. Lt. Col. Gudin de Vallerin writes in *Obstacle, Conduite et Style*, "preferably the two partners should have a long acquaintance, and a good horse should not change hands. The dialogue can then become more intimate and more sophisticated, more discreet and more precise, more elegant and more academic. Horse and rider become one; like the legendary Centaur, they think, feel and act as a single creature."

All great masters agree on the need for knowing how to yield in time. Beudant said that he obtained so much from his horses because he yielded a split second before they did. He meant that, since his equestrian tact allowed him to sense when the horse's will had surrendered to his, he did not wait for this submission to materialize before he yielded.

The physical possibilities are another point in question. No more than all humans can be expected to perform as only a few champions could, can all horses be required to be cracks. But even where the physical basis is present, do not hasten to accuse your horse of ill will when he fails to perform as expected. This is the easy, all too easy, solution of mediocrity. Rather distinguish between two cases:

Either the movement required is new. As long as the horse has not performed it two or three times in response to the same aids, nothing guarantees that he has understood. If it is so, the rider's blame should fall upon himself, because he failed to make his meaning clear.

Or the movement required is known. It takes a thoroughly experienced rider to affirm that the demand has been well-made and that the fault lies with his horse. And even so, a doubt should linger in every horseman's heart; for, being mute, his horse cannot tell when he is under some physical discomfort which, though perhaps passing and not serious, causes him suffering.

Smugness has never been the genuine horseman's vice. Everyone admits that artists are a rare species and that the very gifted are not in the majority. Why should it then be different in equitation? Why, lacking the essential, indispensable foundations, foolishly try to imitate a very brilliant horseman? Why not stay in one's place? I think I have at least a partial answer to this question. Take a painter or a writer, neither can found his renown on anything but his own ability, while the lucky rider, even when mediocre, has a mute companion on whom he counts to make up for his shortcomings and set him off. If the result is good (rare but not impossible), the credit goes to him; if, on the contrary, the outcome should fall short of expectation, the blame falls on the horse. An artist could hardly accuse his brushes, a writer his pen.

Quadriga Driven by Victory, **red-figured, fifth century B.C. (Courtesy Metropolitan Museum of Art, New York)**

# Contents

# I. Dressage

## Introduction

Calme, en avant et droit
General L'Hotte

Before we speak of the education of teacher and rider, let us discuss the education of the horse. This discussion will aid your understanding of the parts which follow, because their principles are built, and depend for their success, on the way the horse has been trained.

Dressage of a young horse means giving him education combined with good manners, helping him develop his physical and moral qualities, hence rendering him easy to use and pleasant to ride. When first we take him over, he knows little of man and nothing of the horseman; and so the very first ground we must gain is of the spirit — winning and keeping his confidence must be our concern at every step along the road.

There is a saying which prescribes "old horses for young riders, old riders for young horses"; and a trainer must be a competent horseman with an emphatic knowledge of animal psychology and a definite sense of what is within his pupil's capabilities. He will then apply the principles of dressage, methodically following a logical sequence, always considerate of the horse's reactions, never openly impatient, yet never retreating into a sterile forbearance which paralyzes all initiative.

Dressage is divided into two main periods—training and schooling. Once more what I said in the Foreword applies: the use of the word "dressage" in speaking exclusively of the show result, is, as with the misuse of Equitation, etymologic nonsense.

Webster's International for 1959 does not mention dressage, except in its addenda, and then as follows: "Guidance of a horse through a set of maneuvers without perceptible use of such aids as voice and reins." The 1964 edition does a little better: "Dressage [F., preparation, straightening, training, fr. *dresser,* to prepare, make straight, train ‡ - age—more at DRESS]: the execution by a horse . . . , etc." * And then it adds a modest also "the systematic training of a horse in obedience and deportment."

The most revealing part in this entry is the etymological parenthesis:

---

*Already somewhat more correct than "Guidance of a horse . . ."

"*dresser,* to prepare, make straight, train." Dressage is (the entire process of) training and a dressage test (adopted and translated from the French, "*épreuve de dressage*") is just exactly what it says: a test of the accomplishments of the horse's dressage.

So let us adopt the term dressage unadulterated and call the two periods making up the process, training and schooling; for in these once more Americans are confused by a variety of more or less colloquial expressions to which each gives his own meaning. I think you will agree with me that the current phrase for the first of the two periods, "breaking in," should be discarded without a second thought; and I feel that training followed by schooling conveys very well their progressive character, "school," as used in equitation, denoting a certain advanced degree of training (such as *basse-école* and *haute-école*).

# Training

Malheur à ceux qui entreprendraient encore de le vaincre par une résistance égale à sa force; toute contrainte doit donc être éloignée du cheval, surtout dans les commencements, si l'on ne veut le rendre à jamais ennemi de l'école et de l'obéissance

—BARON DE BOHAN

### The Preparations

In choosing a horse, good conformation and points are relative to the animal's particular employ, and one must be clear in one's mind as to its future use. We want, physically, a good saddle horse, apt for training up to the isolated flying change of leg and participation in minor jumping events; psychologically, a willing horse, neither timid, nor high-strung. Almost all kinds of saddle horses offer this type of individual, each breed with its virtues and faults.

Remember in examining a horse that, in the words of a French veterinarian, Dr. Nicolas, "he does not travel on his legs alone, but on his heart, his lungs, his digestive tract, his nerves."

Judge, first of all, the general appearance—type, conformation and proportions. Harmony in conformation is of the essence; for what would be the use of powerful hindquarters if combined with a weak forehand? Since the perfect horse does not exist, you are bound to find faults, some serious enough to discard the subject, others compensated by good points of the same or nearby anatomical region.

Next, from a sufficient distance, you inspect the formation of the legs; profile, front and rear view. Approaching for more detailed inspection, begin with the feet. Needless to go any farther if they are in bad shape, for no other good point could make up for shortcomings of the feet.

The conformation of the saddle horse should be as follows:

**The Spanish School. The first riding of young horses. (Courtesy Col. Podhajsky)**

— built in a slightly ascending line with a clearly defined withers which extends well back;
— a short, broad, very muscular back;
— short, broad, straight, well muscled loins;
— a long, muscular, slightly sloping croup;
— a deep, wide chest;
— a medium-long neck, standing out well, with a 45 degree slant, neither too thick, nor too thin;
— a square head, lean, expressive and well set on, a sign of distinction; shun the heavy head;
— a long, sloping shoulder;
— a long, muscular and rather straight arm;
— a rather wide and muscular breast;
— a long, vertical, strong forearm with prominent muscles;

**The Spanish School. Lunging. (Courtesy Col. Podhajsky)**

— the direction of the elbow is important: glued to the body, the horse will be splay-footed, excessively spread, he will be pidgeon-toed;
— a short, dense and lean cannon;
— a broad and neat fetlock;

— length and direction of the pastern are important: it should be rather, not exceedingly, long and sloping;

— a long thigh, almost vertical, with powerful muscles;

— a long, broad and muscular gaskin;

— a lean, neat, wide and open hock;

— the shannon, fetlock and pastern of the hind leg should have the same good points as their counterparts on the foreleg;

— sound feet and normal formation of legs.

The horse should, above all, be examined in action where he must be energetic, yet not excitable. The tail carried aloft is an indication of his vigor. His paces should be easy and fluent on both hands, the set of his legs normal in action as well. However meticulous, this inspection is insufficient without a veterinary examination which alone can give you full guarantees concerning sight and the internal organs.

Aside from purely physical qualities, you must consider the degree of blood;* for no kind of beauty could make up for its lack, and the inherent advantages of all the beauties in the world come to naught unless they are in harmonious proportion to each other.

This complexity makes judging a horse so difficult.

The Arabs have, however, in their proverbs handed down to us some excellent general advice:

Measure your horse from the end of the dock to the middle of the withers and from the withers to the upper lip, passing between the two ears. If the measurements are equal, the horse is good, if the front measurement is greater, he has fine qualities; if it is shorter, there is little to him.

If, when stretching head and neck to drink from a brook on the ground, the horse stands straight without bending one foreleg, rest assured that he is good and all parts of his body are in harmony.

Do not stay on a mount whose fore hooves are under your feet.

The horse with blood under his mass, a well defined withers extending well back, long, sloping shoulders, a well-coupled loin, a deep chest, a well-set-on neck, broad joints and sound tissues is the saddle horse of our choice. Once we have him, we will shop for

The equipment we need:

— a flat lunging rein;

— a cavesson;

— a lunging whip;

— a longish crop;

— a rather thick snaffle bit;

— a double bridle;

*Blood, see Hippology, p.181.

**The Spanish School. The capriole. (Courtesy Col. Podhajsky)**

— a chambon;
— a leather surcingle;
— a saddle;
and, if possible
    — a pair of long reins with collar and surcingle, as well as certain items outside of the actual working equipment, such as
    — exercise and stable bandages
    — leggings and knee-caps,
because a splint is more easily prevented than cured.

The *lunging rein* should be about 25 to 30 feet long and not too heavy. The *cavesson* should be padded and rather wide, adjusted in such a way that the outer cheek strap does not touch the horse's eye, tight enough not to be brutal. The *lunging whip* should be rather rigid from the knob to beyond the middle, progressively more supple toward the slender tip; the knob heavy for better balance and easier handling; the leather thong ending in a lash; the maximum total length 15 feet. The *crop* should be long enough for you to

**The piaffe. Col. Wattel on Clough-Bank. (Courtesy Col. de Saint-André)**

touch the horse's haunches when close to his head, rigid rather than too supple (a switch may be substituted, provided it is not too rigid).

The *snaffle* should be rather thick for the beginnings, inviting the horse to free contact. The *double bridle* coming later, should, like all bitting, be most carefully adjusted. The *chambon* is a training gear which, through extensions of the neck, develops the back and neck muscles. This preliminary work is indispensable for the subsequent schooling, whether academic or over the fences; and while the aim can certainly be reached without this gear, it simplifies the task enormously. Since it is used without the rider on the horse's back, its action is always correct; the horse works it himself through the direction taken by his head and neck. Besides, it can be used when the horse cannot be ridden. More shall be said about it before we set out to use it. The leather *surcingle* carries at its lower part two rings, one on each side, for use with the long reins, and two to four buckles for a proper fit

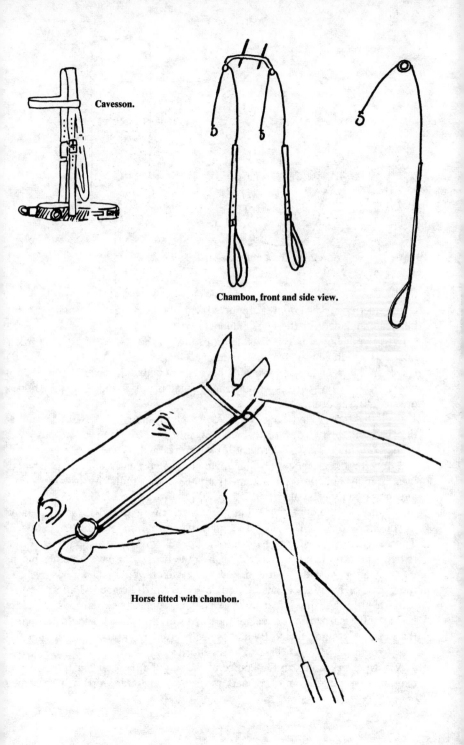

Cavesson.

Chambon, front and side view.

Horse fitted with chambon.

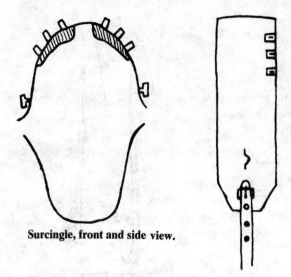

**Surcingle, front and side view.**

of the side reins. The *collar* is employed with the long reins, not indispensable but recommended for the work intended.

When your horse arrives, isolate him to avoid the spread of possible infection and on the morrow exercise him at liberty inside the school. If you leave the head collar on, you will have less trouble retrieving him after a while. Keep a few carrots within reach; sugar is unfamiliar and some horses are slow to accept it.

Call the farrier and have your young pupil shod lightly. Be present at this first, and the two or three subsequent, shoeings; for your farrier, otherwise a fine craftsman, may pay no heed to your dressage.

A few days later choose a stable mate and watch their relationship. Though friendship is not always apparent from the start, animosity usually is and affects the nervous system.

Require no work of your young boarder during this first week; ideally, if you have one and the weather permits, turn him out into a paddock. Take advantage of all the moments he spends with you at liberty in order to acquaint him with your voice. For the time being you have no other means of association, just the caress of the voice which gentles and reassures and the carrot or handful of oats offered with the word, "come." Do not at first stand farther than three feet away from him, sometimes even closer. Before he has fully learned to appreciate the carrot or the oats he should be spared the stress of fetching them. By and by, with growing appreciation of your tidbits, to come to you will cease to be an effort.

Visit him in his box in the course of the day; be there at mealtimes if you can and give him his ration of oats yourself. Your later work will be helped

**Horse fitted for the work on the long reins.**

immeasurably by your voice's power to calm him through its increased effectiveness for frequent association with acts of happy memory.

Carefully watch his feed and droppings during this first week. If all is normal, light work may start which does not overtax your pupil who, at four, is at an age to benefit by it without the risk of blemishes.

A few principles:

— Set yourself a goal and choose the means to attain it, going from known to unknown;

— never fight two resistances at once;

— know how to yield in time;

— know how to limit your demands;

— ask for whatever is new at the end of the lesson;

— use identical aids to obtain identical effects;

— ". . . do not ever ask anything of a horse while he is still vibrating under the impression of a prior demand" (François Baucher, *Oeuvres Complètes*).

The passage. (Courtesy Col. de Saint-André)

# THE EARLY PERIOD

If your horse is hot, exercise him at liberty before you carefully adjust the cavesson, neither slack enough to be severe, nor tight and low enough to keep him from breathing freely, the cheek straps (chiefly the outer) not touching the eyes when the lunging rein tightens, as it will in a moment. Have a helper within calling distance, but if possible give the lesson alone. If your horse is so high-spirited that he is liable to put you on the lunging rein, reduce the school to the desired length by lining fences up across it. It spares him the temptation of walking you all over at his will and assures for the lesson the great calm which is vital in training, particularly in the early period.

Standing by his near side, buckle *the lunging rein* onto the cavesson and hold it at a distance of 20 inches, the rest looped into an 8 in your left hand which holds the lunging whip, the thick end coming out between thumb and index finger, the small end pointing backward and down. Holding the horse this way, describe two or three times a rather large circle. If he tends to bound forward, soothe him with your voice, and with your right hand shake the lunging rein several times; not too hard, for you do not want to teach him fear of advancing. If, on the contrary, he does not walk out sufficiently, rather than staying even with his shoulders, slow down till you are behind them and click your tongue a few times. As soon as he walks out calmly, let slip a little of the rein and take your distance. He will continue to travel the same circle, while you move on a smaller but concentric one. By and by the two of you should reach a distance of 12 to 15 feet. Keep walking on a small circle, in the direction of his haunches to press him forward, in the direction of his shoulders to slow him down. This is the moment for you to transfer the lunging whip, held as before, to your right hand, passing it behind your back so you do not frighten your pupil. Do not seek too much perfection, either in performance, or obedience; the first lessons' intent is to accustom the horse to the lunging rein, the whip, his trainer, in one word, to his work.

After a few times around at a walk, start him into *The Trot,* tactfully showing the tip of the lunging whip, associated with a click or two of the tongue. If the horse has never been beaten and you know how to go about it, he has no more reason to fear this whip than you or the wall. See to it that, if not regular in the academic sense of the word, his trot is at least smooth and calm; encourage him by a slightly drawling, "fine . . . fine . . ." Check once more to a walk, shortening the lunging rein and advancing toward his shoulder, saying, "a-a-at a w-a-a-alk, a-a-at a w-a-a-alk. . . ." Eventually there will not be any need for moving; but since you must teach him to stay on the circle, including at the halt, you had better not begin by teaching him to leave it. Imbue him with respect for the circle as for the track when working at liberty.

In checking to the walk, you have shortened the lunging rein till you are only three feet from the horse's shoulder. By a small vertical vibration of the rein, request *The Halt,* saying, "whoa. . . ." If successful, pat him leisurely and then begin anew; if you succeed again, stop work and take him back to the stable. If not, hold the lunging rein a very few inches from the cavesson. With patience and firmness you will achieve the halt on the circle, standing three feet away on an inner circle.

All of this work should be performed on both hands. During the next lessons you will go over the same work with the same precautions. During one of them, when the horse has proved particularly calm and trusting, accustom him to the touch of the lunging whip by passing its handle over his back, his loins, his croup. Handle and thong in the right hand, so the latter won't flap, the lunging rein shortened to about twenty inches in the left, neither reluctantly, nor brusquely apply the whip to the top of his withers. If he appears worried, soothe him with your voice, then slide the whip along his back and croup. The lunging whip is a working tool which the horse must know; it must inspire respect, not fear, let alone terror.

The horse should be stretching the lunging rein during work. When he moves to an inner circle, drive him back onto the normal one by a horizontal vibration of the rein. The vibration is vertical when requesting a shortening of pace or the halt. A horse's hind legs rarely describe an outer circle in relation to the fore, but the reverse is frequent. Then, with the lunging whip, make him shift his hindquarters into place, so the hind legs follow the track of the fore. Since a horse may be unwilling to submit and take the slightest occasion to "overtake" the lunging rein and kick at the trainer, you must make him stretch it, as if he meant to move away from you, and keep his hindquarters in place. For maximum efficiency, be at the center of the circle traveled by the horse, rein and whip the two sides of a V, its tip coinciding with the center of the circle. This way your horse is framed by lunging rein and whip.

When he begins to obey your voice easily, you may begin *the work at liberty.* While for our specific training aim, the schooling on the lunging rein—which is a means of domination, particularly of the spiritual kind, rather than a training instrument proper—need not be pushed very far: we are great believers in work at liberty.

If you happen to have a large school, fine for work in the saddle, cut it down for work at liberty. A length of 60 to 75 and a width of 35 to 45 feet is sufficient. This way you will have no trouble controlling your pupil without

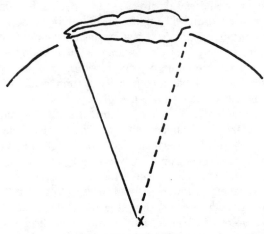

**V-pattern in lunging.**

outside assistance, which is more of a bother than a help, as it would be in winning the confidence of a shy four or five year old child whom you do not at first inspire with a great liking. There, too, you would have far less trouble breaking the ice and winning his trust if acting alone rather than with two or three others.

So reduce the school to a convenient size, set your horse free and let him limber up and relax at a trot. Move on an inner circle, following him and pushing his hindquarters, never letting him leave the track without permission. Demand the same work he did on the lunging rein (walk, trot and halt), as well as the canter, a gait not recommended for lunging.

For the second and third sessions of this exercise at liberty, bit him with a reinless, rather thick snaffle which very few horses seem to mind. For the fourth session return to the cavesson in order to accustom him to the girth. First, exercise him at liberty on both hands; then place the cavesson on him. Holding the lunging rein in the left hand, pat him outright on the back, the flanks, the brisket and again on the back. Keep this up while a helper, this being one of the rare occasions when the need for one arises, is placing a leather surcingle on him, girthing progressively, just as much as necessary to keep it from slipping by itself. Then walk him on the circle. Unless the girth is too tight, he is most unlikely to bound; but if he does, give him a little lunging rein and do not interfere with your hand, except to make sure he does not get tangled up in the rein. Soothe him with your voice; but above all no punishment! Do not let his mind associate girth and punishment. When he calms down, tighten the girth, if necessary, by one or two notches, discon-

nect the lunging rein and set him free. He will buck a few times, but once
he understands that no effort will rid him of the surcingle, he will calm down
by himself. The purpose of the next few lessons is to inure him to the girth;
so do not ask him for anything else as long as he is acting worried during
girthing. This may require three or four sessions, give or take a few. As
soon as he takes the surcingle for granted, bit him again with the snaffle
he knows, and at the next lesson use the *chambon*.

Attach it to the headpiece of the snaffle bridle and take your horse to the
ring where you make the final adjustments. There, place the surcingle on
his back and slip the girth through the ends of the chambon. Now all you
have to do is hang the two hooks into the snaffle rings. It is easy to see whether
the gear needs shortening or lengthening for the hooks to be easily attached
without the horse having to lower his head. Keep the gear rather a little too
long the first few times to prevent any kind of defense, and shorten it progressively to the point of effectiveness. During those first lessons, a helper
is useful, too, because together you can place both snaphooks on at once.

Your particular attention must focus on the horse's yielding to the effect
of the chambon by extending his neck and engaging his hind legs under
his mass. Certain horses hollow out their loins to evade its action, and
the result is diametrically opposed to the one you seek. Hence this entire
work must be carried on in impulsion; the working gait the trot, a calm,
regular, energetic trot.

At the close of this early period, your horse should be working calmly
— on the lunging rein; walking, halting, trotting on both hands;
— at liberty the same, plus the canter;
— should know and obey your voice;
— know the snaffle and the girth;
— be exercised with the chambon which is muscling back and neck
through the engagement of the hind legs.

Even before the beginning of work you have accustomed the young horse
to his new feed and gradually increased the ration of his oats. To avoid
intestinal irritation, give a good mash once a week; and do not neglect very
high-grade hay. Watch his droppings to make sure they are devoid of
worms and the oats well digested. If you find worms, administer a vermifuge;
if you find the oats ill-digested, serve them crushed.

During this period you want to accustom the young horse, without fracas,
to his new way of life. Therefore make sure that whatever you ask of him
can be easily stood and understood; but the suggested means, far from
infallible, are entirely dependent on your manner of applying them.

The advantages of reaching a considerable degree of training before mounting the young horse are that you can teach him new things without the weight

of your body adding to his physical fatigue with its inevitable moral consequences, and that you can observe him and his reactions during the lessons. When exercise and nutrition have muscled up the colt, when he has learned the rudiments of training, when he gives us his trusting obedience, we can undertake work in the saddle. This will be greatly simplified by the results achieved on foot.

## The Work on Foot and in the Saddle

The work on foot has but two objectives: achieving impulsion and the mobility of the haunches. It may precede the work in the saddle and continue parallel to the exercises on the lunging rein. The progression is as follows:

On the lunging rein the horse is bitted with a snaffle to which you add two reins, their ends attached to the buckles of the surcingle. At first they should be barely taut and very even. To keep the horse from rebelling against

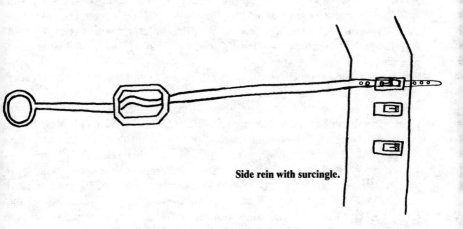

Side rein with surcingle.

the fixity of this gear, the reins should, each in its middle, have a rubber disk affording a certain elasticity, limited, however, by the leather of the rein passing through it. You connect the lunging rein by a forked piece of leather with ends buckled onto the respective snaffle rings. Gesture as little as possible with the lunging rein, content to give discreet indications; use the whip with moderation to back up the clicking of your tongue so your horse stays in a free forward movement at the walk and at the trot.

In the lessons to come you slightly shorten the gear, but not enough to keep the two rubber disks from acting and the reins from remaining elastic at a trot. Placed this way with the side reins on the lunging rein, the horse must step out freely, without the whip, at the simple click of the tongue. Unless this is accomplished, do not go on to the next exercise, which is intended to complete *by the crop,* the work on the lunging rein. Then you will proceed as follows: Bit your horse with his accustomed snaffle and buckle normal reins onto it. Stand at midneck, facing the croup. Take the two even reins with the left hand, twelve inches from the horse's mouth, placing him track to the left at one of the short sides. Take in your right hand a crop with which you have acquainted the horse in the same manner as with the lunging whip. Stroke his neck with the thick end, your voice soothing, gentling. Then, touching, not tapping, his breast with it, request the forward movement by a click of the tongue. If you succeed, pat and take another three or four steps. During these few steps make sure, without aiming for particular firmness, that the horse maintains contact on a taut rein; be content with little. If ever you should wish to push your horse's dressage farther ahead, this request for the forward movement by the crop applied to the breast is the basis of your work on foot. Besides, good results obtained with it during training will assure you, wherever later difficulties may arise, of little trouble in controlling your horse on foot. In fact, good training to the crop facilitates creation of the forward movement by which, once obtained, most difficulties are overcome.

I knew a horseman who trained all his horses, even his hunters, to advance crop to breast. On one occasion when a horse, despite the combined efforts of three grooms, would not climb into the trailer, his master with his crop succeeded single-handedly, the animal subjugated as by a supranatural force. Never an instrument of punishment on foot, it should not frighten the horse.

You will teach him to shift his haunches as follows: Holding the reins as before, you lead him onto a small circle. Walking backward yourself, progressively slow him down, and when the slowest speed short of a halt has been reached, request by small, repeated taps on the thigh an outward shift of the haunches. If the walk is very slow you rarely fail to obtain this at the second or third request. The left hand which holds the reins may further aid the movement by drawing the horse's head slightly to the left. You should, however, succeed without head or neck taking part in the request. Do the same on the right hand, aids reversed.

Before the first mounting lesson you accustom the horse to carrying the saddle, stirrup leathers off, the saddle fitted with a race surcingle so that, at the trot, the flaps will not beat noisily against the sweat flaps.

The mounting lesson should not come as a surprise maneuver which puts you into the saddle against your horse's will, but should be a way of accustoming him to accepting his rider's weight from the beginning, if not joyfully, at least with docility and calm.

If you want these mounting lessons to be profitable, proceed alone. Do not have one or two helpers hold your horse. You teach him nothing in this way. The moment he ceases to be held, he will make the same difficulties and will late, if ever, lose the panic caused by this first lesson where he has been coerced. Another practice to avoid is having an assistant hold a bowlful of oats before his nose. There are only two possibilities here: your horse is either touchy and fearful, or calm and submissive. In the first instance, fear will outweigh gluttony; in the second, there is no need to appeal to it. I am all for an award after a required movement has been carried out, even disproportionate to the movement itself; but I believe neither in bribing the horse, nor in momentarily lulling his distrust which will be encountered again later, manifold. You either know or do not know enough to conduct the preliminary training correctly and then to get into the saddle lightly. If not, you either are not ready for any kind of training, or this particular horse is too difficult for you.

Exercise him at liberty, saddled and bridled, the reins twisted, one of them slipped through the throat latch. Then place him straight into the middle of the school, that is parallel to one of the walls. Act without haste, yet without hesitation. Adjust your reins in the left hand and face the croup. If he should stir, straighten him and start anew. Put your left foot into the stirrup, without taking the upswing. If all goes well, grasp the back part of the saddle with your right hand, very close to the right flap to keep the saddle from sliding on the horse's back. If he has not stirred, constantly soothing him by the sound of your voice, rise quickly, without brusqueness, careful not to let your left toe make contact with his ribs, and touch down into the saddle as lightly as you can. Place your right foot into the stirrup, the leather conveniently twisted beforehand .It usually takes three or four times before one reaches the saddle without the horse's stirring.

In the saddle, wait two or three seconds before you make him step out by a few clicks of the tongue. Then, if successful, pat him and walk him once around. Return by an opening rein to where you have mounted, dismount, pat him and take him back to the stable.

There cannot be during training any question of "discretion of the aids"; so do not feel reluctant to make your gestures ample enough for comprehension.

Sometimes the first lesson does not come off quite so smoothly, the colt makes some bounds and short stops, promptly followed by half-turns. You must stay on; I would say, by all means. If your pupil realizes he can throw you, he will avail himself of every trick he can think up to rid himself of your cumbersome weight. So before you mount, place a collar on him (a well-fitted stirrup leather will do) to steady yourself without hanging onto the reins.

Let the first lessons under the rider sink in for a while, let the young horse get used to the weight of your body, and give him time to find his new balance.

These lessons under the saddle are given *parallel* to the work on the lunging rein, in hand and at liberty. The latter does not require the same moral and physical effort as working in hand, on the lunging rein, or under the saddle. The lessons should never last longer than thirty to forty-five minutes; but whenever possible, ride out with your pupil in hand for an hour or an hour and a half. Though these outings are health exercises, they also familiarize him with the outside world and thus are part of the saddle horse's education; for there are no friendly and frightening, just known and unknown, objects for a horse.

The main purpose of the next lessons is to obtain *the forward movement by the legs* whose back-to-front action must be associated with the clicking of your tongue. Or else use the crop just behind your leg, without great arm motions to scare your pupil, careful not to disturb your seat in the process.

Since the chambon has accustomed him to extending his neck at liberty, you now can achieve the same effect by your hands when working in the saddle.

At a walk *comb your reins* while maintaining the forward movement. Rare is the horse who, after a few minutes, fails to extend his neck; the point is not how completely but that he has understood your request. It will be child's play to obtain complete extensions later.

Having rid yourself of the crop by placing it under your thigh, take both reins in the right hand, separated by your index finger, just as close as possible to the base of the neck, carry this hand to your chest, letting the reins glide through your fingers while maintaining a light tension. While your right hand is approaching your chest, your left gets ready to act the same way. Thus, by the time the right has finished its course, the left has taken over and maintains the contact, the hands acting alternately.

Beware of the horse's finding a resistance when he extends his neck; yield, but maintain contact with the mouth in order to accompany the extension. The other hand should pat him as soon as he begins to stretch his neck. Realizing that the hand is light and having come to trust it, why should he refuse to advance? If you cannot persuade him, his refusal may spring from either a physical discomfort (particularly of the back), or else, ill will. Regardless of the cause, stop the work in the saddle which would do nothing but implant bad habits.

If in doubt, call the veterinarian. If sure of unwillingness, a powerful means, albeit not brutal, will prompt the forward movement. Continue the work on foot for about three weeks so as to habituate your horse to advancing on a taut rein (gear described previously, attached to the surcingle). During the three or four last lessons, bridle him with a double bridle, its reins twisted between the breast and the mouth in such a way as to exert a slight tension on the bits, the throat latch passing between them and keeping them from slackening.

By the time you once again mount your horse, get a pair of *rigid reins,* two wooden sticks almost one inch in diameter, long enough—when one of their extremities is attached by a leather strap to the rings bearing the curb chain hooks—for your hands to hold the other ends, while you keep the upper body straight, the horse's neck and head extended forward.

In your return to the mounting lesson, leave the curb reins loose. When you are up, two aids simultaneously hook in the rigid reins and hand you the extremities. The curb chain is fixed normally. While pressing the horse forward with the encouragement of a few clicks of the tongue, your legs and the rigid reins by a forward shift of both wrists are acting concurrently. Hand action should be moderate; the horse, drawn forward, will yield to it, the hindquarters merely following the forehand. Needless to add that the use of this device is temporary and that you should return to normal aids as soon as feasible. By advancing the outside, and retracting the inside hand, these rigid reins may be successfully employed in making a horse turn who refuses to do so. Their effect is quasi miraculous on restive horses who add all kinds of defenses to the refusal to release their impulsive forces, the worst of which is rearing. With the rigid reins obliging the horse to extend his neck forward by placing additional weight onto the shoulders, any raising of the forehand becomes impossible. This kind of gear is rarely used in training; but it is perfectly functional where a difficult animal must be dominated or a horse having been allowed habitual defenses must be retrained. Though its true place is not in this chapter, I wanted to describe it and its use on account of the domination it brings about in creating the forward movement which often is so hard to obtain.

Let us return to our pupil who is now advancing under the rider's weight. While exercising him in the forward movement, progressively substituting leg action for voice and crop, we are teaching him to yield easily to *the opening and neck reins.* The neck rein, of no special benefit in riding a schooled horse, is useful in the course of training because, contrary to widespread belief, far from diminishing impulsion, it incites the horse to advance.

Train him to the counter-rein (or neck rein) by placing him on a large volte, let us say, on the left hand, by means of an ample left opening rein. Once he has finished two-thirds of the circle, reduce the intensity of the opening rein and, with your right hand, execute a neck rein for the return to the track. Do not be too demanding as to the figure's precision. If he does not seem to understand your neck rein, make two or three consecutive voltes on the same spot by opening rein alone, very calmly, without your legs hustling him, patting him all the while, particularly during the latter third; i.e., your return to the track. When you then ask for the same movement again at the same point, he will surely yield to the neck rein at the end of the volte. Do not forget to pat him if he does and to walk him around once or twice, reins long. Then start over at the same place.

Let me here emphasize the importance of giving a horse time and occasion to associate a new movement with his trainer's caress. We must engrave whatever we wish to teach bit by bit in his head and therefore prevent his carrying out any movement not, or other than, requested by our aids. It would jeopardize or, at the very least, affect the whole remainder of his training.

When applying the right neck rein in the above example, the reins of course separated, make your right wrist act from right to left and back to front, that is, more or less in the direction of the left ear and counter to the direction of the hair of the coat. Since this rein effect acts upon the neck, the rein must naturally in its forward and leftward motion be applied there. Its intensity is determined by the extent to which it bears down on the neck and the number of wrist movements, not by the tension of the rein or the ampleness of the movement. While at first, in order to allow the horse to understand and yield to it, you have to amplify the actions of your hand, including the movements of your forearm, they will subsequently grow well-nigh imperceptible. At any rate, from what we have seen, it becomes obvious that the neck rein, far from impairing the forward movement, is actually aiding it; and the fact that it does not act directly on the mouth is often more than welcome.

So your colt is familiar with mounting, accepts the weight of your body, yields to the opening and neck reins in wide changes of direction, advances or extends the pace at the simultaneous action of your legs.

The purpose of the following lessons is to teach him the canter on a predetermined lead. Up to now, his only canters have occurred at liberty. As usual, you ask him for the new work at the end of a light lesson, so as not to take up the departure at the canter with an already somewhat tired animal.

Every horse has a more or less pronounced facility for the canter on a given lead. You take the track on the hand coinciding with the inside lead of his preference. Do not, like so many novices, try to employ discrete aids for an impression of obedience to light actions; if you want him to associate his canter with your aids, they must be clear enough for him to understand. If we suppose your pupil prefers to canter on the near lead, we take track to the left.

Plan to request the departure at passage of a corner by an increase in leg action and a click of the tongue, and a few yards before, tighten the right rein and slightly retract your right leg so as to aid the near lateral. You have every chance of obtaining the desired result. If not, start over at the same corner. As soon as you succeed, pat him and let him canter once around. Check to a walk and begin again at the same place.

After this second departure, change rein and go around several times at a walk. Using the opposite aids, request the canter on the off lead. If you succeed, do not let him fall into a disunited, or false, canter of the hind legs which your seat should be sensitive enough to feel. If he does, stop him immediately and start over at the same spot. If, despite all your efforts, you cannot obtain the departure on the off lead, the horse's off side must be suppled.

Here are three suppling exercises for this purpose.

1. Develop the off diagonal by posting much more often on it.
2. On foot, have him execute a few steps of right shoulder-in which supples his back in the longitudinal sense and aids the engagement of the off hind. Demand this frequently but never for long. Make sure that the inside hind crosses while advancing.
3. At a free walk (total freedom of neck, only the direction assured), you will take advantage of the naturally produced lateral motion of the spine and accentuate it by a pressure of the leg around which the horse must bend. Practice this exercise particularly on the right curves; if its results are slow in coming, at least it is not liable to blemish your pupil if you are not very skillful. Remember, the more powerful the means, the more delicate its use, and hence the more dangerous in inexpert hands.

## Jumping Lessons at Liberty

Eventually, at the end of a lesson, you place a pole on the ground of the track. Pass it several times at your pupil's side, then make him take it at a trot by himself. Calm is essential if the horse is to know what he is doing and is to focus his attention on this single pole. Depending on his behavior, you may during this first lesson add two more poles on the same side, or wait for the next.

The next time, raise the pole to 30 or 40 cm.* The horse's way of jumping will give direction to your work.

1. He does not take off from too far; his top line during the suspension being slightly convex, he "wraps himself around the jump." That, at any rate for upright obstacles, is perfect.
2. Needing a long trajectory to reach height, he takes off from a distance,

---

*Since all measurements in international equestrian usage are given in the metric system, we are adhering to the same .

his head more or less raised. He jumps with hollow loins, dragging his limbs. His top must be rounded.

3. Though not hollowing out his loins, he takes off from too far, because he does not know how to raise his forehand and must be taught to do so by jumping upright obstacles at a trot.

4. He makes, so to speak, a vertical take-off.

The first horse has a good style for an upright obstacle but may wrap himself only too well around this kind of jump, basculating too quickly, and may well feel uneasy over a spread jump. He must be exercised to extending himself particularly over low, broad oxers. In another exercise, you set up a 40 cm pole and place another, as a sort of false guard-rail, rather far behind on the ground. The distance is determined by the horse and his progress. The work in the saddle will later supplement the work at liberty. If, on the contrary, he also knows how to extend himself over a broad obstacle, you have a horse with good form which, unless devoid of all vigor or proving balky later on, will make a good show jumper.

Let us now try the second horse over a low, broad oxer. He clears it easily, thus ought to have physical ability, but must be taught to use it "rationally." This is done by passing upright obstacles at a trot during the jumping lessons and by frequent exercising with the chambon at liberty, so when mounted he will easily extend his neck at the combing of the reins, whether on the flat or over small fences. Horses with the same faults who, besides, get too close to the obstacle and commit faults with their forelegs belong in this same category. One of my mares used to judge the obstacle by its width, not by its height, when taking off. So she would clear with the greatest of ease an oxer 1.50 m high and 1.60 m wide, while prone to commit a fault on a 1.20 m upright jump. She needed massive obstacles. With this kind, only rather advanced training combined with the appropriate exercises, such as placing a pole on the ground with a guard-rail at a considerable distance, will give any results. Since you unfortunately have no guard-rails at a horse show, schooling must allow the rider to determine the departure; for one can never be sure how, and how correctly, the horse will "judge" an upright obstacle.

The third horse will be less troublesome and clear the upright obstacles correctly as soon as he knows how to raise his forehand and wrap himself around the obstacle by basculating under the hand.

The fourth horse must be accustomed to a distant take-off through the use of spread jumps with greatly spaced guard-rails.

The purpose of this early training over the fences is to improve your pupil's style, a sort of gymnastics rather than true lessons such as will begin with schooling only.

## Rounding Out the Training

If training is to become perfect, you must strive for free contact with the bit, your pupil not pulling, but "resting," on it. The work on the circle or on elements of a circle supples the natural stiffness of the young horse, while the work on straight lines renders him taut. Your main purpose is to supple him, with special attention to the neck which should not be like a piece of rubber bending whichever way you please without effect on the body as a whole and hence losing its role as a rudder. It must be muscled and suppled; and any attempt to supple before muscling would be futile. Only after the neck has grown to be like a flexible steel blade will you be able to begin use of the direct rein of opposition.

When first you teach your pupil to yield to it easily, do not let the rein hand "act;" begin by letting the other "yield." Example: In turning right, instead of increasing the tension of the right rein, yield with the left sufficiently for a right turn through a decrease in the tension of the left rein which frees the near lateral. By and by, the right hand intervenes, but the passive hand should never cease to yield before the other acts. The livelier the action, and/or the shorter the turn, the stronger the intervention of the active hand, and the slighter the yielding of the passive hand.

Rather than request the change of direction invariably by shortening the pace, do so by extending it. Many horsemen tend always to request extension on the straight lines and to practice changes of direction or the passing of corners on a slowdown. This is a mistake. Remember that the hands indicate, the legs oblige and that there cannot be any equitation without the forward movement. So in changes of direction press your pupil into the new direction through additional impulsion; that way you do not tempt him to drop the bit by putting himself behind the legs.

Though you may carry on the entire training and schooling without ever using the long reins, they permit you to overcome certain difficulties with greater ease. The equipment necessary for work on the long reins requires the long reins, a collar, and a surcingle. If no collar is available, you may use a breast-plate by fitting into the two upper rings a fast ring, mounted on a threaded pin which screws onto a felt-and-leather-lined metal piece which keeps the horse from injury and is, in turn, placed between the shoulder and the ring of the breast-plate. This way, the rings of the breast-plate are held between two metal disks of a greater diameter than theirs. In order to make the whole as fast as possible, the breast-plate should be adjusted with the greatest precision. The two small straps of the breast-plate, which normally are fastened to the saddle, are now fastened to the buckles of the surcingle. The rings of the surcingle through which the long reins are sliding should be low enough for these, when held by the trainer, to pass level with the lower end of the buttocks.

In the work on the long reins, as in all work on foot, the horseman has the advantage of seeing the whole horse and his responses to his demands, besides being able more effectively than on the lunging rein to control the direction of the haunches and to obtain free contact with the bit.

The horse, pressed forward by the lunging whip behind and framed by the long reins, will be in the forward movement, straight, and on the way to collection.

When the horse has been trained, which takes eight to ten months, he should

— be in perfect physical condition and well muscled;

— respond to the simultaneous action of the rider's legs by a free movement;

— not evade the bit but, on the contrary, seek it out and keep supple contact with it;

— yield to the first three of the rein effects;

— be calm and immobile during mounting;

— be calm at all three gaits, in the school and outdoors;

— jump calmly a few small artificial and natural obstacles.

# Schooling

Le but du dressage d'un cheval, c'est, au moyen du travail, de le rendre calme, léger, docile, afin qu'il soit agréable dans ses mouvements et commode pour le cavalier. Ceci est valable aussi bien pour le cheval de chasse et le cheval d'armes que pour le cheval d'école.

—DE LA GUERINIERE

## Introduction to Schooling

If they respect the horse's physical and moral possibilities, the exercises performed in schooling perfect whatever he has learned during his early training, lead to greater submissiveness to the rider's will and obedience to ever more discreet aids. The result is
— psychologically, a trusting horse;
— physically, a well muscled horse in fine condition who, having good balance, is light in hand and to the legs which have given him free and easy paces.

Our specific aim is to school him to the point where he executes with impulsion and submissiveness elementary dressage tests which comprise only simple movements not requiring as perfect a collection and balance as does the haute-école.

Suppleness and balance, the two basic qualities* for any kind of work, regardless of the form of equitation practiced, must reach a point of refinement commensurate with the degree of education the trainer wants to give his pupil. To be put into a certain balance by his rider, the horse must be capable of yielding to his indications easily and without physical discomfort. While this ability is achieved by the trainer's constant preoccupation with

---

*Obviously combined with impulsion; without it nothing is possible.

**Col. Gudin de Vallerin. (Photo Jean Bridel, from** L'Année Hippique)

suppling exercises, do not forget for a moment that one instance of excess may ruin the horse definitively and that it is preferable, without exception, to desist too soon than to go too far. Bear in mind that the horse is like a spring leaf from head to tail, not an assemblage of various springs, and that therefore the suppling exercises in affecting the hindquarters have repercussions on the forehand, and vice versa. Always consider the whole, not just one of its component parts. This holds true for the entire dressage which is one unit, not several units added up at random. A trainer must be as much of a synthesist as an analyst.

Schooling may continue the lessons on the lunging rein and the work at liberty which usefully complement the work in the saddle, while the work on foot and on the long reins, which was functional in training, would here overstep the framework of the intended dressage.

You will condition the horse physically by rational work proportionate to his strength; teach progressively, and perfect the new movements through lessons. The work is only performed once daily while the lessons, provided they are short, may be given profitably two or three times a day.

The *bits*. Up to now your horse should, in principle, have been kept in a simple snaffle; with at most temporary use of the double bridle, and this with the following precautions:

A bit with a slightly curved (half-moon) mouthpiece and medium-long cheeks is best for most horses. Actually, the bit should bear on the bars, not on the tongue. If the chin groove is sufficiently hollow to lodge the tongue easily, or almost, the half-moon mouthpiece is fine. Otherwise you need a port-mouthed bit, the dimensions of the tongue passage depending on the thickness of the tongue if compression is to be avoided. While its height must fit the thickness of the tongue, its width must conform to the distance between the bars on which the right and left ends of the mouthpiece should rest squarely. The width of the bit should be that of the mouth, plus one-sixteenth of an inch on each side, the length of the upper cheeks about 1¾ inches and that of the lower, about 3½.

Preferably pick a slender bridoon which takes up as little room as possible. When the bars on both sides of the joint are in straight alignment, its width should be the same as that of the curb bit. There are double-jointed snaffles, otherwise no different from the ordinary, which are recommended in conjunction with a port-mouthed curb bit. Others have a short upper cheek ending in a small ring to which the cheek strap of the snaffle is buckled, keeping the snaffle in place and limiting any sideward sliding (Baucher Snaffle).

A bridle is well adjusted when the bars of the snaffle bit are in contact with the corners of the lips, causing little, if any, wrinkling; but the location of the curb bit bar is the predominant factor and determines the position of the snaffle which must be higher in the horse's mouth than the curb. Do not hesitate to punch additional D's into the cheek straps for maximum precision. The curb chain, an integral part of the curb bit, must always lie flat, fastened so it touches the curb groove when the cheeks of the bit are at a 30 to 35° angle. Keep a horse with a sharp curb groove from being injured by attaching a small leather disk to the curb chain for softer contact. Also add a lipstrap so he will not get into the habit of seizing the cheeks of the bit; a game at first which later turns into an outright defense.

A fine way to accustom your horse to the curb bit is to bridle him without reins in his box and to put a bit of oats in his manger. The Weymouth bit, used in aiding the mobility of the jaw, should be discarded for two reasons. It makes for less precision of hand action, because of the play between cheeks and bar, and prompts a false relaxing at the jaw, given without the rider's invitation and liable to make a formerly "mute" mouth overly fretful.

The horse must get acquainted with the spurs and learn to respect them. In the beginning "Prince of Wales" spurs are preferable, provided the end of the neck is rounded, not tapering. He should accept them very quickly, depending on the tact with which the rider employs this powerful means of domination. Use should not become abuse, lest your pupil soon grow inured to it, the first step toward restiveness. The spur intervenes, by brief contacts to reinforce the action of the leg, only when the latter is impotent to make itself obeyed. In order to achieve eager obedience to leg action, *the lesson of the spur* should be given as soon as possible, with authority, yet without brutality. The reins in a single hand, the other for security on the pommel — to be sure you will not in the slightest oppose the forward movement—make your legs act by taps, followed by a short but energetic attack of the spurs. Simultaneously relax the bridle hand forward and, except for gentling him, play possum on his back. Though you should not rein him in too soon, there is no sense in letting him canter too long; just about fifty yards. The lesson, if well given, will hardly ever have to be repeated during schooling; however, do not hesitate to do so if the horse should grow *cold to the legs*. The forward movement must never be neglected and, whenever affected, be re-established on the spot.

### Suppling Exercises

Since the principal seat of resistance is in the haunches, take maximum control of them by teaching your horse to yield easily to the single leg. Furthermore, only disposition of the haunches will permit you to *impose* a change of direction, while the disposition of head and neck can but *aid* or *indicate* it.

A slow and prudent progression, though, will have to lead to a raising of the neck combined with the corresponding head carriage and relaxing at the jaw. This is how you will bring the *horse in hand.* An exaggerated raising of the neck without regard to the flexibility of the hindquarters and without seeking head carriage will lead to a result diametrically opposed to the one you are looking for.

The following suppling exercises, grouped here according to the regions to be suppled, must be carried on concurrently and interrelatedly; for, let me repeat, their repercussions are reciprocal.

## SUPPLING OF THE HINDQUARTERS

We distinguish between *longitudinal* exercises—which aid the arching of the spine and, consequently, lead to the engagement of the hind legs and prepare the collection through the development of the sacroiliac and coxofemoral joints—and the *lateral* exercises—which aim at greater ease, a lightness in the lateral motions of the haunches.

**The Cavalry School of Saumur. The half-pass. Col. Margot, ex-Equerry in Chief,**

## Lateral Suppling Exercises
*(Schooling to the single leg)*

*On foot.* Continue to work toward an even greater mobility of the haunches which the horse must eventually shift at a mere touch of the crop's pommel at the spot where your leg will later act (drawing it clearly back at first for better understanding), *i.e.*, at about mid-barrel. Work the more rigid side more often and always in the forward movement to prevent any budding backward flow of energies.

*In the saddle.* Your reins in a single hand, associate heel and crop action; and be at first satisfied with little. Gradually, heel action alone will suffice to obtain a shift of the haunches which can later be achieved by a leg acting at its normal place, the manner of its use being far more important than the place.

In the beginning there cannot be any question of regulating the movement determined by the single leg with the other which should, on the contrary, remain absolutely passive.

In order to accustom the horse to shifting his haunches promptly, make broken lines, changing direction by the exclusive action of the single leg. As the horse progresses, the broken lines are shortened to the point where the haunches can, so to speak, be gently swung from heel to heel without the slightest difficulty or resistance.

The half-volte in reverse haunches-out will progressively lead your pupil to the half-turn on the forehand.

Longitudinal Suppling Exercises

These comprise extending, shortening, and changing of pace, rein backs, and work on the circle, which should be begun by the separate suppling of the hind legs. This will make the other exercises easier for the horse.

To avoid confusion, let us recall the definition of the straight horse: When on a straight line, the left haunch and shoulder and the right haunch and shoulder, respectively, are traveling on parallel lines which ,in turn, are parallel to the axis of the movement which corresponds to the spine's vertical projection on the ground. On a curve, the horse must be bent along the entire length of its spine, its vertical projection on the ground coinciding with the curve to be followed, while his outside and inside* bipeds describe two concentric circles, the former on the outside, the latter on the inside. When these conditions are fulfilled, one says that the horse is adjusted on the curve.

The naturally straight horse is nonexistent; horses are usually bent to the left. Work initially on rather large circles to prevent these suppling exercises from turning into a constraint and becoming, in the long run, rather an evil than a blessing. There is a simple trick to help you with the orientation of your work and let you judge the work accomplished. Trace two concentric circles on the ground with clean sawdust, their distance equal to the distance between the hind legs, plus a small margin. This will let you see not only the work done, but the exact dimensions of the circle which, important as they are, we are in the beginning not always able to judge.* *

There are two manners of adjusting your horse on the circle:

— with the horse's barrel tangent to the circle, press the forehand and

---

* We call outside the convex, inside the concave side. The outside lateral thus is the lateral on the convex, while the inside lateral is the one on the concave side.
* *See third suppling exercise concerning the departures at the canter described in training.

hindquarters onto the circle. Thus the horse bends around the rider's inside leg;

— with the entire horse inside the circle, only the head and hind legs tangent, your inside leg presses his barrel outward in order to place it on the circle, while your outside leg and your hands keep the two ends on the circle.

Let us only consider the first case. Track to the left, you lead the forehand onto the circle by a light left opening rein and right neck rein, the right leg slightly retracted, acting from front to back so as to place the hindquarters on the circle, while the left leg at the girth — around which the horse's barrel is bent—maintains the impulsion. Slightly advance your right (outside) shoulder to keep facing in the same direction as the horse, adjusting *yourself* on the circle. Limit your first demands to a few steps on a circle of large diameter, exercising first the rigid side (the one not incurved by nature).

This work on the circle will not only more or less perfectly straighten the spine, but supple it and bring about a more pronounced engagement of the inside hind. After this exercise has suppled the joints of haunch and hock on each side separately, satisfactory results will be more easily attained when both are worked concurrently.

Extending, shortening and changing paces is excellent; but here as elsewhere progress must be slow. Turn chiefly to the trot; extend, shorten, pass from trot to walk, and vice versa. The extension and shortening of the walk is not at first particularly interesting, and you will find it easier to obtain and maintain tension at a trot than at a walk where the horse can more easily hold back.

*The halts* should during early schooling be used with the greatest moderation, because they tend to enervate the horse. Substitute the half-halt, the rein back, or the half-pirouette. A profitable introduction to the halt can only be undertaken after a tentative suppling of the hindquarters and a partial straightening of the horse. Since hitherto the halt has been for him synonymous with immobility and nothing else, it would be futile to make him repeat to the saturation point a movement he cannot yet perform with any degree of correctness. It would be teaching him to do wrong.

Once you have, by suppling the hindquarters, obtained a certain degree of engagement of the hind legs and the horse has been put between the rider's hands and legs, you will be in a position to achieve, aside from immobility, the rectitude of position where the four feet form the four corners of a rectangle. Going from simple to complex, you will obtain the halt from the walk, then from the trot, and finally from the canter. Once you stop having trouble getting the halt from the walk, hind legs straight on the same line, and the horse keeps them in this position wihout difficulty, you proceed to the following stage: striving for the same halt from the walk, but with a more pronounced engagement of the hind legs.

The introduction to the halt from the trot and canter will depend, above all, on the collection you have attained at those paces. As long as the trot and canter are not sufficiently improved, you had better perform one or two intermediate beats at a walk to obtain a correct halt. Wanting to go any farther would entail disorder and, far from improving the work, only make the horse unlearn the first lessons of the halt.

To achieve a straight halt, walk at a slow, measured pace, keeping your legs in place. Having brought your horse in hand, request the halt by finger pressure on the reins. The halt obtained, the hands cease to act; and though the legs cease likewise, they do not yield but resist, so as to keep the hind legs in place and to maintain the collection adequate to the pace. If the horse at first does not remain straight, straighten him *by placing the shoulders before the haunches,* not vice versa.

In order to lighten the forehand and prompt the engagement of the hind legs, we shall make use of *the half-halt,* which, preserving the forward movement, does not impair the activeness of the hindquarters. It should be performed on a taut rein, with a moderate elevation of both wrists on a vertical plane. Its action may be of varying intensity, depending on the subject and his prior schooling. A lively and brief hand action, or else a simple upward finger pressure on the reins, these are the two extremes.

*The rein back* is another of these exercises. Prior to beginning the rein back in the saddle, the horse should be schooled to the retrograde movement on foot. Facing him, grasp the reins with both hands close to the snaffle rings. Make him advance two or three steps and, through successive oppositions of your hands, ask for one step back. Do not place his head too high; leave him, on the contrary, plenty of latitude for placing it. The most important is, at first, for him to understand your request and to be permitted to respond with the greatest possible ease. During this entire preparatory work on foot, always request the rein back as follows: three steps forward, one step back, three steps forward. You must from the first impress on your pupil that the slighest backward step is immediately followed by the forward movement. In short, the horse must be taught to back physically with the impulse to advance.

Besides, viewed as an exercise, the value of the rein back lies in the transitions from walk to backing, and vice versa. When requesting it, lighten the back to a maximum by greater pressure on the stirrups; shorten the walk to a maximum by alternate actions of the hands; subsequently, increasing these actions, request the rein back. Though obviously the horse is not ready to pass from the walk to the rein back without marking a slight halt, this pause must be reduced to a minimum. Most resistances are caused by the rider's overloading of the hindquarters. The goal to reach is for the horse to back straight, each diagonal beat commanded by a hand action on the rein corresponding to the diagonal in action, moving forward by himself as soon as the hands cease to act.

## SUPPLING OF THE FOREHAND

The principal purpose of suppling this region is to lighten it by progressively *raising the neck*, complemented by the corresponding *head carriage,* on the one side, and the *mobility of the shoulders* to yield easily to the neck rein, on the other. These different exercises and those of the hindquarters, which cannot be disassociated, will be supplemented by the shoulder-in and the half-pass which are the subjects of a later section.

In your pursuit of *the mobility of the shoulders* you will make changes of direction by neck rein, your legs acting at their normal place, with strictly equal intensity, in order to keep the forward movement alive. The haunches will thus always take part in the changes of direction, the horse turning by both ends. As he yields more and more easily to the neck rein and the single leg action, you endeavor to keep the haunches from participating in the changes of direction by exerting a *wall-like resistance* with the single leg. You return to the exercises on the broken lines, modifying at will the angle and length of their straight elements as progress occurs. When your horse has come about a certain dexterity, you require him to execute ever tighter half-voltes, holding the haunches, the ultimate expression of it the half-turn on the haunches. The forehand can thus be gently swung from rein to rein, the way the hindquarters may be swung from heel to heel.

## SUPPLING OF THE NECK AND MOUTH

If your hands are to exert effective and useful action on the whole horse, the head must be drawn back to a position approaching the vertical, without ever going beyond. Placed this way, it allows the bit in action maximum effect and precision. This head carriage, if it is to keep its full value, must be attained through a progressive raising of the neck which becomes rounded, particularly in its upper part, the poll remaining its highest point.

Correct head carriage is the consequence of a flexion of the joints of the first vetebra (atlas) with the occipital bone, on one hand, and with the second vertebra (axis), on the other. Thus a complete and correct head carriage is quite obviously not easy to obtain, since in addition to the trainer's skill the horse must have the qualities which make it possible. The horse with a thick lower jaw or overdeveloped parotid region will be troublesome when introduced to head carriage. Here, too, your pupil's physical possibilities must be borne in mind; it is preferable to obtain correctly a less pronounced

**Head carriage with raised neck.**

head carriage with a moderately raised neck than a more accentuated but false one, for its value lies in its effect on the entire horse rather than in the shape it lends to the neck.

During training and early schooling, you have been requiring your pupil to flex his neck. This has developed muscles along its entire length; and, instead of thrusting in the withers between the shoulders by a premature raising of the neck, you have, on the contrary, contributed to a good muscling of its base.

Head carriage without raising of the neck would almost certainly result in a horse behind the bit through overbending; raising of the neck without this head carriage would lead to the collapse of the base of the neck with its disastrous consequences for the hindquarters—hollow loins, hocks crushed to the utmost. You must therefore strive for raising of the neck and head carriage progressively and simultaneously.

It must be achieved by an advance of the body toward the head, not a retreat of the head toward the body; for although you can obtain the same result by both procedures, the consequences of the resulting head carriage are diametrically opposed. With the first procedure, the horse goes into this head carriage by forward movement, capital element never to be lost from sight. The least of the evils resulting from the second would be to teach him to yield to a traction of the bit by retracting head and neck. Rarely can the trainer's skill arrest the retraction at this point, which usually spreads all along the spine and arrives at the retraction of the entire body, the feet remaining at their place—the backward flow of energies. It therefore is preferable to choose the slightly longer, but safer road.

*Relaxing at the jaw* must be discussed before we attempt to introduce the horse to lateral and direct flexions. A horse's jaw may be contracted for two reasons: either through muscular tension in some region of the body, with repercussions in the mouth; or through a contraction originating in the mouth itself.

Relaxing at the jaw is conveyed by a slight opening of the mouth, permitting the tongue to move up and take the bits which fall back into place with a clicking sound; the same tongue movements as in deglutition. It is obtained little by little by the rider's tact. From the moment of its first timid appearance, he encourages it every time through a release of the reins without loss of contact. You will try to achieve this at slow gaits, working on straight lines, but chiefly on the circle. Proving the absence of contraction, relaxing at the jaw is the outward sign of lightness.

You may find *weight resistances* springing from bad balance. These are to be counteracted by half-halts. *Force resistances* springing from muscular contractions are to be counteracted by vibrations on the snaffle bit. These vibrations, without participation of the wrists, are made by a swift and smooth back-and-forth motion of scant sweeps, fingernails down.

The horse can be taught and exercised on foot to relax at the jaw by local exercises of the mouth. Difficult, however, to do well and requiring a great deal of tact, the effect of these exercises may be more harmful than good. Do not embark on this before you are sure that you can prevent the horse from backing and prompt him to move forward freely at your slightest appeal.

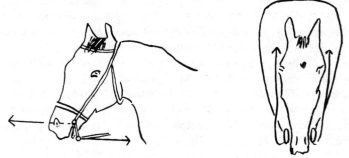

**Two exercises for relaxing at the jaw.**

In the first exercise you make him half-open his mouth in order to obtain mobility of the tongue by an inverse traction exercised on the curb reins. Standing at the near side of his head, grasp the right curb rein with your right hand, the left with your left. Exercise with your right hand a slow and continuous traction in the direction of the neck, while the left hand exerts equal traction in the opposite direction.

In the second exercise you place the seam of the snaffle rein on the horse's poll (right behind the headstall) and, making the reins slide through the snaffle rings, exercise an almost vertically upward traction. Wait for the mobilization of the tongue.

In both exercises yield as soon as the horse yields and be content with the smallest sign of obedience. At the slightest backing, stop immediately, make your horse walk out and start all over a little farther ahead. In these exercises the exact direction given to the tractions must be of such precision that they will not act on the neck and, above all, not on the entire horse.

The third exercise I am going to describe is less academic, yet less dangerous. Before meals, place a double bridle with very short curb bit cheeks on your pupil. His relaxing at the jaw will be perfectly correct without the risk of any backward flow of energies. In this case, give him his oats crushed, because he cannot chew quite as well as otherwise.

Lateral Flexions and Direct Flexions

Before requiring direct flexions, you should supple the poll region by lateral flexions which consist of a slight rotation of the head around a vertical axis. The tips of the ears must thus always be at equal height, lest there be a twisting of the poll and the flexions be false. Here, too, you should limit your demands, the more so if your pupil has a heavy lower jaw or an overdeveloped parotid region.

After you have raised his neck by lifting your hands vertically, request him to relax at the jaw on a taut rein, your legs opposing the slightest retraction of the body. At the smallest sign of obedience, desist and pat. If in the beginnings you have trouble obtaining direct flexions, you may gentle the poll with one hand, while the other makes the request on the reins. Do not abuse this procedure which, through repetition, may cause overbending.

Both lateral and direct flexions may be requested on foot, but this requires a certain skill and is not devoid of danger. Initially requested at a halt, they will subsequently be executed at a walk. By a slow progression you will thus arrive at bringing the horse in hand at the three gaits.

## The Work on Two Tracks

The work on two tracks, where the forelegs advance on a track of their own parallel to that of the hind legs, has a triple purpose:
— to make the horse more dexterous and consequently better balanced by teaching him to advance laterally and to pass swiftly from one side to the other;
— to supple the whole horse;

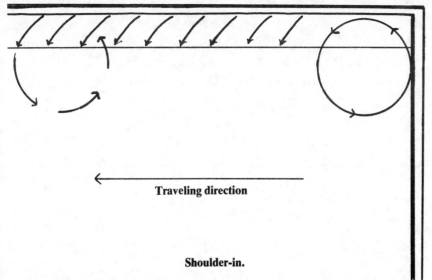

**Shoulder-in.**

— to obtain engagement of the hind legs.

It complements the work on straight lines and on curves by putting into play certain muscles which in work on a single track were playing but a secondary part, but to which falls the principal task in work on two tracks.

We shall restrict this study to *the shoulder-in* and to *the half-pass*.

According to the inflexion given the horse in lateral work and the direction followed, the different limbs are required, one by one, to furnish the chief effort. Work on two tracks can be undertaken profitably only after the horse has been thoroughly exercised in work on the circle with the consequent engagement of the inside hind.

## The Shoulder-In

In the *shoulder-in*, the horse is bent all along his spine and moves in the direction of his convex side. "Adjusted" on a circle, and thus bent, he leaves this circle traveling parallel to himself and maintaining the same bend (fore and hind legs remaining on their respective tracks). The circle should at first be very large, and you will be content to obtain the *Schulter vor* (shoulder in front) described by Steinbrecht.* In this exercise, the track** of the inside hind coincides with that of the outside fore, and this with a minimum bend.

---

*G. Steinbrecht, German horseman and author (1808-1885).
**One says the horse moves "on one track" when the track of the hind legs coincides with that of the forelegs. Actually, there are two tracks: that traveled by the near lateral and that traveled by the off lateral. The same observation applies to the definition of "two tracks" which means that the track of the hind legs is distinct from that of the forelegs. Actually, as before, the track of the forelegs is composed of two tracks; that of the near

**Schulter vor.**

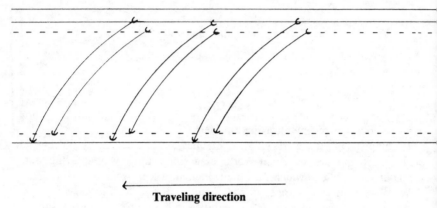

←————————————

**Traveling direction**

**Left shoulder-in.**

To perform *the left shoulder-in,* place your horse track to the left on a circle of a size corresponding to the extent of bend you wish to obtain in the shoulder-in. At the moment of the hind legs' arrival at the point of tangency (with the track), request a few steps of shoulder-in, then cease the movement while finishing the circle element you have begun.

The aids applied are:

*The left rein:*
fifth effect acts on the entire body of the horse, who bends;

*The right rein:*
limits the inflexion of the neck and is at the same time the guiding rein which keeps the forehand on its track;

—————————————

fore and that of the off fore. The same applies to the hind legs which travel each on a track of their own. So there are four different tracks. This figure comes down to three in the case of the *Schulter Vor,* where the track of the inside hind coincides with that of the outside fore.

*The left leg:*
around which the horse is bent, acts close to the girth from back to front;

*The right leg:*
keeps the off hind from deviating;

*The body weight:*
is rationally distributed with a slight accent on the right.

Unless the shoulder-in is requested departing from the circle, keep the inclination with respect to the direction followed from becoming too pronounced; about 30 degrees.

You must constantly watch the inside hind to which falls the hardest task (staying the mass under which it must engage itself by a bending of the haunches) and which will try to evade the effort by skidding inward. On the other hand, this hind will find it easier to cross the outside hind than the inside fore to cross the outside fore. In fact, let us consider the above example (left shoulder-in): The horse is bent to the left and moves right. The left bend will cause the bringing together of the limbs of the near lateral and the distancing of the off lateral. The near hind thus finds itself naturally in front of its off counterpart and the crossing is thereby aided. The same does not apply to the near fore which finds itself behind its off counterpart and in crossing without striking it must stretch far forward in a rounded motion. To allow the inside limbs to place themselves in front of the outside limbs and, all the more so, to cross, your outside leg — which happens to be the right — must, by keeping the off hind engaged, prevent its evasion to the right; the right rein, which for the same reasons watches over the off shoulder, is the guiding rein.

The most serious faults to be avoided are:

— loss of impulsion;
— bending of the neck alone, without participation of the entire body;
— evasion of the hind legs, particularly of the outside hind, which is hardest to detect.

The shoulder-in, considered to be the overall suppling exercise par excellence and also a potent means of control will

— free the shoulders;
— lighten the forehand;
— supple back and loin;
—engage the hind legs under the mass.

In the words of La Guérinière, the lesson of the shoulder-in is "the most learned of all in equitation and the one best suited to acquaint the horse with the reins and obedience to the legs."

## The Half-Pass

In *the half-pass* the horse is kept straight from head to dock with the head flexed slightly in the direction of the movement, his position slightly oblique in relation to the direction followed, the forehand in advance of the hind-quarters; such is the classic half-pass. It may, however, if performed during schooling for the purpose of further suppling, be executed with a slight bend toward the side of the movement.

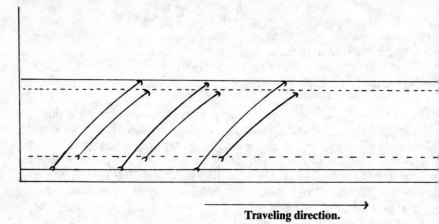

Traveling direction.

**Half-pass to the right.**

Performing *the half-pass to the right, the right rein* with light opening effect to place the head, is the guiding rein. *The left rein* is a neck rein driving the shoulders toward the right (direction of the half-pass). The left leg is the determining aid driving the haunches toward the right, acting in the di-rection of the half-pass. *The right leg* maintains the impulsion and watches over the off hind, prevents any evasion to the right and keeps it engaged. *The body weight* is accentuated on the right.

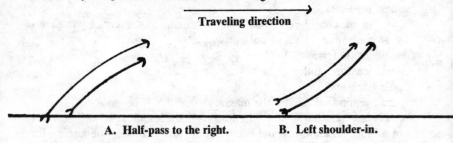

Traveling direction

**A.  Half-pass to the right.      B.  Left shoulder-in.**

In the right half-pass (example above), the limbs of the off lateral are drawn together, while those of the near lateral are drawn apart. The near hind has to make a greater effort than in the left shoulder-in to cross its counterpart; chiefly if the latter is kept engaged through the action of the rider's right leg. By contrast, the crossing of the off fore by its near counterpart is easier than in the left shoulder-in.

As in the case of the left shoulder-in, it is thus the crossed limb which regulates the work of the crossing limb. You must therefore prevent any lateral evasion and adequately regulate the advance of the crossed limb; otherwise the work on two tracks loses practically all its value and does no more than perhaps give the horse a certain dexterity in moving laterally, at the risk of blemishing his limbs which strike each other on account of a wrong position.

What we have seen leads to the following conclusion. In the shoulder-in, the crossing effort is greater for the forelegs and lesser for the hind legs. In the half-pass, the crossing effort is greater for the hind legs and lesser for the forelegs.

## The Work on Two Tracks on the Circle

To habituate the horse to the half-pass and to develop his action, you should resort to *the work on two tracks on the circle* which includes:

— *the half-volte haunches-in,* its limit the *half-turn on the haunches;*
— *the half-volte in reverse haunches-out,* its limit the *half-turn on the forehand.*

These exercises are complemented by:

—the *volte haunches-in,* its limit the *pirouette;*
—the *volte haunches-out,* its limit the *pirouette in reverse.*

Their purpose is to make the horse, in the lateral work, as dexterous in his forehand as in his hindquarters. The trainer, working particularly the more rigid side, will see in the degree of homogeny attained in the movement on two tracks the measure of his skill.

This work on the circle is in turn complemented by the *half-pass*:

— *head to the wall* where the forelegs are traveling on the track, the hind legs on an inner track parallel to the former;
— *tail to the wall* where the hind legs are traveling on the track, the forelegs on an inner track parallel to the former;
— *on the diagonal across the arena;*

and by

— *counter-changes of hand on two tracks* which may be performed either departing from the track, or from the center line.

We shall examine each of these exercises separately and see what may be expected of them.

*In order to avoid unnecessary repetition, we shall suppose in the different examples that at the beginning of the movement we are track to the left. Depending on their nature, the inside during execution will be either left or right. The aids and their effects should be inversed when track to the right.*

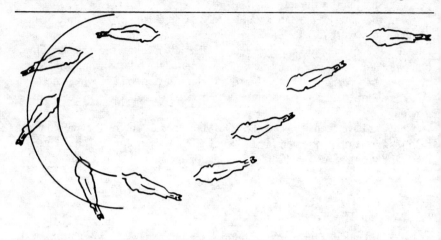

**Half-volte haunches-in with return to the track by half-pass.**

The half-volte haunches-in has certain advantages:
— it prepares the half-turn on the haunches (half-pirouette);
— it lightens the forehand by shifting the weight to the hindquarters;
— it amplifies the action of the forelegs in crossing.

In order to place the horse on the half circle, you must by *the right (neck) rein* first drive the shoulders to the left; *the left rein* places the head to the left and serves as guiding rein; *the right leg* intervenes to shift the haunches toward the left onto an inner track, though only after the horse, through the shift of the forehand toward the left, is placed on the intended angle (an inclination of about 25 to 35 degrees). *The left leg* maintains the impulsion; *the body weight* is accentuated on the left.

In accordance with the intensity you give your aids, particularly to the tension of the reins and to the opposition of the right leg, the horse executes an ever tighter half-volte haunches-in, eventually arriving at the half-pirouette.

In this exercise, the principal task falls to the off fore. By the way you place your horse, you may at will diminish or increase the effort of the off fore in crossing. The more the horse is bent around your left leg, the more ample is the crossing; the more he is placed in the other direction—as in the right shoulder-in—the greater is the effort of the foreleg and the shoulder. Practiced thus—that is, on a curve track to the left, the placing as for the right shoulder-in—this exercise takes the name of *counter-shoulder-in.*

The near fore is worked in the same manner in the half right pirouette.

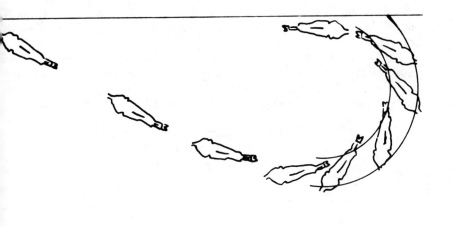

**Half-volte in reverse haunches-out.**

The Half-Volte in Reverse Haunches-Out has certain advantages:

— it prepares the half-turn on the forehand (half-pirouette in reverse);

— it amplifies the action of the hind legs;

— it aids the engagement of the hind legs.

The forehand, however, is more burdened, as is the case whenever the hindquarters rotate around it.

On a half-volte in reverse at the end of the oblique, having placed the fore-legs onto the half circle, the action of *the right leg* sets the hind legs onto an inner track parallel to the one followed by the forelegs. *The left hand* places the head to the left. The rein effect is an opening rein, also supposed to guide the forelegs onto the track and limit, if necessary, the shoulders' leftward shift by moving to the right. *The right hand* shifts the shoulders leftward by a neck rein. *The left leg* at the girth maintains the impulsion and keeps the near hind from skidding to the left and engaged. *The right leg,* being the determining aid, drives the haunches leftward, acting in the direction they are following. *The body weight* is accentuated on the left.

As in the preceding exercise, you may increase or decrease the crossing effort by the way you place your horse. In the present case the work of crossing falls to the off hind. The more the horse bends around your left leg (placing to the left), the greater the crossing effort; the inverse placing diminishes this effort.

Responding to the intensity of your aids, particularly of the tension of the reins, of their opposition to the leftward shift of the shoulders, and of the action of your right leg, the horse will execute an ever tighter half-volte in reverse haunches-out, eventually arriving at the half-pirouette in reverse.

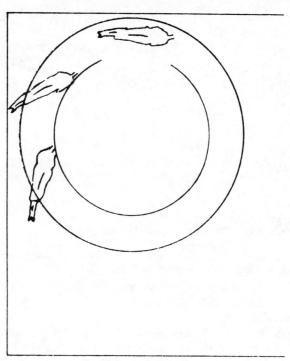

**Volte haunches-in.**

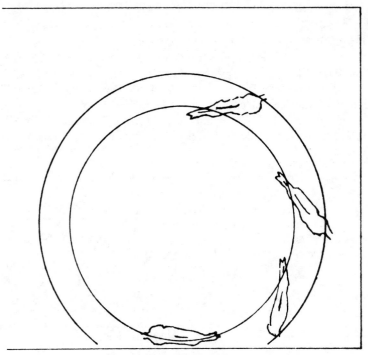

**Volte haunches-out.**

*The Volte Haunches-In and Haunches-Out.* When your horse is thoroughly exercised in these two maneuvers, you will repeat them on a complete circle, requesting them now haunches-in, now haunches-out. Practiced this way, the forelegs remain on the same track which coincides with the circle, and it is the hind legs which are shifted to an inner or outer track. The purpose is to increase the suppleness and activeness of the hindquarters which grow light to the action of the single leg and are, so to speak, gently swung from leg to leg.

The volte haunches-in, when practiced with an eye to an eventual pirouette, should be requested on departing from an inner track (about 5 meters from the wall), applying the same procedure as in the half-volte haunches-in. The same applies to the volte haunches-out when requested with an eventual pirouette in reverse in mind.

The aids are those of the classic half-pass, the head flexed in the direction of the movement (to the right for a left volte haunches-out).

One important observation: in all this work on two tracks on curves, make sure that the haunches, in their lateral movement, are not ever in advance of the forehand, because the forward movement has not lost a whit of its importance.

## The Half-Pass on a Straight Line

*The half-pass on a straight line* is taken up *head to the wall*. The forelegs travel on the track, the hind legs on an inner track. The oblique on which the horse travels should, at first, be at an angle of 30 degrees and by stages reach 45 degrees. It would be harmful to demand an excessive obliqueness from the start which, furthermore, would impair the forward movement which must remain intact in the work on two tracks. Keep this in mind during the entire progression.

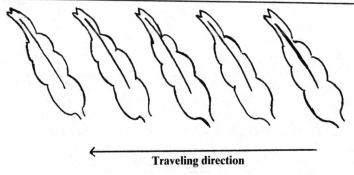

← **Traveling direction**

**Head to the wall.**

After shortening the pace in order to set the hindquarters onto the inner track by the action of the right leg, the aids employed are the following: the left (opening) rein places the head and also serves as guiding rein; the right (neck) rein drives the forehand leftward and limits the placing caused by the left rein; the left leg close to the girth maintains the impulsion; the right leg drives the haunches in the direction of the half-pass; the body weight is accentuated on the left.

To straighten, the action of the left leg places the haunches back behind the shoulders.

Preferably make use of the corners to place the horse into the head-to-the-wall position, lest right-leg action cause a rotation of the hindquarters around the forehand.

The *tail to the wall* movement is a little more difficult, since the wall cannot be used for guidance any more. Here, too, the inclination should at first be slight, a maximum of 45 degrees. The forelegs are on the inner track. The results obtained by this exercise are a measure of the horse's obedience to your reins and legs.

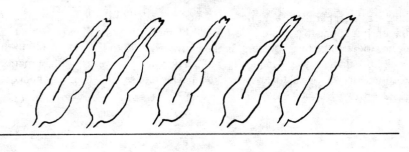

**Traveling direction**

**Tail to the wall.**

In order to lead the forelegs onto the track, you may, while passing a corner, slow down the forehand which describes a smaller circle than the hind legs which are driven by the left leg.

When the horse is placed in accordance with the intended oblique act with the usual aids. *The right rein,* which places the head, is also the guiding rein, its role more important here than in the foregoing exercise where in guiding the forehand it was aided by the wall. Do not forget to change the placing which, before passing the corner, was to the left (track to the left) and while passing the corner and during the half-pass to the right must be to the right. This way of doing, alas, makes the hindquarters pivot around the forehand. Academic equitation disapproves of it and provides us with another method:

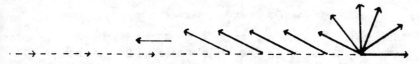

**Tail to the wall.**

At the end of one side, execute an element of a volte haunches-in. The head was flexed to the left (track to the left). While turning, haunches-in, it is likewise flexed to the left. When the horse has been placed on the oblique for the half-pass tail to the wall, *the left rein* draws the shoulders to the left which are driven in this direction by an effect of *the right (neck) rein* while *the right leg* requests the same movement of the hindquarters. *The left leg* maintains the impulsion and regulates the horse's bend. *The body weight* accentuated on the left, aids the entire horse's movements to the left.

In *the half-pass on the diagonal,* the forelegs travel on the diagonal, the hind legs on a parallel track; the entire horse parallel to the long sides. During the early period, it is preferable for the haunches to stay slightly behind, so as not to overtake the shoulders; in the half-pass, head to the wall or tail to the wall, this danger was practically null. You must, however, obtain perfect rectitude if you wish to arrive at the next exercise, the counter-change of hand on two tracks.

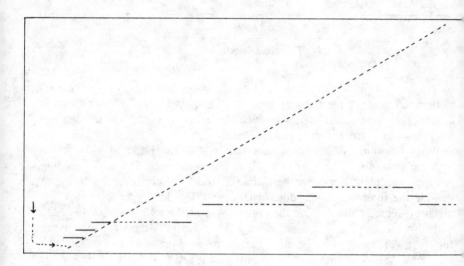

**Preparation for the half-pass on the diagonal.**

Before initiating the half-pass on the diagonal, wait for the entire horse to be parallel to the wall of the long side, place the head for the half-pass and request the shift of the shoulders before that of the haunches. The interval between the two requests should be minute. When you take the opposite track (the forelegs must be on the track 6 meters before the corner), do not discontinue right-leg action before the hind legs have placed themselves behind the shoulders. You want to have your horse prefectly straight before you pass the corner, which otherwise you could not do properly because the horse could not be adjusted on the curve.

To prevent him from anticipating the movement and to accustom him to being ever ready to obey your aids, besides preparing him for the counter-changes of hand on two tracks, you should discontinue the half-pass at varying points of the diagonal and request a few straight forward steps; then continue the half-pass in the same direction. Subsequently, in the course of a half-pass from right to left, you request a few straight forward steps during which you place your horse perfectly straight and parallel to the walls of the long sides; inversing the aids, request a half-pass from left to right. Do not always make your requests at the same points; thus by and by and very naturally you will arrive at *counter changes of hand on two tracks.*

**Counter-change of hand on two tracks on one side of the school.**

These are initially requested departing from the track. Track to the left, request three or four steps of the half-pass to the left, one step straight forward, and return to the track by the same number of steps, half-passing to the right. Needless to say that the horse must be straight from haunches to shoulders and parallel to the walls of the long sides. The head is flexed slightly in the direction of the movement without any participation of the neck. If you can obtain this by a light opening effect, you avoid a repercussion on the haunches.

Then you pass on to counter-changes of hand departing from the center line. Having placed your horse on a turn down the center line, half-pass three steps to the left, one step straight forward, half-pass three steps to the right to return to the center line, plus three more steps to the right.

In sum, the exercise is as follows: Departure from the center line; three steps to the left, six steps to the right, six steps to the left; three steps to the

**Counter-change of hand on two tracks on the center line.**

right to return to the center line. One step straight forward is necessary before each change of direction. Only later, when the horse is in perfect balance through collection, may the counter-changes of hand be obtained without transition; for the moment it would only touch off a scramble.

All these exercises on two tracks are performed at the walk and at the trot, except for the pirouettes and half-pirouettes, in reverse or otherwise, which the rider cannot carry out at the trot before knowing how to perform the piaffe. The half-pass at the canter is discussed under the heading of that gait.

The impulsion must remain intact during the work on two tracks; do not hesitate to discontinue the movement in order to re-establish it.

In the shoulder-in do not look for an excessive bend and, if this exercise is to keep its full value, make sure the outside lateral (the off lateral in the left shoulder-in) does not deviate.

Placing in the classic half-pass should do no more than draw the head slightly to the side to which the horse is moving, sure that the action of the prompting hand does not hamper the movement of the outside shoulder or counteract the shift of the haunches.

The distribution of weight on the legs changes and influences them in accordance with the inflexion you give the horse for the direction he is following. When he moves to the left by a right shoulder-in, he is bent to the right, and the off hind determines the movement to the left but is overburdened (concave side). In the half-pass to the left, the same hind determines the movement to the left but finds itself on the convex side and is lightened to the same extent. In the above example, the near shoulder is lightened in the shoulder-in, while in turn it is overburdened in the half-pass.

## The Work at the Canter

The main purpose of cantering lessons is to exercise the horse in cantering with equal ease on either lead, which will make the introduction to the departures infinitely less troublesome. Eventually, after we obtain smooth departures on either lead, we can undertake the isolated flying changes of leg, our final dressage goal in this case.

The principal difficulty in the work at the canter is partly caused by the horse's natural inflexion in addition to the deviation caused by the gait. You must therefore by appropriate suppling exercises

— straighten as far as possible the side of the natural bend;
— obtain near-perfect symmetry of the diagonals;
— develop the action of each limb.

These suppling exercises, discussed in an earlier chapter, will be complemented by lunging on the circle at the canter, particularly on the hand opposite the horse's natural bend. Let us take the example of the horse with a naturally leftward bend.

Using surcingle and side reins and a snaffle,* shorten slightly the right rein to place the head slightly to the right. The horse must be on a circle to the right with a radius of about 5 meters. Place yourself at one end of the school so as to have him travel a circle tangent to two sides of the hall. This way you limit any evasion of the haunches to the outside of the circle. The horse at a trot, make use of his passing the corner to request a departure at the canter at the voice which, in the beginning, may be reinforced by the lunging whip. If the aids have been too weak and the horse only responds by extending the trot, your first preoccupation will be to shorten the trot and to recommence with a new request at the same point and with more energetic aids. You will proceed likewise if he strikes off on the false lead or into a disunited canter. His behavior should be your guide in the fit of the gear; it varies from horse to horse and even with the same individual in accordance with the results attained. When you have obtained a departure on the off lead, let him work into his gait several times around and intervene as little as possible. You return him to the trot, ask for a new departure at the canter at the same point and, if you succeed, terminate the lesson and send him back to the stables. The purpose of this exercise is to obtain at the voice a calm canter

*See "Work on the Lunging Rein" in Chapter 1.

on the off lead. Repeat the same lesson in the saddle. Request by voice as before, and gradually substitute your legs and hands.

The departure at the canter seems to be much rather an acquired reflex than the result of a movement determined by position. Training has accustomed the horse to striking off into the canter on a predetermined lead, without hesitation, by simple aids and without impairment of rectitude.

The aids best suited to these requirements are the lateral inside aids: left rein, left leg to obtain departure on the near lead. You cannot force a horse to strike off into the canter if he is unwilling, unless—a means we shall not take into consideration—you push him beyond his maximum rate of speed at the trot. Thus it is above all a matter of education and balance.

When you are sure to obtain the canter at the voice easily, and the canter on the off lead on a circle without constraint, the introduction to the departures by the inside leg and hand is only a matter of time, depending on your skill and the extent of the horse's schooling.

*Cantering on the near lead* on a left circle, there must be slight tension of the left rein (head flexed as for the left canter being the signal), action of the left leg at the girth, associated with the voice requesting the canter. By and by the heel will replace the voice, and without the latter's assistance you will be able to obtain the departure at the canter requested on the track and, eventually, on the center line.

Do the same work track to the right on the off lead.

A particular leg action is needed to avoid confusion in the horse's mind as to this request and that for the half-pass; but is not all of equitation a matter of shades as soon as one goes beyond the simultaneous action of both legs to press the horse forward and of both hands for the halt? It is up to you to establish a clear and precise language between yourself and your horse; and without loss of clarity or precision, this language will grow more and more discreet as you progress.

Take advantage of hacking or outdoor work, with no wall to help you any more, to give your horse assurance in his right or left canter, whichever has been troubling him. When he is supple and nearly as comfortable on one lead as on the other, you request *the departure on the center line*.

For this, track to the left, make a turn down the center line where you will request a departure on the near lead; before arriving at the opposite track, request the walk; take the track to the right. On a new turn down, request a departure on the off lead. Do not alternate regularly between near and off—and request more departures on the lead on which the horse seems less dexterous.

This is where many horsemen, who during the entire dressage have made a great show of patience, cannot resist the temptation to request flying changes of leg or, out of ignorance, believe that they have entered the field of *haute-école* because they obtain a flying change of leg on the diagonal. There is no truth in this, and such delusions only close the door on the future of your schooling and on official dressage tests which, without exception, require, if not always the countercanter, at least work with foundations resting on this principle. The same applies to those who teach their horses the passage by means which are, to say the least, dubious. One of them is the departure from the counter-changes of hand on two tracks at the trot. By shortening the lateral shifts the horse rocks from right to left and from left to right between his rider's legs. If the result is likely to dazzle the layman, it is not liable to fool a horseman. It means depriving yourself of the satisfaction of work well done, for you will always be aware of having cheated.

*The countercanter* is above all a matter of your tact and of your horse's balance. If he is cantering well-balanced and your aids are not, meaning to help, bothering and confusing him, this exercise is not very difficult, provided you do not ask your pupil for more than he can give.

You begin, track to the left, by requesting a departure on the off lead on the quarter line. By and by your requests are made closer and closer to the track where, eventually, you obtain a departure on the counterlead (off fore, track to the left). Do not ask him to pass the corner at a canter. Return to your work far from the walls. On an element of a straight line, cantering on

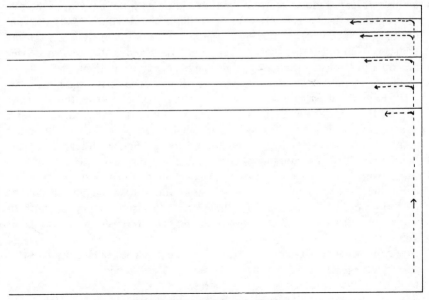

**Introduction to the countercanter.**

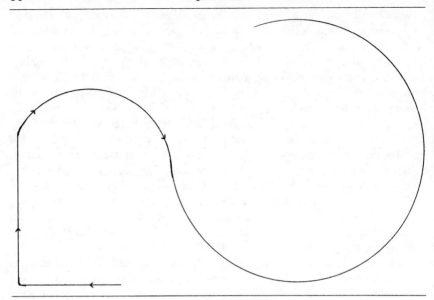

**Introduction to the countercanter.**

the off fore, request a change of direction to the left, following an element of a curve of large radius; return to the right. Little by little, mindful of the rate of progress, use elements of curves of a diminishing radius. Make cautious use of your aids when requesting changes of direction, chiefly when shifting your seat. Do not forget that the head must be flexed to the side of the leg on which the horse is cantering: right canter track to the right—head flexed to the right; right canter track to the left—head flexed to the right.

If the horse were to give you a flying change of leg during this exercise, request the walk and recommence the same work at the same place. Return, if necessary, to less accentuated curves, but no punishment which the horse would remember when introduced to the flying change of leg. Since the purpose is a kind of gymnastics to permit the horse to go around at a countercanter with ease and good balance, do not attempt to solve the problem by constraint. Maintaining a slow progression, you will eventually be able to perform a complete serpentine on the center line (large loops); at the half-volte and half-volte in reverse without flying change of leg; ending with the volte.

Having accomplished this last exercise, you can fearlessly take up *the flying change of leg*. On the center line, at a walk, request a departure on the near fore, for example, after three or four strides, check to a walk. Calm is of the essence. Request the departure on the off lead, and so on. If you obtain cor-

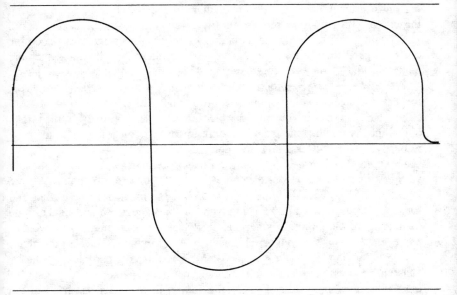

**Serpentine at the canter.**

rect departures, the horse is ready for the flying change of leg; else he must continue to work the departures.

To prompt the flying change of leg (not to wrest it from the horse):

— request, on a left circle of a radius of about 5 meters, the departure on the off fore (*i.e., countercanter*);
— cadence the canter by the right rein (which determines the placing);
— let the left leg remain passive;
— change the placing, and left leg action (aids of the departure on the near fore);
— let the right hand and leg remain passive;
— let the seat remain passive.

The horse will give the flying change of leg from the outside to the inside, maybe botching it a little, but he will have understood. Pat him at length and begin the same work again on the same circle on the same hand. Since the ease of the flying change will depend on the balance and the work done on the departures at the canter, you must, if you have trouble with the flying changes, go all the way back to the departure at the canter.

Once the first point has been attained, it is a matter of doing the opposite: that is, to pass from the inside leg (canter on the true lead) to the outside leg (countercanter).

Track to the left, cantering on the near fore, request the flying change of leg on a straight line; continue to canter on the counterlead after passing the corner. Progressively request the flying change closer to the corner till you obtain it while passing the corner. Once more take up the exercise on the circle, large at first, alternating the request and alternating the hand they are made on; that is, the near fore being now the inside, now the outside, leg.

*The half-pass at the canter* should in itself not pose any serious problems; for, being a succession of oblique forward bounds, the horse performs it more easily than at the walk or trot to which exercise he is already trained. The only difficulty could come from his confusion as to the leg actions requesting, respectively, the half-pass and the canter.

*Example:* The horse is cantering on the off lead, track to the right. You wish to execute a half-pass at the canter on the diagonal across the arena from left to right. You will use your left leg to press the haunches to the right and forward. If you were to make it intervene at the same place and in the same manner as in obtaining a flying change of leg, the horse might well wonder and even give you the change, although the head remains flexed to the right.

The leg action is not the same: When requesting the half-pass, it acts by consecutive pressures, respecting the cadence of the canter, its contact with the flanks enveloping; in requesting the canter, its action is restricted to the lower leg and takes the form of a small attack. To make things easier in the beginnings of the half-pass, you should, however, slightly retract the outside leg (the left in this instance).

## Conclusions

In following this road, you are giving the saddle horse an elementary dressage. Although you need not pass through the entire progression in order to utilize him and certain omissions are permissible, I have felt that we should dwell on certain points in order to give this elementary dressage a solid basis, if ever you should wish to push your pupil's education further, in order to give you a better understanding of the direction in which you should work, and lastly in order to make the horse agreeable, not only usable.

So far I have not mentioned outdoor work which technically is very nearly a repetition of the work done in the school. Hacking will let you keep an easy check on the progress made through the lessons in the school; so take your young horse out as often as you can, not only for health reasons, but to give him keenness, balance, wind and muscle and to keep from breaking his spirit by forever locking him in between the four walls of school or box. And finally do not forget that hacking is the complement, not the continuation, of the lessons which will bear better fruit if you do not keep your pupil in a perpetual state of subjection.

During this period of schooling with its work on one and two tracks you have achieved smoother gaits with a beginning of collection. The horse's top line, haunches and shoulders suppled, able to engage his hind legs at the request of your legs, the mouth resting trustingly on the bit and yielding to the indications of your hand, the horse will combine tension, impulsion and lightness at slow and lively gaits.

Extending a pace will no longer be the result of a precipitation of the movement, but of the amplitude of the action. The ultimate expression of an extended pace is the "extended trot." A pace is not shortened through decreased impulsion but, on the contrary, under full impulsion, gains through a flexion of the joints in height what it loses in extension—its expression par excellence the piaffe.

This result can be attained only through daily work over a period of many months (about two years in addition to the training period), based on patience, perseverance and firmness. If it is pleasant to ride a well schooled horse, this pleasure is doubled when the schooling is the fruit of your personal work.

## Schooling Over the Fences

The training our pupil has received, far from harming the schooling over the fences, will make its first steps easier, for successful jumping requires the very same kind of frankness, obedience and keenness as the other disciplines. Progressive work must now give him a style allowing him to jump safely and with a minimum of effort.

Provided the horse does jump and is usable under the saddle, the first quality he must be given is balance. Since the jump is the result of a release of the springs (hocks), sufficient tension must be created to allow this to occur, *i.e., collection.*

These two chief qualities have been obtained inside the school; now the physical capabilities must be developed which will enable him to round a course without harm to limbs and inner organs. Our "work" will pursue this aim in rather slow canters of a progressively increased duration on ground neither too hard, nor too boggy, till we arrive at 2,000-yard canters at a rate of 400 yards per minute, the rate of speed on the course. In this work the horse canters with extended neck and the head slightly flexed. Although the contact must be firmer than in the school canter, it must never become a handicap in guiding your mount or prevent him from yielding to your indications.

---

*There is in English no designation for the French "trot en extension" which, in contrast with "trot allongé," does not imply a precipitation of the cadence, but a development of the gesture. Here the truly "extended" trot is meant, not a "rapid" trot.

The pas d'école. Col. de Saint-André, Chief Equerry of the Cadre Noir, Cavalry School of Saumur, on Azur. (Courtesy Col. de Saint-André)

The Spanish School. The right shoulder-in. (Courtesy Col. Podhajsky)

At this point you are standing at a crossroads from where you may lead your horse in four different directions.

1. He seems gifted for dressage and you have, yourself, a penchant for this specialty.
2. You want to put him on the road to show jumping.
3. You wish to stay where you have arrived, that is, to be satisfied with minor horse shows and the perfecting of the previously obtained results in the school, whether because the horse by his nature does not permit you to go any farther, or because you yourself consider your aim achieved.
4. Because the horse is not qualified for any of the three, you may want to put him into the ranks to be used in the instruction of your pupils.

Let us here examine the main difficulties you will encounter on the course, should you take roads 2 or 3.

— The height and width of the obstacles. This problem can only be solved by the horse's power in combination with his style, natural or acquired through training.
— Management difficulties which schooling must solve.
— Psychological difficulties due to the horse's lack of experience (negotiating water jumps, banks, the arrangement or color of certain obstacles) which are overcome by training and by practice on the course.

Making him jump a pole with a good guard-rail and a square oxer, you have no trouble judging your young horse's power. Although it can be increased by muscling, training and experience, there is no mistaking the obvious ceiling to be respected during the first horse shows.

In West Germany, where for some time I trained young horses and riders, I was greatly helped by a classification which, to my mind, was very nearly perfect in that it allowed both horse and rider to get their practice in the field. Although horse and rider should be trained on the flat, the schooling over the fences and its application in public events will teach them how to jump.

Let me give you an outline of the classifications:

| | | |
|---|---|---|
| Class A. Beginners | Maximum Height* | 1.10 m |
| Class L. Easy | Maximum Height | 1.20 m |
| Class M. Medium | Maximum Height | 1.30 m |
| Class S. Difficult | Minimum Height | 1.40 m |

The last class in turn is divided into several categories. We shall speak of the first two only where the width of the obstacles is limited, respectively,

*Of course, only half of the obstacles reach maximum height.

to 1.20 m and 1.40 m, and their number to from 8 to 12 and from 12 to 16.

Curb bit and special rein devices are banned, so that the horse must at least have received a correct elementary schooling and the rider cannot avail himself of artifices letting him dodge certain difficulties. Such special gear is authorized only for use with difficult horses, or those whose schooling is not as yet on a level with their jumping ability which, however, allows them to face considerable difficulties under experienced riders. I would personally make an exception of the running martingale, which does not have the bad effects of most of the other special gear, and, if adjusted correctly, reinforces the action of the snaffle.

This categorization affords beginning horses and riders effective practice without requiring the horse in his first shows to give a maximum which might mar him in body and spirit. Moreover, so as not to disgust the young horseman, there are certain tests reserved for him, where the horses themselves are subject to categorization. In the beginners' events, which require chiefly a free jumper, the management difficulties are held to a minimum and the obstacles are inviting, preferably broad so the horse must stretch to clear them (oxers are not square, their second element is somewhat higher than the first). Double obstacles do not hold traps. The idea is to encourage the young horse to jump, not dishearten him. The "easy" class, where the obstacles are barely higher or more numerous, improves the horse by requiring more submissiveness, acquainting him with new (the water jump) or less inviting obstacles than those encountered in the "beginners" class. The width of the oxers increases faster than the height. For many horses and riders this class remains the last where they may continue to jump with pleasure and without breakage; for the "medium" and "difficult" classes require qualities which not all horses and riders possess.

Therefore, prepare your horse for show-jumping by as intelligent a training as you would carry on for dressage events, and adopt as a model progression for the schooling over the fences the norms of the first two categories ("beginners" and "easy") where the difficulties are restricted to a minimum. When the horse is ready in body and spirit—that is, neither disheartened, nor the least fatigued after a jumping lesson—then, and only then, may you take up the difficulties of show-jumping and overcome them one by one.

In training your horse as explained, including schooling over the fences at liberty,* supplemented by the same exercises under the rider, you will be leading him toward events such as I have described.

Since this book is intended to guide trainer, teacher and pupil in their first steps, it deals with the problems of horsemanship within a general

*See Training.

framework and ignores all specialization. Therefore the future show rider and teacher of show riders should turn to a literature which deals specifically with jumping technique and with the preparation for show-jumping.*

*In preparation by the author.

# II. Instruction

The Manège, by Hoppe, 1798. (Kupferstichkabinett, State Art Collections, Kassel. Retzlaff Archive)

The teacher who is attempting to teach without inspiring the pupil with a desire to learn is hammering on cold iron.

—HORACE MANN

## Introduction

There comes for all of us the first lesson we must give alone. Our fear of not living up to the hour, our uncertainty of the next moment are painfully obvious; self-consciousness of tone and gesture betray our inexperience. In an effort to conceal it or, at least, attenuate the effect, we are talking, talking far too much. Our words first astonish our pupils, then daze them, daze us and, short of dazing the horses, create an atmosphere so charged with electricity it sparks ideas of independence in some, while others are falling into a dolce far niente and stop in every corner. Only a thorough, if theoretical, knowledge of the do's and don't's can somehow help us overcome the difficulties bearing down on us from all sides at every moment; unless—the height of ill luck—a couple of horsemen happen to be watching from the visitors' gallery.

This is how most of us react; though there are some who rebel against this initial fumbling—the way timid people, under certain circumstances, may make a show of most unfortunate daring—attempting to impersonate, while only mimicking, an instructor who has all the know-how they are lacking.

No matter what you do, you will not fool a seasoned horseman, let alone an experienced teacher; the best is to be natural and not to "play-act." It is just as normal for a teacher to "give" as for a pupil to "take" his first lesson; and if at this moment you are standing in the middle of the school, it is because experts have discovered in you the essential qualities which will make a good instructor.

The list of these qualities, apt to become impressive through sheer length, is headed by the innate love of teaching which will permit you constantly to perfect others. Next are the gifts of being
— a good horseman;

— methodical;

— clear in your explanations;

— patient;

— capable of judging a situation rapidly and finding instantly the required solution;

— a living example to your pupils.

One of these must be developed through experience: to judge a situation rapidly, one must learn to observe, and to be able to observe one must not talk a great deal. An instructor's role is not to spill out wholesale to his pupils all he knows, but to expose clearly what he expects of them and then to pass on to performance where he must see what is amiss and recognize the essential point where emphasis is due, discarding details to which he may return after the crucial idea has been thoroughly understood and performance has become satisfactory. One of France's great masters of equitation, General L'Hotte, has written of the need "to speak little but pertinently." Using a metaphor, one might say that an instructor must not only be a broadcaster but also a receiver and base his broadcasts on reception.

Your first aim is to capture your pupils' confidence. While this is not attained, everything remains to be done; for you can ask, but not demand, to be obeyed. For your lessons to be profitable, your pupils must derive satisfaction from carrying out what you request. Discipline is necessary in equitation; but outside of the army, where often the outward signs suffice to enforce it, you must gain ascendancy over your pupils through your own personality, a sort of obedience which is harder to attain but, freely granted, far more complete.

Of equitation it may be said—as Napoleon said of war—that it is "an art made up entirely of execution." To understand means to feel; so you must teach your pupils how to feel. You will choose the most suitable mount for each; for in the last analysis it is the horse who is the greatest of his teachers. You will not shy from striking their imagination through metaphors which keep their attention wide awake during lively and varied classes; for boredom is your worst enemy. If you have a sense of humor, use it within the limits of good taste, but keep a humorous dart from turning into a poisoned arrow. Above all, know how to laugh when the joke is on you.

The material side of your problem is of like importance. Where should you stand during a lesson? Wherever your presence is most useful. If, teaching a class of accomplished horsemen, you place yourself near a corner, you will practically never lose sight of them, except during the brief moments when they pass behind your back. This spot is not recommended, though, if, by yourself, you have beginners on the track; for they would not stay there long. Then your place is in the middle, where there is a device which will let you see everything at once. Do not let your eyes follow one pupil while you lose yourself in a long speech addressed to him. A brief remark will be better understood, will straighten out a critical situation and allow you, by a swift half-turn, to pass on to another. Without looking like a marionette, you can keep them all within nearly constant sight. A mirror is very helpful, if placed at the center of one of the long sides at a correct angle to let you see the riders as they pass behind your back. Facing it, you can, without changing place, supervise one long side, the two short sides and a part of the long side behind. Your place is also in the middle if the hall is very large, because everyone should be able to hear you easily from where you are, regardless of their stations.

I strongly advise you against engaging any assistants in conducting a class; the only help you may accept is from a head rider whose sole task is to draw the rest of the class along at the desired pace. I for my part have always managed alone and have never seen a class run smoothly where several teachers were counseling at once. What is true for the pupils is true for the horses. Some of my friends used to call upon an army of assistants when exercising a horse at liberty. The outcome was wont to be the opposite of what was intended, and I would venture to say that the negative result was in direct proportion to the number of assistants involved. If three people can move about a riding school so that each one's moves help and reinforce those of the two others, each one could surely put a horse through his paces without anyone's help. But we already have dealt with this subject in the chapter on dressage.

Should you conduct your class on horseback or on foot? Without a moment's hesitation I answer, on foot. Except for the instructor's additional fatigue, it has all the advantages, none of the inconveniences. If it should ever become necessary for you to ride during a class and one of your pupils "lends" you his horse, your demonstration will, at least psychologically, carry more weight, for it might otherwise occur to the pupils that whatever you are showing is far better than what they could do thanks to qualities of your horse absent in theirs. Falls occur, mainly during beginners' classes, a girth may have to be tightened, etc. If you are in the saddle, your horse will be more of an encumbrance than a help to you. If, on the other hand, you are holding a class for proficient horsemen, you will tend to busy yourself a little too much with your own affairs and not enough with theirs. Keep your horse for hacking and for jumping lessons in the outdoor ring.

One of a teacher's invaluable aids is the proper use of his voice. As the occasion requires, it should know how to command, to scold, to calm, to reassure, to stimulate and to reward. It should not be wasted, always be used knowingly. Do not give way to shouts, a proof of ill-breeding and a confession of weakness. Whoever is accustomed to commanding takes obedience for granted, does not worry about seeing it refused. Only the fear of disobedience requires shouting, with humans and horses alike.

If you make it a point to speak slowly and clearly, your pupils will understand you very well; and with a little practice you will quickly acquire a voice which carries. If the school is very large, take advantage of the moments of rest to group your riders around you for conversational advice and explanation. The same applies when explaining a new movement. To bring them within closer reacn of your voice, you may place them on a circle around you, in the center, or at one end of the school where, the circle tangent to three walls, guiding their horses is simplified. If they are beginners, you lessen the risk of disorder by making them close ranks on the track, halt, and then approaching them.

Standing in the middle, no school is too big for your commands of pace. change of direction or movement to be heard. If you want them carried out correctly, give them correctly; that is, prepare your riders for what they will be required to do by a preparatory clarifying command, followed two or three seconds later by the command proper. It is understood that for maximum precision the last syllable of the command prompts the movement. To sum up, a command consists of

— a preparatory command;
— an executory command.

For example, the class is at a walk and you want it to break into a sitting trot. Preparatory command: "Prepare for the sitting trot." Executory command: "Trot!" When making a half-volte, the riders remaining one behind the other in the same sequence, preparatory command: "Prepare for the half-volte consecutively." Executory command: "Half-volte!" If the same movement is to be performed by all riders simultaneously, each making an independent half-volte, the preparatory command is: "Prepare for the half-volte individually." The executory command "half-volte!"

A word about the lunging whip. Some say it does more harm than good and thus should be discarded; others cannot get along without it and use it profusely. The truth, as with everything else, lies between the two extremes. Discarding it completely, you are depriving yourself of an invaluable aid; to employ it wrongly or without rhyme or reason is disastrous. Unless you are familiar with its handling, though, I advise you not to use it on one particular horse; you only risk disorder or even falls, and your pupils will be well aware that all this has been caused by a blunder on your part. If one of your horses cuts his corners or walks on an inner track, show him the tip of the lunging whip from where you stand (that is, from the center of the school), at most take one step in his direction, no more, toward the haunches, not the shoulders. This gesture is a call to order addressing spirit rather than body. If insufficient, your horse must be retrained and ridden by you to be reminded of his duties, Normally, a circular motion performed while pivoting a full turn around yourself, the tip of the whip toward the ground, should be enough to make your horses understand that work has begun and that they must maintain the pace you set for them and stay on the track until further notice. Any cracking of the lash is outlawed. Obviously your horses have been trained to the lunging whip before their utilization in class.

Before now entering the school for your first lesson, let us quickly survey the problem: what is it all about? You are supposed to teach others what you already know; how should you go about it? Just as naturally as possible, from the simple toward the complex. Remember your own beginnings in equitation; your problems were the same as those with which your pupils presently will have to cope. How will the horses react? Largely the way they will feel you to be. Be calm, patient and gentle without weakness. If a moment of disorder occurs in the class, remain "orderly" and do not lose your head. A fully experienced teacher is not safe from such contingencies, and only his way of re-establishing order points up the difference between him and the neophyte. Finally, any time you want to speak, give a moment's thought to what you want to say and judge yourself if the remark is of the essence. If not, abstain. Even so, at the end of the hour you will still have talked too much.

Now, if you know your subject, enter self-assured and with an easy manner; and if you are able to put, along with your technical knowledge, a little of your heart into your classes, you will soon have won over pupils and horses and have reached your aim: to create, increase and maintain mutual understanding and trusting harmony among horses, pupils and instructor.

### The Walk in the First Lesson

So here you are in the middle of the school. If it is large, you will have your horses better in hand if, for the first few lessons, you reduce its length by setting up a barrier across.

If you do not want to lose control of your beginner's class in this first lesson, your pupils should not be more than a dozen. The horses are lined up in the center, held in hand by their prospective riders. Have one break rank and place him in left profile about 15 feet in front of the others. This way your explanations can be rendered clearly to all at once. Eventually mount for a demonstration of the movements making up your lesson. Use clear-cut, somewhat conspicuous aids so they can see your hand and leg action. Otherwise, not understanding a great deal, they will tend to believe that at least part of horsemanship rests on principles of witchcraft. Before sending them onto the track, correct each one's position, check all girths and the length of all stirrups. It is preferable to have a head rider draw the rest of the horses along for you, but not indispensable if you have a reliable old leader.

Your aim during the first lessons is essentially to give your pupils a sense of security by addressing yourself to their reason and accustoming their bodies to being on horseback.

Show them that they can easily manage their horses by simple and logical means. Constant practice will eventually make it normal and natural for them to sit in a saddle, to have a horse between their legs and reins in their hands; yet it is important to give them during the very first lesson a good position which will afford their awkward aids the maximum effectiveness you can expect. Its cornerstone is the head: carried high at all times, it allows the rest of the body to be correctly placed as well.

Your pupils will learn to press their horses forward from the halt by simultaneous action of both heels, to halt, and to turn them at a walk; above all not at the halt! Do not stifle the forward movement.

Having clearly explained in a few words how to use the heels to create forward movement and the role of the hands permitting it, send them onto the track. Have them walk straight ahead from the halt on the center line up to the track where they turn in the direction you indicate. To help this straight forward movement, place yourself behind the horses and increase the effect of their leg action by a few clicks of your tongue.

Once on the track, be content to ask them to press their horses forward at the walk and to make them stay on the track and ride out the corners. Do not plunge right away into great explanations; let them get used to their new situation. By a short, concise sentence correct particularly deficient positions, and relax a bit yourself.

Teach them from the beginning the right way to halt. It is far more complicated to teach beginners to raise their hands vertically, without pulling, than to close their fingers over the reins, keeping their wrists in a straight alignment with their forearms, elbows close to the body, and to resist in their shoulders. It must be impressed upon them that one does not halt by traction but by a wall-like opposition of hands and shoulders. If the word "resist" seems too technical, say, "straighten the upper body"; everyone will understand, and in so doing they will resist in their shoulders. Thus you will teach from the very start the shoulders' important part in equitation. Re-emphasize that a head carried high will immediately and greatly improve their position and facilitate the changes of direction.

As to the latter, be at first content with little, do not enter into the details of rein effects, not even of the opening rein. What matters is that your pupils, from the first lesson on, be able to halt, re-start at a walk and make a few easy changes of direction. At the end of the hour you will have demonstrated that they can communicate with their horses by simple means. Thus, to turn right, for example: "Look to the right, in the direction you want to go, shift both wrists in the same direction, to the right, and forward. Finally, use your legs to push your horses forward in this same direction." In a few clear words you give them the means to manage their horses, without losing yourself in long explanations doubtlessly comprising many a "but." Moreover, this system prevents them from pulling on the reins; and you thus prove to them that a horse obeys hand action without need for traction on his mouth. To employ a classic rein effect would be to ask them for proof of an independence of aids you cannot expect till several lessons later. So in the meantime you would be teaching them to do wrong; for asking their right hand to act in a right opening rein, their left would automatically act and counter the other.

You will avoid accidents during dismounting if at first you have your pupils drop both stirrups. Later, when they are a little more adroit, you may teach them the classic manner. Boys should be taught to vault into the saddle, and then into it and out in rapid succession without pausing on the ground.

## Suppling Exercises

This first class includes a few of the simplest suppling exercises. They are important and should be performed at every lesson for months on end. There being many, you can easily vary them in order to avoid monotony. It is up to you to prescribe to each according to his shortcomings those exercises he should practice specifically; without stirrups, never lasting too long, but well done. The principal ones are:

*Arm rotation.* Here the arms are rotated alternately, one after another. Make sure that the arms are stretched and vertical when up, in other words, that they describe a circle on one and the same plane. You may add *head rotation,* requiring the eyes to follow the hand.

*Shoulder rotation,* raising the shoulders, drawing them back while lowering them.

*Trunk rotation,* for suppling the loins. Arms stretched out horizontally, the rider twists alternately to left and right to look at the rider following him.

*Trunk flexion,* bending forward and back alternately, keeping the legs in place. While bending forward, the head is raised to maximum height to keep the rider from stooping, while bending backward his back should almost touch the croup, but not to the point of resting on the loins and croup; in this position the knees must not be raised. There is a variation of this: touching the horse's right point of the shoulder and left point of the buttock with the right hand, without the legs participating in the bust and arm movements.

*Raising of both thighs,* followed by *a sharp downward kick of the heels.*

*For placing the rider's seat* well forward in the saddle there is an efficient means which is to lean back from the waist up, one hand grasping the pommel, and to pedal toward the horse's ears. When legs and upper body resume their normal place, the seat must not be allowed to slip back toward the cantle.

*Stretching one arm out in front* horizontally, *with the foot* of the same side *touch the hand,* the arm remaining motionless. Doing the opposite, by a forward flexion of the upper body the left hand touches the left toe, the leg remaining at its normal place.

*Leg flexion,* raising the heels as high as possible without touching the horse, keeping thigh and knee in place. This exercise may be combined with the rotation of the arm of the same or opposite side.

*Foot rotation,* inside out and outside in.

Some of these exercises may be taken up again at the trot and at the canter. Those requiring a forward or sideward bend of the upper body must be done when the active side coincides with the inside of the school, so that in case of a fall the rider will not land between horse and wall. Each should be done four or five times, no more, but in such manner that an effort is supplied and a resistance overcome.

## The Progression

To determine an exact and precise purely theoretical progression would be to make a wager no riding master could win. The quality of his pupils, the frequency of their lessons, his own pedagogical gifts are as many equations to be solved separately and as a whole, each one in relation to the other. I am therefore suggesting a typical progression for medium pupils riding regularly two or three hours a week in a homogeneous class.

This progression is presented in the form of a table consisting of six periods. For clarity's sake I have made some arbitrary separations, though actually they are closely interrelated and, in practice, cannot be walled off from each other.

Our aim is to train, in two or three years, horsemen with a position and seat permitting them to perform creditably in minor horse shows, to give them the knowledge and constant practice of the elementary principles of classic equitation which will enable them to take part in simple dressage tests, and to develop in them the kind of dedicated enthusiasm which will let them enjoy the work involved in the perfecting of horsemanship.

The chapters subsequent to this progression table will deal only with the new subjects encountered, examined from the viewpoint of instruction, and this only in so far as they may present the instructor with difficulties of application during the lessons. The rest is dealt with from the viewpoint of elementary equitation in the third part of this book.

## *Progression Table**

### FIRST PERIOD

(Giving your pupil a sense of security)
— Position.
— The walk.
— The halt.
— Turning (only by shifting both wrists in the new direction).
— Holding the reins separately or jointly in a single hand.
— Introduction to the sitting and posting trot.
— Introduction to figure riding at a walk, consecutively (voltes and turns down the center line).
— Introduction to the canter.
— Introduction to figure riding at the sitting trot (add the half-volte and half-volte in reverse).
— Negotiating a pole placed on ground level at the sitting trot.
— At the end of this period start hacking (after 15 to 20 lessons).

### SECOND PERIOD

Once your pupil feels secure, your next step is to give him self-assurance. It is for you to judge if, for best results, you should assign major or minor importance to outdoor work. A teacher must not only attend to his pupil's physique, but also to his morale. Some, fine inside the school, turn into sorry horsemen outside, and vice versa.

— The holding of the four reins.
— Introduction to the opening and neck reins.

*While it is not hard to estimate the approximate number of lessons for the 1st period, it is impossible for the subsequent ones. The outdoor work is, of course, continued regularly during all, its frequency determined by the pupil's disposition.

— Breaking into the trot from the halt.
— Posting trot without stirrups.
— Improvement of the posting trot (how to recognize the diagonal one is posting on and how to change from one to the other).
— Introduction to the action of the single leg (shifting the haunches) = half-turn on the spot.
— Introduction to the action of the single leg (creating impulsion).
— Introduction to breaking into the canter from the sitting trot.
— Negotiating a foot-high pole in the center of the school (with and without stirrups).

## THIRD PERIOD

This period is given to improving whatever the pupil has learned. It is the ideal moment for increased outdoor work, whether in open country, passing logs and small ditches, or in the outdoor ring where, in the course of the class, a few fences may be taken. Accustom your pupils to saddling and bridling.

## FOURTH PERIOD

— Improving the three gaits.
— Figure riding at the sitting trot (consecutively and individually).
— Introduction to the three reins of opposition.
— Coordination of the aids.
— Half-turn on the forehand.

## FIFTH PERIOD

— Improving the rein effects.
— Increasing precision of movements.
— Introduction to the rein back.
— Introduction to starting into the canter on a predetermined lead on the center line.
— Introduction to rounding small obstacle courses.

## SIXTH PERIOD

— Improving what has been learned during the fifth period.
— Half-turn on the haunches.
— Striking off into the canter from the rein back.
— Schooling over the fences.

## The Posting Trot

At the first lesson of the posting trot, the movement should initially be performed at the walk. It will give your pupils a notion of what they will have to do once the horse breaks into the trot. Since it is, more than anything else, a question of rhythm, some will get the cadence very quickly, others will take longer, a very few will not, despite the best will on your part and theirs, be able to rise in the saddle. Several "devices" can remedy this situation. The first is to give them a horse of a somewhat harsh gait which better makes them feel the two beats of the trot and by the amplitude of the reaction aids them in rising. It may not work if the pupil does not hold up his loins properly which, as he touches down into the saddle, instead of allowing him to be lifted by the following shock by transmitting it to the entire upper body, absorbs it. Thus he remains in the hollow of the saddle. Such pupils are usually gifted for the sitting trot. To help the pupil rise, you may place a stirrup leather, like a collar, around his horse's neck by which his hands can draw him up. As soon as he has sensed the rhythm, this leather must be discarded, because it makes for a false position and should therefore be used as late as possible and discarded at the earliest possible moment.

## The Sitting Trot

When you demonstrate on horseback what is expected of your pupils at the sitting trot, do not hesitate to exaggerate the leaning back and the settling down of the loins; your first aim is to supple them sufficiently to absorb the shocks of the gait. As progress continues, you will become more exacting as to position, as to the straightness from the waist up. But if you demand too soon, albeit in the beginning, an impeccable position of the upper body, your pupils will contract the dorsal and lumbar muscles and bounce around in the saddle for lessons on end, without understanding what it is all about. They must be made to realize—that is, to feel—that by letting their loins play freely they can absorb these shocks from the beginning. It will automatically bring about a better seat and spare them the unpleasant feeling of constantly losing their balance and expecting a fall at any moment. So I prefer to see a pupil, at first at least, relaxed in the hollow of his saddle, letting his loins work correctly and holding on to the pommel, both reins in the other hand, rather than reins separated, hanging on to the horse's mouth, sitting on the cantle, legs sliding back.

The most important thing in learning is to grasp the essence of the problem; for time will do no more than develop and establish the movement, and no one ends up by doing things right through practicing them wrong, neither horse, nor rider. By "wrong" I mean, striking out in the wrong direction due to misconceptions, and not imperfect performance of a movement through mere lack of experience and training. In the first case, the more you advance, the farther you draw from your goal, the closer to it in the second.

When your pupils have become somewhat familiar with the sitting trot, you ask them to lean far back, holding on to the pommel, raising their spread knees, only balance and suppleness of loins keeping them in the saddle; a strenuous exercise which should, at first, be limited to just a few beats of the trot.

## The Canter

You face your most serious difficulties when first you want to teach the canter, for those of a psychological nature are now added to the purely technical. Actually, most beginners believe this gait, being the swiftest, to be the most difficult.

Though you certainly can make a pupil canter during his very first lesson, on the lunging rein, with a horse which smoothly takes and holds this gait, to make a whole class of beginners canter at their second or third lesson is out of the question. Before coping with this new difficulty, they must have a measure of control over their horses and perform the posting and sitting trot easily, if not correctly.

Besides, you run up against the problem of those who "do not want to." You may insist on their cantering, or you may wait two or three lessons. If you do send them onto the track for a canter, you must be sure that they are capable of it and that all will go smoothly. For, should you fail, restoring confidence would call for a much longer waiting period and make your subsequent task a great deal more delicate.

However, certain pupils are like invalids who only want to be reassured. They would like to try, but they do not trust themselves and believe that they "cannot." If you do not insist, you confirm them in their belief; the longer you wait, the harder it will become, because they will gradually lose the little self-assurance which they possessed to start with.

So it is for you to choose the right moment for the first cantering lesson. There is a last resort for nearly hopeless cases, the lunging rein. At the end of the class, retain the pupil who "does not want to" or who "cannot," and by a few turns around at a canter on the lunging rein rid him of his complex.

There are two methods you may follow when giving your first cantering lesson, each with its pros and cons:
— all riders canter simultaneously;
— each rider canters individually.

In the first case, your difficulty lies in making all horses strike off at once; your advantage, in letting them canter long enough to give your pupils a chance to settle down to the pace, the horses cadencing themselves while you have time to make your comments, without all kinds of fits and starts.

In the second case, the only advantage is yours, at least when dealing with beginners, for you only have to worry about one horse at a time. You make your riders close ranks. At your command, the first alone strikes off, canters up to the back of the file, and so forth. You may keep your class at a walk or at a trot. The drawback is that the individual canter does not last long enough for the pupil to sense the cadence of this gait, so he retains in his memory nothing but a less than smooth departure and the transition from canter to trot which can hardly be called pleasant. Besides, working this way, horse No. 2 often feels like following when the one in front of him canters off and, when his turn finally comes, may anticipate your command, single-mindedly bent on catching up with the group as fast as he can, scaring his rider, who feels the horse out of his control as well as yours, out of his wits. This difficulty should be saved for later when your beginners have progressed to where they can impose their will upon their mounts.

Two points require your attention:
— Avoid giving a beginner a horse who does not canter on the true lead of his own accord. There is no sense in further complicating the lessons for the pupil. Just try, yourself, to canter a riding school horse on the outside lead and see how comfortable it is, chiefly while passing the corners. The false canter stems from a lack of suppleness and has nothing to do with the countercanter of a well schooled horse for whom this exercise is proof of suppleness and balance.
— Your pupils must, from the first, canter on both hands. Some have a marked preference which must be fought from the beginning.

One last word of advice. You had better not let one or several unwilling pupils come to the center of the school while the others are cantering. In the first place, you will be encumbered by the closeness of their horses; secondly, there will always be one or two smarties among your animals who leave the track to come and take a rest beside their friends in the middle. The consequent disorder can easily be avoided if—with some of your beginners willing and able—you wait till near the end of the hour and then send the horses which are not to canter back to the stables. This way you are skirting the difficulty, because all your horses are on the track. Though once you acquire the knack you will take such troubles very lightly, for the moment it is better to be on the safe side.

The position of the rider on the course. The horse is at the left canter, at the end of the second beat (off diagonal on the ground). The near fore is already on the ground, which, when bearing down fully, will constitute the third beat. (Photo Michel Alexis)

## The Departures at the Canter

When your pupils begin to start their horses into the canter by their own aids, teach them first the academic way which applies the lateral inside aids. Let them acquire considerably more experience and be imbued with the importance of keeping their horses straight before you teach them to use the diagonal aids which will enable them to ride with perfect ease imperfectly trained horses. For the moment they cannot graduate hand and leg action correctly, and you would see horses completely traversed having trouble breaking into a canter, while everything would have gone smoothly with the lateral aids.

You will, however, by and by explain to them that a horse learns to strike off on a predetermined lead at first at the demand of the lateral outside aids; that, to strike off on the near fore, one uses the right rein and leg, the former to restrain the off lateral, the latter to keep the haunches in place and to aid the engagement of the off hind which will lead off the first stride.

This method tends to traverse the animal and draw his muzzle to the right, while it should be to the left; but it is the most readily accessible to the natural understanding of the green horse.

As soon as he strikes off easily into the canter at the prompting of the outside leg, one proceeds to start him by the diagonal aids which should only be a transitory means en route to the departure by the lateral inside aids. In order to pass from the lateral outside to the diagonal aids, one decreases the intensity of the effect of the right rein and slightly tightens the left, to draw the muzzle to the left to assure correct placing. This achieved, one gradually replaces action of the right heel with that of the left acting at the girth. Thus the right heel, the action of which had at first determined the departure at the canter, at present plays but the passive part of warning the horse that he will be asked for a departure on the near lead. The left heel now determines the striking off into the canter.

Progressively one reduces the role of the right heel, till the moment when the horse strikes off on a predetermined lead at the prompting of the inside leg alone. None but this way of striking off allows the horse to remain straight.

I am passing on to you this simply phrased explanation because, in conjunction with demonstration and practice, it has usually clarified the process for my pupils.

## Beginners and Tack

Riders ought to learn as soon as possible to manage four reins, and yet their hands are awkward and should not be entrusted prematurely with a double bridle. You can spare the horse's mouth and yet have the rider cope with the four leathers by placing a second rein on the snaffle bit, the upper rein standing for the snaffle, the lower for the curb, rein. Accustom them to shifting the four reins from hand to hand, to separating them, and so forth. Later, when you feel they can handle a curb bit, show them a full bridle in the tack room and explain its workings.

For several lessons running let them personally adjust the curb chain and the throat latch before mounting. Eventually they should be taught to saddle and bridle correctly and to take care of their horses. Have at first one pupil practice at a time, so you can watch him and avoid accidents. But the average rider with two or three years of experience should be able to take part in tours of several days' duration in which, under the supervision of an instructor, each one is taking care of his own mount.

## *Hacking*

Your classes should be as homogeneous as possible and their progression based on the weakest member. However, as, one by one, the participants acquire a little form, they should ride outdoors, for that is where they have a chance to gain the characteristic "mettle" of the horseman.

For those first rides, gather as many proficient riders as beginners; it will make your group considerably safer. Maintain regular paces which give horses and riders a sense of order and discipline. Trot at a free and sustained pace and canter at first for only short stretches and not too fast, unless you want to see one of your horses overtake you with several others in hot pursuit. Once this happens, you are defenseless, with but one course of action: to stop, in the hope that the runaways, realizing they have lost their stable mates, will also stop and wait for them, grazing a little farther on, friendship winning out over the charms of the stable. But the harm is done and there is nothing you can do about the rest; whereas knowing how to organize your ride, assign the horses, and regulate the pace is up to you and only you.

For just about the same reasons, do not by any means permit stragglers. Your horses should be grouped as closely as safety rules against kicking allow. When most of your company is composed of beginners or semi-beginners, you had better place them in single file and urge them to keep their horses' noses behind the croups of those before them. This will prevent the dangerous overtaking during canters. A pupil's horse is less liable to bolt if the horizon before him presents a croup rather than a straight, unobstructed bridle path. Also, placed this way during walks, your pupils cannot become engrossed in conversations which, with their lack of experience, would keep them from noticing that their neighbor's horse is teasing theirs and that a kick is in the making.

As soon as they acquire the necessary skill, you should organize rides in the open country. I know that nowadays it is not easy to find, close to big cities, woods appropriate for this kind of sport; but if you look around, you may find, if not the ideal spot, one which will familiarize your pupils with small declivities to scale and to descend, logs, and small natural ditches with and without water.

Rides along bridle paths and across country should not be considered a distraction useless for training. Though working and learning take place in the school, performance in the open is of equal importance. You can train neither horse, nor rider by shutting them up forever between four walls. Aside from the purely material aspect, there is a question of psychology. A pupil too long accustomed to the school may be bewildered by the livelier action outside and liable to lose confidence; while others, stiff and self-conscious in the riding hall, are able to relax and forget themselves outside. It is for you, their instructor, to judge and to know how to dose the outside work for each according to his shortcomings and disposition.

## *Jumping*

With the coming of self-assurance and the gradual disappearance of stiffness, there come the first jumping lessons. Just at first, a pole placed on ground level and cleared at a trot without stirrups is enough. Very soon you combine this with suppling exercises; the pole—formerly placed on the track and passed in a group—now placed on ground level in the center of the school and taken individually in a combined suppling and management exercise.

Do not teach your pupils too soon to lean forward and rise in the saddle. When the time comes, the rider's position over the jump will be easily explained, while it is most important and takes more learning to lead one's horse to the obstacle with the necessary impulsion, cramping him as little as possible, and with the maximum efficiency of aids for which they must be well seated in the saddle.

Make them understand that on a course the moment of the jump is something very fleeting where the rider can do but one thing, go with his horse; while between jumps he can and must take care of impulsion, rate of speed, balance, direction and the best place for the take-off, and that therefore it is not by staying frozen in the same position, no matter how perfect, from one end of the course to the other that he is most efficient.

When the pole on ground level in the middle of the school has been cleared without stirrups at a trot and at a canter, you repeat the exercise over a 60 to 90 cm bar. Then you have them take their stirrups and show them how to lean slightly forward and rise in their stirrups at the moment of the jump. Teach them from the start to press their mounts forward with their legs up to the last stride before the jump. Unless the horses bore at the obstacle, they may let go of the reins, either at your command or at the moment of the jump, which is extremely useful for acquiring the reflex to relax the fingers rather than clutch the reins. Another good exercise is to set up in the center of the school a pole with a guard-rail on each side (generally known as an "A-Bar," because in profile it forms an A), careful to place the pole so it drops out easily in both directions. You have the rider describe a figure eight for an oblique approach to the jump requiring greater precision of management. This, by the way, is even for the skilled rider a device for a perfect take-off without having to alter the horse's strides. To the extent he opens or closes the angle of the jump in relation to the direction followed by the horse, he shortens or lengthens the distance between himself and the jump and prepares the change of direction required afterward.

True jumping lessons, however, must wait till your pupils have a good seat, good pliancy, and the gymnastics of jumping have become familiar to them. Then they may round courses designed, more than anything else, as exercises in management. Far better to teach them to control their horses' pace and changes of direction in jumping 60 cm, or less, than to make them jump 1.20 m, or more, on a course which only puts to the test the horses' abilities, requiring of themselves little but to follow haphazardly their mounts.

A word about the tack is necessary here. Even though the pupil is by now familiar with the handling of the curb bit, the horse should be bitted with a simple snaffle in addition to a running martingale and a noseband. I know that, in a reaction to past abuse, it is the currently adopted policy of many national federations to ban any kind of special rein devices. But (as I was saying with respect to the lunging whip) why deprive ourselves of a valuable aid? Some purists claim that he who rides in shows should be horseman enough to ride with a plain double bridle or even snaffle only, without recourse to any other gear. Horsemanship is difficult enough without willfully making it more so. There appears in this book a photograph of Col. Danloux, taken when he was Chief Equerry of the Cadre Noir, riding his show jumper bitted with a snaffle (a double snaffle, I do believe), plus running martingale. This picture has been chosen from among dozens to illustrate the "Danloux positon". I feel, as many other horsemen do, that the running martingale and a well-adjusted noseband are the natural complements of the snaffle.

Although we shall more appropriately return to the matter of tack in the part dealing with hippology, I want to give you an example of the merits of the running martingale as concerns the subject at hand. A horse show, where French riders competed against German, included an event reserved for juniors up to sixteen years of age. One of our horses, although a free jumper, had two annoying faults: a troublesome tendency to evade the bit and to bore at the obstacle.

I entrusted him to a boy of fourteen entering his first competition and who finished second among fifteen after rounding a course where the horse had not once evaded the bit or seemed the least unmanageable. In the afternoon, a young lieutenant rode the same animal over an almost identical course on the same grounds, without the running martingale. At mid-course, the horse, having knocked down two or three jumps, ran out at a tangent and was eliminated. The experiment was conclusive.

When ridden by beginners, horses tend either to refuse almost constantly, or else to bore at the obstacle. Why? I think, probably because of their riders' "freewheeling" style of going. In teaching them to use their hands and legs, I apply a progression with a time-table which depends on the quality and work of each pupil; for never should a greater difficulty be taken up before the preceding one is overcome.

I have about ten well-spaced 60 cm jumps set up in the outdoor school, sometimes an 80 cm triple bar; at first at least no two consecutive jumps in straight alignment, which prevents the riders themselves from "boring at the obstacle."

I make them jump each fence by itself and interrupt this work by some walking and trotting. Then they jump them all in a row, though checking to a walk after each. Once this is done calmly and smoothly, they check to a trot instead of a walk and eventually round the entire course at a canter, though slowing down after each jump.

This exercise teaches your pupils to control their mounts and shows them from the beginning that they need not canter for speed if they rein their horses in after each jump and so avoid great curves in turning, that this way they gain time by not losing any. It also teaches them to use their legs; for checking their horses to a walk after each jump, they must restart them every time into a canter and press them toward the next. It also keeps you from shaping riders who round an obstacle course as if running a hurdle race and to whom whatever lies between the starting and finishing lines are but incidental problems to be surmounted or muddled through, as the case may be.

With their horses at a walk between two jumps, they settle back into the hollow of their saddles; and early in the game you make them practice meaningful "intervention" without great harm to their horses' mouths and by and by permit them to acquire good reflexes. Take them always, the same as your horses, "from simple to complex."

From the first lesson on insist on one capital point, the position of the head. Teach them to look at the obstacle they are about to jump and to aim at its middle. As soon as their horses are placed in the right direction, have them look at the next, and so forth. Do not permit them to turn around to see whether they have committed a "fault." A horseman looks straight ahead; what has happened has happened and has lost all importance, since it cannot be helped, while whatever lies ahead must be well done.

For these jumping lessons give preference to horses with natural impulsion, keen at the jump, even if a little too much so, over excessively calm horses who only seek a pretext to refuse or run out. With the latter you teach your pupils nothing, are liable to disgust them and, moreover, encourage your horses in their disobedience. Keep them, if they jump at all, for more seasoned riders.

### The Half-Turn on the Forehand
### (or Half-Pirouette in Reverse)

Before you broach the subject of the half-turn on the forehand you should teach your pupils to turn their horses by means of their legs. Their hands will surely help them at first, but the progression is as follows:

When you have reached the subject of the opening rein, teach them to use the leg on the same side, so that their horses turn by both ends, and there and then explain the coordination of the aids. It is the easiest example to understand and carry out. To make things even easier for them and maintain the impulsion, have them perform these half-turns at a walk. Track to the left, about 15 feet from each other, direct them to keep their horses at a walk while they perform a half left turn by left opening rein and left leg, and to return to the track.

By the time this exercise is performed with ease and leg action is becoming more efficient, you pass on to the second stage which you reach very naturally once you begin figure riding. Have them perform an individual half-volte in reverse, far enough apart not to interfere with each other. Subsequently ask them to make their legs act at the end of the half-volte in order to place the hindquarters on the track. The role of the hands in this maneuver is essentially passive, its sole aim to keep the neck strictly straight. Progressively advance the moment of leg action, till they describe the half-volte in reverse by shifting the haunches.

As they progress, the shortening of the walk becomes even more marked, so as to allow for greater amplitude in the crossing of the hind legs. It is, moreover, a splendid way to make them understand that in shifting the haunches the leg must not perform continuously but by successive actions which make themselves felt when the horse starts to lift the hind leg on the side of the acting leg. To help them get to "feel" this moment, you watch one rider and say to him, "leg . . . leg . . . leg . . . ."every time it is supposed to intervene. You take on the next, and so on. It is a striking example in emphasizing the importance of timing. Actually, regardless of the intensity given to the leg, its effectiveness would be null if it were used while the corresponding foot is firmly on the ground. Moreover, during this exercise the rider perceives most easily in his seat the play of the hind legs, learns to generally feel what is going on under him, *i.e.*, develops the tact of his seat.

Though in performing the half-volte in reverse haunches-out the leg indubitably constitutes the active aid, the hands, passive aid, have their part to play. Aside from the slowdown they demand to allow the hind legs to cross, they limit the shifting of the forehand and cause a correct placing of the head.

For example, track to the left, you command a half-volte in reverse. As the horses are starting in on the half circle, the hands request, without altering the cadence, a shortening of the walk. By a counter-rein of opposition in front of the withers the left hand limits and regulates as convenient the shift of the shoulders to the left and gives the correct placing to the left; because the head should indeed be flexed in the direction of the shift of the hind quarters. The right hand drives the shoulders to the left by a neck rein and limits the action of the left which determines the placing. Thereby the neck is kept straight. The left leg at the girth maintains the forward movement. The rider's weight is accented to the left.

In no case and at no moment of this maneuver must the haunches be in advance of the shoulders. The roles of hands and legs depend on the horse in question. If his hindquarters are active and his forehand sluggish, the right leg action and the left rein effect must be light, while the right rein must be of maximum effectiveness in pushing the shoulders to the left. In the opposite case, the actions of the right hand are attenuated and those of the right leg and left hand increased.

The same aids are used in the half right turn on the forehand, except that the right hand need not push the shoulders to the left, the off fore serving as a pivot. The action of the left hand is lighter and the counter-rein of opposition is replaced by enough of a neck rein to determine the placing and to prevent the forehand from shifting to the left. The leg action is the same. The seat is weighted to the left. For this movement to be well done, the foot serving as a pivot (in our example, the off fore) must be raised at each step and touch down again on the same spot, and the off hind must clearly cross in front of the near. These two conditions imply that during the entire half-turn the horse is in the forward movement. To safeguard this, any halt should be avoided before the half-turn on the forehand which should be linked to the preceding movement and the following.

## The Half-Turn on the Haunches
### (or Half-Pirouette)

Like the half-turn on the forehand, the half-turn on the haunches (also called the half-pirouette) is a movement which must be preceded by a progression which prepares horse or rider to carry it out. Your pupils will not cope with this difficulty before they have become familiar with the half-turn on the forehand and their tact has developed a little further.

Track to the left, command a half left turn at a walk, without the left leg, by means of the hands alone; that is, by the right neck rein. Once this exercise is performed with ease, explain that, before the neck rein acts, they must shorten the walk by resisting in their shoulders. Then talk to them of the outside leg (in this case, the right) which must resist in order to prevent the hindquarters from shifting to the right. This way you arrive progressively at the half-turn on the haunches at a walk.

The right counter-rein takes effect at the moment the off fore is raised, its action similar to that of the single leg in the half-turn on the forehand. Help your pupils use it with good timing, as you did for the action of the single leg in the half-pirouette in reverse.

Thus the time will have come for the half-volte haunches-in. For example, track to the left, ask for a half-volte. The hands slow down the walk. In order to start the half circle, left hand action to determine the placing and right neck rein to set the forehand on the curve. Right single leg, so as to maintain the hindquarters on an inner circle parallel to that on which the forehand travels. The left leg at the girth maintains the impulsion. The seat is weighted to the left. The right leg should not intervene too strongly lest it cause too pronounced an inclination.

In this exercise, the principal role falls to the hands. The horse's forehand is constanly swung gently from hand to hand, the right determining the leftward movement, the other regulating and controlling the shift of the forehand.

In a half-pirouette well done, the horse must be balanced and the rider have a sense of this balance. The inside hind which serves as a pivot must be raised at each step and touch down on the same spot. If, on the one side, the horse leans the least bit on the forehand, his haunches will shift; if, on the other, the hand action is too strong, he will back or his energies will flow backward. Hence you had better wait a while before you require your pupils to perform this movement.

### The Rein Back

Wait even longer before you demand the rein back, and then not of everybody at once on the track. Call your class, one by one, to the middle of the school there to rein back one or two steps. Keep the halt separating forward and retrograde movement down to a minimum and require the forward movement to follow immediately upon the end of the rein back. Put your horses back into the forward movement after these lessons by a few departures at the canter; have your riders restart on the track and command the canter—a few extensions and a few slowdowns. When the horses maintain good contact on a taut rein, command the walk and the halt, a half-turn on the haunches and a strike-off into the canter. Repeat this two or three times on each hand. At the second strike-off your horses will "bound" forward. For maximum effectiveness, the canters should be brief.

My method of teaching the rein back proper is to shorten the walk by alternate hand action (finger pressure on the reins). Through continued action of this kind the horse comes to a halt and begins to back; as soon as two retrograde steps have been accomplished, hand action ceases and the horse is once more pressed forward. Done this way, there is not really a moment's halt between the forward and retrograde motions.

I advise against teaching the rein back by means of the legs. This manner—which incites to the retrograde movement by pressing the horse forward through leg action and making him run up against a wall-like resistance of the hands—has at least one great drawback; it uses identical means to demand a movement opposite to the forward. Later maybe, but not yet. Moreover, you run the risk of confusing your horses. Leave for the moment to the legs their sole task of creating the forward movement when acting simultaneously, which by itself is quite a job.

## Conclusion

The advice I have given you is no more than a marker here, a marker there along the road of a progression that you will have to establish yourself, taking your inspiration from the great principles of classic equitation. I have briefly touched on points which, being secondary, might otherwise have remained in the shadows , have dwelt on others at some length because, being truisms, they tend to be overlooked. Nothing in either instruction or equitation can take the place of timing, a faculty no one can help you develop, gradually refined by your own growing experience.

Successful teaching requires good teaching aids. Horses are  yours, and if one day you should have to buy them, be clear in your mind as to their purpose. A good riding school horse is harder to find than you may think. In addition to the qualities inherent in his conformation, he must be very gentle; well-bred, without the slightest trace of nervousness (do not confuse a well-bred, with a hot, horse); naturally well balanced and of a forth-right disposition. It then is up to you to develop these qualities through train-ing, to ride the horse regularly, if, as an instrument for instruction, you want to keep him in the groove or, if need be, return him to it. If your pupils are to progress, your horses must be more knowledgeable than they.

Prepare the progression for your lessons carefully, not rigidly. As useful as it may be to determine the stages through which you want to take your pupils, so that your lessons link up within a logical framework, do not set yourself a deadline for a certain goal. With some pupils it will take longer than with others; so build each lesson mainly on the preceding one.

Let me now draw your particular attention to a point of great importance. Do not attempt to turn each pupil into your alter ego. You do not "break" but train your horses; just so you must leave to each pupil his personality. Everyone does not have the same qualities or faults; try to develop the former to a maximum and to attenuate as much as possible the latter, without over-stepping the framework of classic equitation. Just as one may say that two people resemble each other without having identical features, you may say that a group of pupils bears the mark of their teacher without therefore having to ape him. I often remember my teacher's answer, "ride him as you feel him," to my questions of how I should act on horses I was riding for the first time. In a few concise, imaginative words he made his comments after the maneu-ver, without having to enter into details, because his remarks were clear and made you "feel" what should be done and not be done. To make your pupils "feel" is the key to the teaching problem.

Also remember, however, that you must be a living example. Not every instructor can be expected to be a champion; but your pupils, beginners and proficient riders alike, must want to learn to ride like you—in the school, over the fences, in the park, or across country. When you explain a movement, do not hesitate to demonstrate it on horseback; even if to do so you must ask a pupil to dismount. A live example is worth more than any amount of explana-tions; and you must be able to say with self-assurance: "Look at me, do as I do."

True self-confidence can only come from mastery of one's subject, which in your case happens to be the practice and pedagogy of equitation. This self-assurance will then bring with it a natural authority which never swag-gers, never sneers and gives your actions a calm which, a positive force, never appears solemn or jaded. Thus your own confidence, translated into au-thority and from authority into calm, will communicate itself to your horses and your pupils.

# III. Equitation

## Note

The following pages treat the subject of equitation in accordance with the possibilities of the pupil whom we are taking up in his beginnings, much as we did the colt, to make him pass through the different stages of the first three years. Therefore I have purposely discarded all but the essentials, giving, however, some details which are constantly mentioned in the ring, yet hardly ever written down. My double aim is for the pupil to read and reread the advice he receives verbally in the school and for the instructor to acquire a better technique in conveying his meaning. Therefore this third part ought to be as useful to the teacher as Dressage and Instruction to the learner whom they help, I hope, to understand the underlying logic of the instruction he receives.

Each point you found in the *Progression,* with the notable exception of *Jumping,* is discussed as a unit; that is, from first mention all the way through the *Sixth Period.*

God forbid that I should go to any heaven in which there are no horses. . . .
—Robert Bontine Cunninghame-Graham in a letter to Theodore Roosevelt in
1917.

## Introduction

Horsemanship offers us in its variety a wider choice than any other sport.
Yet it is "one," despite all this diversity, and based in all its parts on a close
entente between horse and rider. The mutual trust and comprehension from
which it springs must be constantly perfected, regardless of the type of
equitation practiced. The winning of one's horse should not be difficult, because instinctively and with a capacity for attachment he seeks the company
of man and takes an interest in what we do with him. Frequently polo ponies
follow the ball and play the game themselves; many a show jumper's satisfaction during the ceremony of awards is evident, if only to his rider. Equally
able to convey his meaning in the negative, he will at times return to the paddock with brilliant action, full of life, after refusing, seemingly sapless,
three times at the same jump. History, not only literature, bears witness to the
initiative of horses who helped their riders out of tight spots and sometimes
earned their almost brotherly friendship. Depending on their gifts, horse
and rider can reach a higher or lesser level of rapport and performance, some
reaching the point of equitation as an art which, like all others, is infinitely
perfectible.

All stages along this road have their own joys, none ever growing stale;
"for nature will never disclose all her secrets to us, and the horse will forever
have in store for us novelties, surprises, springing from life itself." (Gen.
L'Hotte, *Questions Equestres.*)

Your teacher will help you to communicate with your horse by instructing
you in the use of your hands and legs which are your means of expression.
Your practice, combined with his advice, will improve your seat and pliancy
which, in turn, will let you feel and, feeling, understand your horse. If you
are gifted, you will eventually use your aids with good measure and tim-

ing; and they will convey to you the slightest of your mount's reactions. This is then, in terms of equitation, "the equestrian tact."

Equestrian tact is the hallmark of the artist, from which it does not follow that horsemanship is closed to others. Since a century ago it was as usual and normal to ride a horse as nowadays it is to drive a car, you should not let the mistaken idea discourage you that sound equitation is a sport for a minority. It would deprive you of a pleasure, a pastime, a sport, which can afford you the greatest of joys.

Let us here study together the rudiments of classic equitation, which do not require any particular disposition on your part, provided you like horses and show a little good will. The other qualities will be given you by practice and Saint George.

## The First Lessons

This may be the first time you have ever ridden, perhaps the first time you have held a horse. You are standing at his near side*, the two reins separated by your right index finger, held at about six inches from his mouth. You are speaking to him gently and pat his neck before mounting.

## MOUNTING

Still and always at his near side, you shift both reins to the left hand, the right rein somewhat shortened to draw your horse's nose to the right. Facing the croup, you place your left hand, which holds the reins, on the crest and your right hand helps your left foot place itself all the way into the stirrup. Standing as close as possible to the horse, you place your right hand on the cantle and, bearing down on the stirrup, rise lightly, bending forward from the waist. Do not let your left toe touch the horse's side.

While your right leg is sliding over the croup, you place the right hand on the pommel and then touch down into the saddle just as gently as you can and finally place your right foot into the stirrup and separate your reins. That is, you take one into each hand so it will pass under your small finger and come back out between index and thumb, the latter holding it flattened against the index. The fingernails of both hands face each other, the wrists about eight inches apart. If your horse walks out, just close your fingers over your taut reins and straighten up. You will be surprised how well this single gesture will check him.

---

*Near = left; off = right.

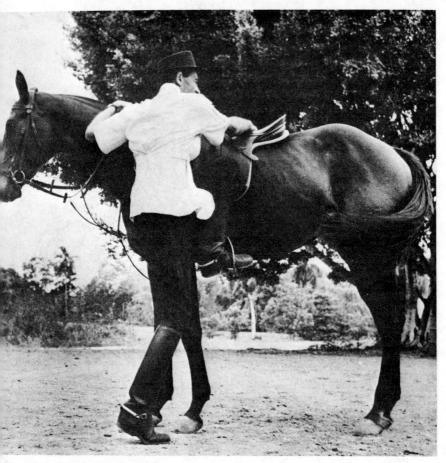

**Mounting. First movement: horse at a straight halt, the right rein held slightly tighter than the left. (Photo Michel Alexis)**

## THE RIDER'S POSITION ON HORSEBACK

For maximum comfort with maximum effectiveness of hands and legs and without loss of elegance, there exists a basic position from which one cannot deviate without infringing on comfort, effectiveness, elegance, or all. You should be seated

— plumb, your weight equally distributed on both buttocks which are pushed forward to a maximum;

— the flats of the thighs turned in, the backs of the knees in pliant contact, the legs stretched naturally downward;

**The position of the rider on horseback.**
**Above: wrong.**        **Below: right.**
**(After a sketch by Major Licart.)**

**Mounting. Second movement: the reins are tightened by a simple twist of the left wrist. (Photo Michel Alexis)**

— the stirrups placed under the balls of your feet will permit you to keep your heels down;
— the loins supple but held up;
— the upper body erect but at ease;
— the shoulders drawn back and down in an even line;
— the head straight and clear of the shoulders;
— the arms dropping naturally, elbows bent and close to the body, wrists held up in straight alignment with the forearms, that is, about four inches above the withers, thumbs up, fingernails facing.

In sum, your shoulders, hips and heels should be on one and the same perpendicular. This way your position is good; the difficulty will lie in holding it when your horse begins to move; and it will take you months of practice, or even longer, to do so with ease at the different gaits.

## YOUR MEANS OF COMMUNICATION WITH YOUR HORSE

Your means of communication with your horse are the hands and the legs.

*The role of the legs is to create the forward movement* when acting at their normal place (slightly behind the girth) simultaneously by taps, reinforced if necessary by the heels which—toes turned out so the heels approach the horse perpendicularly—act by light attacks. Do not make them brush backward.

*The role of the hands* is twofold: *to shorten the pace and to halt; to control the direction.* To shorten the pace and to halt, your hands act by finger pressure on the reins. To change direction, both hands shift in the newly chosen direction.

For the horse to perceive and understand the indications of your hands, your reins must be taut and even. They are taut when your hands, being at their place, feel the contact of the mouth, even when taut, your hands being at their place, the neck is strictly straight, adjusted when taut and even. This is a *conditio sine qua non* while you work. During the moments of rest, the fingers relax and, at the horse's request, give him the reins.

In sum, the legs demand the forward movement, the hands shorten the pace and halt, or else direct. The obvious conclusion is that you must *never oppose your hands* (brakes) *to your legs.* When your legs request the forward movement, your hands must "open the door" to allow the horse to move forward. When your hands request a shortening of pace or halt, your legs must cease to act.

Your hands and legs will, however, act concurrently when the former request a change of direction, when they do not command, but only indicate the new direction to be taken, and the legs, pressing the horse forward in this direction, permit this to be carried out.

Whenever you make your legs act, require your horse to move straight ahead up to the track; there, look to the left, shift both wrists leftward and forward in order to turn left. Do not look at your hands, but far ahead in the direction you want to take. Carrying your head aloft facilitates management, allows for a correct overall position, and lets your hands do their work a great deal better.

AT A WALK on the track now, you must pay attention to three points:
— to keep a constant distance of about six feet between yourself and the horse in front of you;
— to press your own horse forward;
— to watch your position.

The safety factor in the first point is obvious. As to the second point, you

**The position of the rider on horseback. Col. Margot, ex-Equerry in Chief, Cadre Noir, Saumur. (Photo Blanchaud)**

press your horse forward by alternate leg action; and if you are not tense, you will clearly perceive a slight lateral swinging under your seat. Your legs are alternately shifted to right and left. For a few seconds keep your legs still to let them sense this slight lateral shift, and then put to use the shift to the right to increase the pressure of the left calf, without letting the right intervene which, in turn, will act when you feel the shift to the left while the left remains passive, and so forth. If, too tense, you cannot manage to feel and grasp this moment during your first lesson, you will most certainly during the second or third; just remember to try.

As concerns the third point, your position, it is, at least at a walk, less difficult to hold than you would think, far more natural than it would appear from its dry and arid definition, and very close to that of a person seated at table, at least as concerns the upper body and the arms. Sit comfortably and naturally, not just poised on the seat bones. As at table, do not slump, sit erect, without seeming to have swallowed a stick. Do not stiffen the loins, hold them up, and remember the very British saying that a gentleman keeps his elbows close to his body at table, in conversation and on horseback.

## EXTENDING AND SHORTENING THE PACE

To extend the pace slightly relax the lower fingers (fourth and fifth) and increase the force and rate of leg action. To shorten the pace, cease leg action and increase rein tension by alternate pressures of the fingers. Exert pressure with the fingers of one hand without letting those of the other act, then slightly relax those which have just acted and exert pressure with the others as if you wanted to squeeze the juice from a lemon in each hand alternately. Each increase and decrease of pressure lasts but a split second. This simple hand action suffices to obtain the shortening of the pace, provided you keep your elbows close to the body and your shoulders drawn back. When the desired slowdown is attained, cease hand action but keep your reins a little tauter than before and make your legs act anew.

## HALTING

To halt obtain first of all a shortening of the pace, then close the fingers of both hands at once over the reins. *Keep your elbows close to the body,* shoulders resisting. Once the halt is obtained, cease the hand action which has prompted it, your lower fingers relaxing very slightly, reins kept taut.

Three points should be borne in mind:
— the preparation of the horse for execution of the requested movement;
— the important role played by the shoulders;
— to yield when the horse yields.

## THE PREPARATION OF THE HORSE

An animal with a will of his own, susceptible to distraction, the horse must be kept attentive to what he is supposed to do during work. Such attention cannot be expected over exceedingly long periods of time, and therefore working sessions must be interrupted by rest periods in which body and mind may relax. Even when attentive to his rider's orders, he cannot perform a new movement instantaneously without preparation. Humans are no different; in accordance with their intellectual level, they are capable of more or less sustained attention; but the saturation point will forcibly be reached sometime. Neither can they react properly without a minimum of preparation. Imagine a person having to perform a variety of movements on orders conveyed by gestures, without warning, some of them subject to confusion by their great mutual resemblance and by the additional fact that they are made by someone who is still learning and cannot yet carry them out correctly. Whatever performance, if any, might follow these signals would be jerky. This is the very result we want to avoid, seeking, as we do, effectiveness in order and harmony.

This explains the warning (preparatory command) your instructor gives you before each executory command, so as not to surprise you and give you time to warn your horse. The more knowledgeable a team of horse and rider, the shorter grows the time of preparation and the more discreet, even imperceptible, the rider's action, to the point where the impression is gained that, in the words of General L'Hotte, "the horse moves under its rider as if of its own accord."

## THE ROLE OF THE SHOULDERS

If you want to be in a correct and hence efficient position, your elbows must be kept close to the body and your wrists in straight alignment with your forearms, so that the tension of the reins can only be altered by the action of your lower fingers. If you want to add force to this action, have recourse to your shoulders which may choose to "permit," by yielding, or to "create a wall," by blocking themselves as long as required to oppose an initiative taken by the horse; and between the two extremes you have a whole spectrum of different shades. There must not be any contraction, because the shoulders are, so to speak, the extreme end of the reins and their slightest contraction is felt by the horse's mouth. The horseman's arms and forearms are the live prolongation of the reins, with the hands as a very subtle keyboard; so in reality, the reins extend from the horse's mouth to the rider's shoulders.

## YIELDING WHEN THE HORSE YIELDS

For you, who are using schooled horses who know how to perform any movement you may demand, this concept has but one meaning: to cease leg or hand action as soon as the horse has fully carried out the request, that is, all the way to the final point.

Let me explain. You want to halt. You demand a shortening of the pace and then the halt. If, having obtained it, your hands continue to act, the horse will start to back, a movement you had no intention of requesting. Consequently you will make your legs act once more to press forward a horse now at a loss to understand your contradictory language. Once you obtain the halt, therefore, cease hand action; yield, if you want to prevent an overly prolonged action from prompting a movement not intended. By the same token you are giving your mount a mark of approval. Thus the yielding has two motivations, one concerned with his body, the other with his mind.

On the other hand, accustom yourself from the beginning to finishing a movement completely; do not cease action sooner than you should, even if the horse has already understood and half carried out your demand. It is a serious fault, very hard to shed later on, and its evil consequences will but grow with growing horsemanship.

## SUPPLING EXERCISES

Like all sports, equitation initially requires unaccustomed muscular efforts; and so you should be prepared to do suppling exercises. These have four aims:
— to give you the necessary suppleness;
— to help you find a good position;
— to help you acquire complete independence of your four limbs;
— to give you ease, which is indispensable.
You may read a description of these exercises in Instruction.

If you want to "find the hollow of the saddle" and your legs to "descend," you must at every session and at all gaits work without stirrups. In this work the rider's position remains unchanged, except for a wider leg angle and feet hanging down naturally, the toes lower than the heels.

And now turn, let us say, left, and come to a halt on the center line.

## DISMOUNTING

Your horse at a halt, drop both stirrups, pick up both reins, taut and even, in your left hand. Place the right hand on the pommel, lean forward and to the right from the waist up, slip the right leg over the croup, and slide to the ground. Standing to the left of the horse's neck, take both reins in the right hand, about six inches behind his mouth, fingernails down, index between the two reins.

At the end of the first lesson you will obviously not be able to put this whole long theory into correct practice; not even at the end of the third. But you now know what to do and what to expect. Only perseverance in your personal effort will let you progress. If a person is to derive any benefit from a gift, he must accept it with interest. Just so it is up to you to accept your teacher's advice, to believe in it and to try to put it into effect. It is his offering, but its assimilation can only be the fruit of your own work.

Begin at the earliest to have a definite purpose in mind. If during your lessons, aside from heeding your instructor's observations, you pay particular attention to some detail you have previously pinpointed for yourself, you will be surprised at your rapid progress.

Once you have made up your mind to learn to ride, I suggest that you take your first ten or fifteen lessons in as close a succession as possible and that you ride regularly thereafter. Ten lessons in three months do not have the same result as the same number in a fortnight, above all in the beginning.

I have entered into certain details to make you better understand the why and how, and to keep from returning to the same movement in different chapters. If I were you, I would once read all of Equitation and then return to the different parts as they come up in your progression, which for the rest follows the model progression defined in Instruction.

## The Trot

At a trot, you have two possibilities: at the posting trot you rise in the saddle at every other beat; at the sitting trot you remain in the saddle. Each has advantages and disadvantages. The posting trot is less tiring for horse and rider. Actually, the horseman eludes, by rising in the saddle, every other reaction and spares not only his, but his horse's loins and back. The gait can be maintained longer at a fast pace than can the sitting trot. It is chiefly an outdoor gait which is used in the school to limber up the horse but cannot be employed at a slow cadence, at the risk of looking ungainly, and deprives the rider of at least partial precision in the use of hands and legs and of the suppleness of his seat.

The sitting trot is far more tiring for the horse and for the rider who is subjected to all the reactions which his loins strive to absorb. The position of his upper body causes his entire weight to burden the back and, by repercussion, the loins of the horse, in addition to the jolts which cannot be totally avoided, no matter how supple he may be. It does, however, permit him to be much better joined to the movements of his horse and to use his legs and hands with maximum effectiveness. Also, performed without stirrups as an exercise, it supples the loins and thus develops the seat. It is chiefly a school gait.

At the posting trot, you lean slightly forward from the waist, without hunching. Raise your head, "leading with your chin," and keep your shoulders drawn back. The inclination of the upper body comes from the loins' slight bend at the waist and must not cause a backward motion of the pelvis.

**The posting trot: rider rising, seat barely leaving the saddle. Principal difference to the eye between this and following photo is the evident forward movement of the seat. (Photo Michel Alexis)**

Supporting yourself lightly on the stirrups and keeping your knees in contact with the saddle, use one shock to leave the hollow of the saddle and touch back down softly at the following; do not drop back. The extent of your rise should be restricted to the minimum necessary to avoid every other reaction, much rather a consequence of this reaction on the horse's part than of any rising motion on yours. The better you hold up the loins, without stiffening

**The posting trot: rider sitting in the saddle. Inclination of torso corresponds to the speed of the trot. (Photo Michel Alexis)**

them when touching back down, the easier will be the subsequent rise. Once you have grasped the mechanism of the posting trot, you must for months on end perfect the movement which should be conspicuous only for its ease and lightness.

As soon as you know how to post at your ease, you must learn to recognize the diagonal on which you are posting and to pass from one to the other. So, come to think of it, how does your horse trot?

The limbs of the horse are, for easier study and explanation, grouped by pairs of legs and each combination bears a name.

### Six Bipeds

| | |
|---|---|
| Fore biped | = the two forelegs |
| Hind biped | = the two hind legs |
| Near lateral biped | = near fore and hind |
| Off lateral biped | = off fore and hind |
| Near diagonal biped | = near fore and off hind |
| Off diagonal biped | = off fore and near hind |

The side of the foreleg determines the appellation of the diagonal.

The trot is a jogging two-beat gait on alternate diagonals, one on the ground while the other is in the air.* Thus, everytime you are seated, one of the two diagonals is on the ground; and this is the diagonal on which you are posting. To determine which it actually is, use your eyes till the day when the tact of your seat will let you feel it. For now, watch the tops of your trotting horse's shoulders which move slightly in opposite directions, one forward, the other back. When the top of the off shoulder advances, the corresponding foot is on the ground, and vice versa. You can watch the shoulder without changing position, but not the foot.

Once you find it easy to recognize the diagonal on which you are posting, you will find it easy to change it. For example, posting on the off diagonal, you want to pass onto the near. Stay in the saddle one extra time (that is, a total of two times), then rise again. During the two times you have spent in the saddle, the horse has had the off diagonal on the ground (first beat in the saddle) and the near diagonal (second beat in the saddle). When you rise again, the near diagonal will be in the air, and once more on the ground when you touch back down into the saddle. So now you are posting on the near diagonal.

This knowledge is important, because the diagonal on which you are post- ing tires more than the other, making it imperative to change from time to time and to spare the horse needless fatigue. Furthermore, since the diagonal on which you are posting covers a little more ground, posting forever on the same would render the trot unsymmetrical. Since in the ring you always post on the outside diagonal (the one close to the wall) for reasons of balance in passing the corners, your work in the school should be divided as equally as possible between the two hands.

Your aim during the first posting lessons is to grasp the cadence. If you

---

*For the breakdown of all gaits, see Hippology.

**The posting trot: rider sitting in the saddle. (Photo Michel Alexis)**

have trouble, place your hands on the horse's neck and seize a handful of mane. Since you are supposed to rise on every other beat, count, "one . . . two . . . one . . . two . . ."; at one, lean on your stirrups, lift your seat and at two, touch back down into the saddle. A little energy and good will can cope with this difficulty. Above all, keep from raising your hands and hanging on to your reins; if you do, your upper body, thrown back, makes it even harder for you to rise; you will pull on your horse's mouth (not recommended) and cause not only him, but the entire class, to stop.

**The sitting trot: example of taut horse. (Photo Michel Alexis)**

As soon as you have grasped the cadence, begin to straighten up, leaving the upper body slightly inclined, in a return to a more academic position.

The sitting trot may be performed with or without stirrups. Before you can execute it correctly with stirrups. you must be trained to do so without. Actually, as long as you have not come by a little seat and your legs have not begun to "descend," you experience a certain stiffness at this gait which makes you press on the stirrups, an action which, rather than help you, only adds to your discomfort and is of scant assistance in recovering your balance

**The position of the rider without stirrups: horse halted straight and brought in hand. (Photo Michel Alexis)**

when you come to lose it. So, at first, at any rate, look upon your stirrups as unreliable friends and, later on, as "an ornament for the foot."

The sitting trot without stirrups is tiring, and a good balance should be struck between use and abuse. At first you do but short stretches at a slow cadence, which little by little may be lengthened and increased in cadence without harm. After a year and a half of practice, you should be able to

**Sitting trot without stirrups. (Photo Michel Alexis)**

follow an entire class hour without stirrups. Later on you may practice it while hacking, a few minutes at first, longer every time, till you get to where you manage a two-hour ride without stirrups. Since the progression followed in this should be slow and rational, you are far better qualified than your instructor to tell what you can and cannot do. But remember that progress does not come by itself and that each lesson should take you one step ahead. For a long time to come, your main worry will be to keep your balance; till you are able to free your mind of this, you cannot broach the true problems of equitation.

To sum up, the sitting trot without stirrups is the exercise which will best supple your loins and which, performed correctly, is the proof that muscle contraction has disappeared. It is the exercise par excellence for giving you the seat and pliancy which are indispensable for horsemanship.

Except for the lack of stirrups, you are placed as usual. So as not to worry about balance, at first take both reins in the hand close to the wall and hold on to the pommel with the other. Exaggerate the backward slant of the upper body, relax your shoulders, leave your loins supple, settle down into the saddle, push your seat forward as much as you can, and let your legs drop of their own weight without either spreading them, or pressing on your knees. The shocks you receive at the trot will tend to push your pelvis toward the cantle and make you lean forward from the waist. To counteract this, push your pelvis to the front by a forward motion of the loins at every shock. To aid this play of the loins, keep leaning back and use your hand on the pommel to help your pelvis advance. This position has obviously but one purpose: it leaves your upper body and limbs fully supple for your loins to react to and absorb every shock, your pelvis swinging out from under your hips at each. As soon as you have grasped the movement, begin to straighten up and let go of the pommel; but first of all acquire suppleness of loins.

After you have come to perform the sitting trot more or less correctly without stirrups, you pick them up, without pressing on them, for you will hold them without trouble through the free play of your joints, chiefly those of ankles and knees, and the dead weight of your legs.

## The Canter

At the canter, contrary to what you might think, you are at the smoothest and, at least for the horseman, most restful gait. Instead of a jogging two-beat gait by successive diagonals, as the trot, it is a jogging and basculating three-beat gait, each stride comprising three beats and a period of suspension, which results for you in a sensation of being rocked forward.

As with the sitting trot, the movement is more easily grasped without stirrups. Actually, if you do not drop them for your first cantering lessons, you are liable to stiffen up and bear down on them to keep from losing them, and therefore bounce in the saddle. If, on the contrary, you are relaxed, you will settle into the hollow of the saddle and, at the stage you are in, your knees will rise a bit with the motion, with the result that you will lose your stirrups. So why not let go of them before you start and have one thing less to worry about?

**The horse at the left canter finds itself, at the third beat, on the near fore, ready to go into suspension. (Photo Michel Alexis)**

To strike off into the canter, keep your reins taut and your hands low so as not to job the horse in the mouth. At the command for the departure, use your legs, holding the upper body at a slight backward slant. If your horse does not immediately break into the canter, shorten the trot by tightening the reins a bit, and as soon as your hands cease to act, use your heels twice sharply to start him. Do not be afraid to use them quite energetically; half measures when demanding the canter result but in an extension of the trot

**The horse at the left canter finds itself, in suspension, ready to place the off hind on the ground — first beat of the stride. (Photo Michel Alexis)**

which only complicates the situation. Remember for the moment that you must request the departure at the canter from a slow trot, which avoids all problems of seat and allows your legs maximum effectiveness, your hands maximum fixity; and that if your first request does not start the horse into the canter, consider it badly made, your departure a definitive miss; recommence with a new, more energetic demand. Do not attempt to prolong the actions of the first to which the horse's only response would be an extension of the trot.

As soon as he is at the canter, let your loins swing forward so as to remain with the cantering movement, your upper body slightly back. Make your loins act as if to wipe the saddle back to front with the bottom of your breeches, while your legs keep your horse at a canter.

When you want to check to a trot, discontinue leg action, increase rein tension, and resist in your shoulders. Since the transition from canter to trot is pretty rough, the first few times you had better keep these trotting beats by which you pass to the walk down to a minimum, though later it will be a fine exercise for improving your seat.

I have spoken a great deal of leaning back from the waist, of settling down in the saddle, of making yourself heavy, of taking your feet out of the stirrups and even of holding on to the pommel, with a view to overcoming the difficulties encountered by all beginners, or to fighting certain natural tendencies plaguing all of them. Our eventual goal is, however, to acquire an erect, free and easy position at all gaits.

## General Information

You are now "broken in," and the next lessons must improve your position at all gaits before we can go any further in your equestrian education. This breathing spell gives us time to take a look at some important matters, such as the bridle.

Since you manage your horse by the reins and the bit or bits, you should, if you want to use them competently, have an early acquaintance with their structure and action.

There are two kinds of bits: snaffle bits and curb bits.

The snaffle bit usually consists of two smooth mobile parts joined in the middle by a small ring, each bearing at the other end a larger ring where the reins are attached. This bit acts directly upon the corners of the mouth.

The curb bit consists of a rigid, slightly curved bar, called the mouthpiece, and two lateral cheeks (or arms) with mobile rings at their lower ends where the reins are attached. The upper part of the cheeks end in fast rings (cheek strap rings) by which the bit is attached to the bridle. These two cheek strap rings carry two hooks for the curb chain and below two D's where the lipstrap is attached. This bit is far more powerful because it acts like a lever on the tongue and bars of the horse, the curb chain serving as a fulcrum. "It therefore is a mechanism designed to allow the rider to produce a given intensity of effect by a lesser intensity of effort." General Decarpentry, *Equitation Académique*.)

The curb bit is mostly used in conjunction with a snaffle (which is then called a bridoon), while the snaffle may be employed alone. So when a horse is bitted with a simple snaffle, you have two, with a double bridle four, reins.

During the first few months you will encounter only the two, but very soon your teacher will accustom you to handling four, maybe without actually bitting your horse with a curb bit.

## HOLDING THE REINS

### A. Snaffle Bit

1. *Both reins in the left hand.*

   The left rein under the fifth finger (little finger), the right rein between the fourth and fifth, the end coming out between the index and the thumb which is on top, closed over the second joint of the index to keep the reins from slipping.

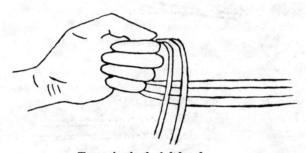

**Two reins in the left hand.**

2. *Both reins in the right hand.*

   Pick up the reins with your whole hand, separated by the index, fingernails turned down.

3. *Reins separated.*

   Both reins in the left hand, place the right hand slightly in front of the left, pick up the right rein with the right hand so that, passing under your fifth finger, it comes out between index and thumb, your hands about 8 inches apart, fingernails facing.

### B. Curb Bit

1. *The four reins in the left hand.*

   Left snaffle rein under the fifth finger; left curb rein between the fourth and fifth fingers; right curb rein between the third and fourth fingers; right snaffle rein between the second and third fingers. The four reins come out between index and thumb.

2. *The four reins in the right hand.*

   Right snaffle rein between the fourth and fifth fingers; right curb rein between the third and fourth fingers; left curb rein between the second and third fingers; left snaffle rein between index and thumb. The end of the reins comes out under the little finger.

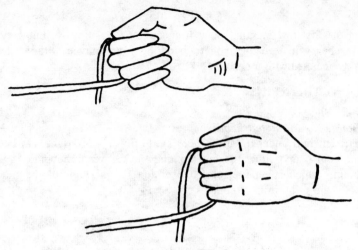

**Two reins separated.**

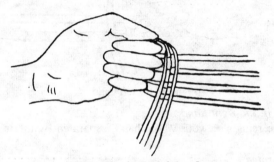

**Four reins in the left hand.**

3. *The four reins separated.*

   The four reins in the left hand, place the right slightly in front of the left, separate the right reins by the fourth finger and make the ends come out between index and thumb.

In all cases, the ends of the reins fall to the right of the horse's neck.

You approach your horse whether to mount or to bridle, from the near side. He has been so accustomed since his first contacts with man. Pat his neck with the kind of forthright gesture to which he is responsive; it is futile to express your friendship by kissing him on the nose or calling him by an array of pet names to which only lap dogs are accustomed. Let all your gestures be sober, and, while with him, do not launch into conversation, crop waving at the end of one arm like a semaphore.

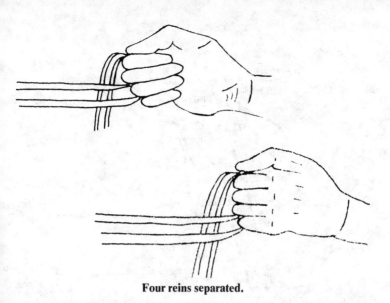

**Four reins separated.**

Check your tack as far as you are able. See if the girth is tight enough ithout slicing your horse in half. When in doubt, consult with your teacher. his is for now all you can check by yourself; but you may "adjust," at least ntatively, your stirrup leathers before mounting. Facing the horse's near de, grasp the floor of the stirrup with your left hand and place it under your ght armpit, the right arm stretched out, fist closed and placed on the stirrup ar. If the length of the leather corresponds to the length of your arm, all is ell; else you lengthen or shorten it. Twist the leather, which will make it

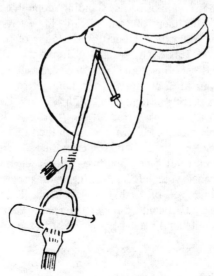

**Twisting the stirrup leather.**

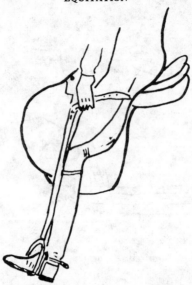

**Adjusting the stirrup on horseback.**

easier to pick up your stirrup during class: grasp it with your left hand at a point about six inches up and hold it flat, while you take the floor of the stirrup with your right hand and give the leather several twists to the right. You pass in front of your horse to do the same on the off side, of course in the opposite direction. During these operations you obviously have slipped your reins over your left, then your right, arm. Remember that, unless haltered or in his box, a horse cannot be left standing alone like a bicycle.

For a truly correct adjustment of your stirrups, however, you must be in the saddle. At first, let yourself be guided by the floor of the stirrup which should be just below your ankle when your leg drops naturally. Later, when your leg has "descended" and has found its place, you will keep your foot in the stirrup and turn your knee out to let your hand get to the buckle of the leather, adjusting your stirrup instantly and with a single hand in a matter of seconds.

The same is true for regirthing. Learn to do it in the saddle as early as you can, because many horses, particularly mares, do not accept sufficient girthing on leaving the stable and it must be done two or three times. Take the reins in the right hand, advance your left leg, raising your knee till it is in front and above the flap which you lift with your left hand. Then slip this same hand up to the billets, the flap held up under your arm. Take up one or two notches, starting with the front billet (the one closest to the horse's shoulder).

**Re-girthing on horseback.**

## Hacking

You begin to ride out for pleasure, to become accustomed to the livelier paces, and to acquire, eventually, the mettle of the horseman. Locked in between four walls, forever returning to the same point, horses tend to grow jaded and to advance joylessly, if not unwillingly. Outdoors, on the contrary, in ever changing surroundings, where the horizon is more than a wall, they become alert, eager to go ahead.

Far yet from being an accomplished horseman, gracefully submit to your teacher's orders, do not fancy yourself smarter than anyone else; every day at every hour in every country there are riders on runaway horses. This sort of incident usually ends well, the rider being more frightened than injured; but it does happen that, in crossing a street at full speed, the horse stumbles or a vehicle runs into him, and this is almost bound to entail broken bones.

Riders on the Beach, **by Max Liebermann. (Rheinisches Bildarchiv, Cologne)**

Most of such mishaps do not occur with horses of a difficult reputation whose experienced, knowledgeable masters take their precautions, but with easy horses whose mediocre riders do not "sense" what may and may not be done. Riding accidents, like the rest, are more often than not "silly accidents." Bravery does not require one to take risks one is unable to evaluate, but to know how to weigh the pro and the con, how to calculate the risk and then to take it lucidly if the chances for success appear to justify it. Your teacher is there to give you the benefit of his experience and to guide you in your early steps; trust him. Once your equestrian tact has developed and you have gained some experience, you may take the initiatives you deem right, none but you bearing the consequences.

A few requirements of savoir-faire, however, cannot be ignored, indeed have the force of law. By the time you ride out alone, be sure not to cross another horseman at a canter, but to check to the slower gait and, if trotting, to shorten the trot. Do not ever overtake another at a canter, never at any gait, without requesting permission.

In any case, remember to salute. Take reins and crop in the left hand, your crop staying to the right of the horse's neck (a crop is normally carried in the right hand) and tip your headgear "generously" with your right. Our forefathers, the knights, of whom horsemen are the most direct descendents, have passed on the salute to us, a tradition which should not be allowed to wane. So when I say, generously, I mean, not sketchy and as if grudgingly. Remember to hold the crop in your left hand, lest it follow the right in its course and frighten not only your own mount but that of the person greeted, robbing your salute not only of grace, but of propriety.

A lady salutes, after passing the reins to the left hand, by raising the crop, which her right is holding at about six inches from the knob, vertically, tip downward, to her forehead, wrist at nose level. For lack of a crop, she gives a slight nod.

When riding in company, do not fail to warn your companion before a change of gait; and if deference is due, where the bridle path is running along a road, place yourself between it and his or her horse.

## The Figures

A riding school is rectangular; the center is its geometric center; the center line divides it into two equal parts down its length. The quarter line runs parallel to the center line, dividing each half of the school into two equal parts. So there is just one center line but two quarter lines. The track, where the horses travel, runs along the wall. A distinction is made between the outer track, defined above, and the inner track, parallel to it but 3 meters from the wall. A rider on the track having the center of the school to his left is riding on the left hand or rein, or track to the left; the other way around he is riding on the right hand or rein, or track to the right. To turn left or right is to make a change of direction to the left or right. The parapet is a slightly outward-sloping wooden wall running all around at about ankle-level of a man on horseback, its purpose to protect his leg and, particularly, ankle, from the wall, should the horse get too close to it or viciously try to press him against it.

The figures are a group of well-defined movements letting riders work off the track without creating confusion. Their purpose is twofold: to exercise the rider in the management of his horse; to supple the horse.

*The volte* is a circle tangent to the track, 6 meters* in diameter. Obviously this figure does not cause a change of hand.

*The half-volte* is composed of a half circle, 6 meters in diameter, followed

*All measurements in international competition adhering to the metric system, the rider must be accustomed to their use.

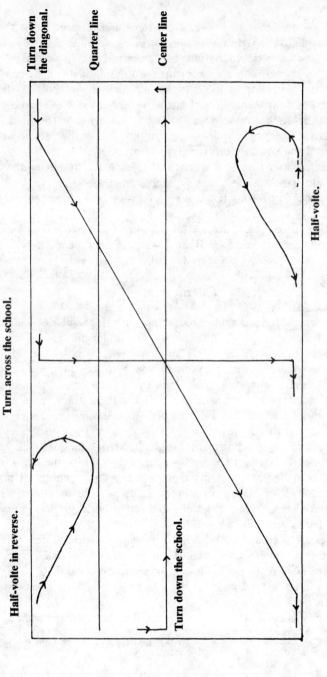

Turn down
the diagonal.

Quarter line

Center line

Half-volte.

Turn across the school.

Manège figures.

Half-volte in reverse.

Turn down the school.

by an oblique return to the track. It causes a change of hand.

*The half-volte in reverse* is composed of an oblique followed by a half circle, 6 meters in diameter, which must end upon arrival at the track. It also causes a change of hand.

*The turn down the center line (or school)* is composed of a quarter-turn (left or right) by which you leave the track, a straight line, and another quarter-turn by which you take the opposite side of the track.

*The turn across the center line (or school)* is the same kind of movement, performed through the width of the school, at any point of it, likewise with or without change of hand, depending on the command.*

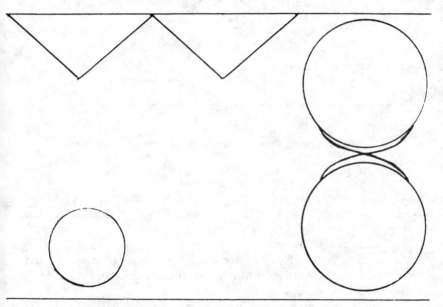

**Manège figures: volte, broken line, changing circles.**

*The diagonal change of hand* is a straight line crossing the school almost diagonally, the rider leaving the track only when he finds himself 3 meters beyond one corner and taking the opposite side of the track 6 meters before the other. In this figure, as its name indicates, a change of hand is mandatory.

*The broken line* is composed of consecutive obliques, their tightness depending on how often they are repeated on the same side of the school and how far they advance toward the center line.

*For example: "Prepare for the turn down the school . . . turn!" Or else. "Prepare for the turn down the school . . . and change hands . . . turn!".

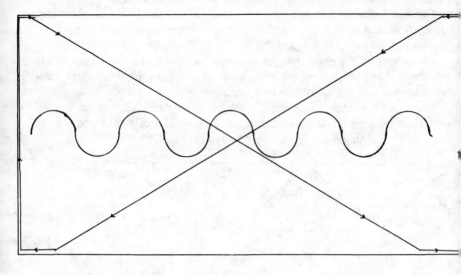

**Manège figures: serpentine on the center line, figure of eight.**

All these movements may be performed consecutively, that is, following the head rider, or (except for the diagonal change of hand) individually, that is, simultaneously. One of the main difficulties is to advance straight when leaving the track, and the best means to achieve it is to fix a point in the direction you are following and to keep your eyes on it as long as you are engaged in this. Another is to maintain the horses at an even pace, with no alteration in cadence.

The dimensions given are of the classic volte and half-volte; but your instructor may have to adjust them to the size of the school and the number of riders.

### The Aids

The aids, the different means available to the rider for managing his horse, are divided into two groups: Natural aids—legs, hands, body weight— and artificial aids—principally the crop, the spurs, the lunging whip, and the voice. The independence of aids is the ability to make each aid act independently of the others, legs from hands, hand from hand, and leg from leg.

The role of the hands is to regulate the pace and to control the direction. They may act, resist, yield. They act to shorten the gait, halt, rein back or change direction. They resist to oppose an unrequested movement of the horse. They yield when they cease to act, or to resist, and thereby convey the rider's approval to his mount.

They act by finger pressure on the reins, by raising the wrists vertically, by adding the body weight to the action of the fingers on the reins. In these different activities, they *never* exert backward traction. The reins resist when, having acted, they continue to exert a given tension on the reins, neither increasing, nor decreasing the intensity. The reins yield by the relaxing of the fingers and by the lowering of the wrists.

The hands can act simultaneously or singly. They are acting simultaneously when engaged in a change of pace or a rein back. They are acting singly when engaged in controlling direction. When acting singly, a distinction is made between the active hand (which acts) and the passive hand (which resists). The latter's role is restricted to complementing, reinforcing, or limiting the action of the former.

## THE FIVE REIN EFFECTS

*The opening rein* (1st effect) has a natural action upon the horse. It consists of drawing his nose in the direction one wants to take. To turn right, make your right wrist pivot a quarter right turn, thereby turning your nails up, and shift it to the right, keeping your elbows close to the body.

*The counter-rein* (2nd effect) also called, the neck rein, acts upon the base of the neck which it nudges in the proposed direction. To turn right, make your left wrist act from left to right and from back to front. It is the only rein effect permitting you to manage your horse with a single hand. Unlike the opening rein, the horse, able to evade it without trouble, must be trained to obey it.

Both rein effects act on the forehand which takes the new direction, while the hindquarters are content to follow the shoulders in this change. Since the action does not interfere with the forward movement, the horse does not tend to slow down.

By contrast the following three rein effects address the hindquarters. By a rational disposition of his reins, the rider opposes the shoulders to the haunches, whence their appellation of reins of opposition. This opposition impairs the forward movement which the rider's legs must painstakingly keep intact or restore whenever it tends to disappear; and the effectiveness of these reins is commensurate with the degree of activity the rider creates in the hindquarters.

*The direct rein of opposition* acts upon the haunches. *The counter-rein of opposition in front of the withers* (4th effect) acts upon the shoulders. *The counter-rein of opposition passing behind the withers* (5th effect or intermediate rein) acts upon the shoulders and the haunches.

**Francis, Duke of Alençon (the future Francis II). French School (sixteenth century). (Photo Giraudon courtesy Musee Conde)**

*The right direct rein of opposition* makes the horse turn right by pushing his haunches to the left. In performing this rein effect, the rider tightens the right rein in the direction of his right knee, after slightly relaxing the fingers of his left hand so as to make the horse understand more easily the action of the right. With this effect the reins remain parallel to the horse's axis.

*The right counter-rein of opposition in front of the withers* makes the horse turn left by throwing his shoulders to the left and his haunches to the right; the horse thus pivots around an axis passing approximately through the vertical of the stirrup leathers. In performing this rein effect, the rider, increasing finger pressure on the right rein, shifts his right wrist to the left, passing in front of the withers.

*The right counter-rein of opposition behind the withers* displaces the whole horse toward the left. This rein effect is intermediate between the direct rein of opposition, which only acts upon the haunches, and the counter-rein of opposition in front of the withers, which only acts upon the shoulders. It thus falls to the rider, in shifting his right wrist toward the left, to determine how far behind the withers the right rein should pass in order to act with equal intensity upon shoulders and haunches; because the more this intermediate rein tends to approach the direct rein of opposition, the more it acts upon the hindquarters and, on the contrary, the more it tends to approach the counter-rein of opposition in front of the withers, the greater its effect on the forehand.

Some people add a sixth rein effect, calling it, the "intermediate rein," and placing it, ill-advisedly, between the two counter-reins of opposition (fourth and fifth effects). It is hard to see what result this effect could have that could not be achieved by one of the two counter-reins of opposition. On the other hand, the appellation of "intermediate rein" takes on meaning when given to the fifth effect which is truly intermediate between the direct rein of opposition acting upon the haunches and the counter-rein of opposition passing in front of the withers and acting, if done correctly, upon shoulders and haunches with equal intensity. Since the position of the rider's wrist is definitely intermediate between those it holds in the direct rein of opposition and in the counter-rein of opposition in front of the withers, I am inclined to adopt this definition given it by Major Licart, ex-Equerry of the Cadre Noir of Saumur.

In the figures below, "a" represents the active hand, "p" the passive hand, "S" the shoulders, "H" the haunches.

*The role of the legs* is to produce the forward movement and to shift the haunches. Like the hands, they may act, resist, yield. They act simultaneously slightly behind the girth, always forward, to prompt, maintain, or increase the forward movement by pressures, taps, heel attacks. They act

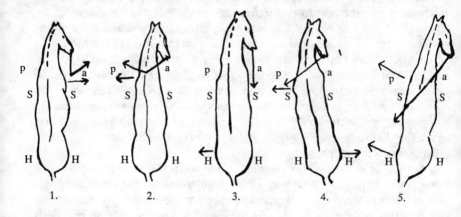

**The five rein effects: 1. The opening rein. 2. The counter-rein or neck rein. 3. The direct rein of opposition. 4. The counter rein of opposition passing in front of the withers. 5. The counter rein of opposition passing behind the withers.**

singly slightly behind the girth, always forward, to shift the haunches by pressures or heel attacks. They resist to oppose an unrequested shift of the haunches, or to limit such a shift if prompted by the rider. The legs yield when, neither acting nor resisting any more, they cease to make their effect felt on the horse's flanks (they must, however, stay in contact).

The leg acting singly, called the single leg may act in two different ways, depending on the place and manner of its action. Acting slightly behind its normal place, back to front, it causes a shift of the haunches. Acting at the girth, back to front, it creates and maintains the forward movement and prompts the engagement of the hind leg on the same side, without altering the direction of the haunches.

*The role of the body weight.* By a rational distribution of his weight, the rider acts upon the horse's balance and can thus reinforce the action of his hands and legs. For example, in order to charge the off side of the horse, he has but to weigh more on his right buttock. This increase of weight on the right is all the more evident to the horse because logically his near side is lightened by an equal amount of weight. Any shift of the upper body is forbidden during this action.

You cannot use your body weight effectively before you have acquired a good seat; else you will act "out of step" and handicap, rather than help, management.

*The crop* is carried tip down in the right hand in front of the knee. The manners of its use are as different as its well-defined purposes, its handling often delicate; so that for the learner it can be but a sort of artificial leg. After you pass your reins to the other hand to keep from chucking your horse in the mouth, you must therefore use it as close in front or in back of your leg as possible.

*The spurs* reinforce the action of the legs. As soon as you have come by a little fixity, get accustomed to their use, which is delicate and will in the beginning cause an occasional mishap for lack of fixity or a bad position of the foot, or both. But the sooner you get used to wearing them, the sooner these faults will disappear.

Some spurs have rowels with notches of different length and number. The longer and fewer the notches, the more severe the spur. The length of the neck must be proportionate to the length of the rider's leg. The longer the leg, the longer the neck, so he can touch the horse with a minimum shift of leg and foot. At any rate, the rowel must turn freely. With other models the neck ends in a notchless rowel or simply in an enlargement or ball. These are much less "offensive" and often have good results. On the well-adjusted spur the neck is a little below the buckles where the straps are attached.

*The coordination of the aids is* the correct use the rider makes of his legs, hands, and body weight, so combining them that each complements and reinforces the two others in obtaining precise execution of a given movement.

Although it is easy to define and understand the meaning of the coordination of the aids and to give examples, putting it into practice is not. Once the stage of elementary equitation has passed, it is much rather a question of common sense, reflection and tact than of clearly defined, immutable rules. Moreover, if aids are to be precise, their intensity must vary from moment to moment, because the horse himself, the object of their action, is a living and thus changing being. Besides, more often than not, the moment of action being fleeting, they should be the result of reflex rather than reflection. Hence you must in the beginning apply yourself, with your instructor's help, to losing the bad reflexes and to acquiring the good. Through practice, your aids, awkward to start with, will become less and less so, and your seat will improve, allowing your hands and legs to act with more precision and better timing.

It may therefore be said that you will pass through three stages:

1. The period where your seat is mediocre and you have not rid yourself of the bad reflexes which are the burden of all beginners. You let your aids act only after reflection to prevent a bad reflex from materializing; and you attempt to apply your instructor's advice.

2.   When your seat has improved, when you have acquired a certain ease and ceased to be a slave to your bad reflexes, you try to make your aids act with more precision and better timing.

3.   Imbued with good principles and your seat allowing you to "feel," you are able to make your aids act by reflex. You will always have to think before requesting a movement; but then, having chosen your aids, these will act by reflex at the right moment with the required intensity, neither more, nor less.

In sum, the first stage is the negative period (preventing the bad reflexes from materializing); the second is the zero point (the bad reflexes have ceased to materialize, but the good have not yet developed); the third is the positive period (acquiring and perfecting the good reflexes).

For a long time to come you will have to test the correctness of your choice of aids by cross-checking them; that is, by taking the opposite viewpoint and analyzing their combination for a possible discord among the component parts.

Example of
The Coordination of the Aids and the Five Rein Effects

| | Acting Rein | Forehand | Acting Leg | Hindquarters | New Direction Taken | Aids Applied |
|---|---|---|---|---|---|---|
| I. | Right opening rein | Drawn to the right | Right, pushing the haunches to the left, aiding the right turn. | Pushed to the left | To the right | Lateral* |
| II. | Right counter-rein | Pushed to the left | Left, pushing the haunches to the right, aiding the left turn. | Pushed to the right | To the left | Diagonal** |
| III. | Right direct rein of opposition | Turned to the right | Right, reinforcing the action of the right rein which pushes the haunches to the left. | Pushed to the left | To the right | Lateral |
| IV. | Right counter-rein of opposition in front of the withers; 4th effect | Pushed to the left | Left, reinforcing the action of the right rein which pushes the haunches to the right. | Pushed to the right | To the left | Diagonal |
| V. | Right counter-rein of opposition behind the withers; 5th effect or intermediate rein | Pushed to the left | Right, reinforcing the action of the right rein which pushes the haunches to the left. | Pushed to the left | The entire horse is moved to the left. | Lateral |

## APPLICATION OF THE COORDINATION OF THE AIDS

When the hands act simultaneously in shortening the pace, checking to

* One calls lateral aids the combination of the hand and leg acting on the same side. Example: The right hand and leg are the right lateral aids.
** One calls diagonal aids the combination of the hand of one side and the leg of the opposite. Example: The left hand and right leg.

a slower gait, halting, or reining back, the legs cease action simultaneously lest there be opposition between hands and legs, *i.e.,* no coordination of the aids. As soon as the hands have obtained the desired result, the legs become once more "active" to maintain the impulsion.

Example: You want to shorten the strong trot. (1) Cease leg action, (the legs yield); (2) Increase rein tension by more tightly closing your lower fingers (the hands act); (3) Once the desired shortening of the pace is obtained, the hands cease to act, though they keep the reins tauter than before to maintain the required degree of shortening (the hands resist); (4) The legs become active again to maintain the impulsion (the legs act).

When the legs act simultaneously in extending the pace, the hands cease to act. When the pace is sufficiently extended, the hands act in a slight increase of rein tension, limiting the extension, and thereafter resist, maintaining the horse at the desired speed.

Example: You want to extend the trot. (1) The hands, by ceasing to resist, allow the horse to obey (the hands yield); (2) Leg action increases, causing extension (the legs act); (3) Limiting the extension, the hands act; during the hand action, the legs yield; (4) Keeping the extension within the desired limits, the hands resist; and maintaining the impulsion, once more the legs act. Do not ever, therefore, let your hands and legs act simultaneously, and respect the principle, "hands without legs, legs without hands."*

Later on, when your aids have become more refined, action of hand and leg may follow more closely, yet without mingling. You will give your actions and the movements springing therefrom a greater mellowness and smoothness of transition by reducing the time of intervention of your aids, alternately and repeatedly.

When wishing to shorten the pace, for example, rather than acting in a continuous manner on the reins till you obtain the complete shortening desired, your hands will act on the reins for shorter periods of time, your legs less intensely, ceasing to act to let your hands return to their action which predominates over theirs. The same occurs in extensions of pace with, this time, however, a predominance of legs over hands. This way your horse will, so to speak, be gently swung back and forth between your hands and legs.

It is also possible to coordinate the two reins. Before one of them acts to change direction, the other must yield in order not to counteract it and then resist to give its action maximum effect.

The same goes for the legs; before one of them acts to shift the croup, the other must yield to allow the horse to carry out what has been requested, and then resist to regulate the movement.

* François Baucher, Oeuvres Complètes (1867).

*The forward movement.* While all equitation is dependent on a precise and rational application of aids, its entire foundation rests on impulsion, the forward movement; nothing is possible without it. From the beginning, give it all your attention, all your care; it is the capital point which takes precedence over everything else and will always be your very first preoccupation, though with growing mastery you will learn how to shade your demands. Your aids cannot be effective unless the horse is already in the forward movement; to ask him for anything before it exists would be labor lost and a source of disappointments.

It is your legs which must create, develop and maintain the impulsion, that is, a sharp desire on the horse's part to move forward as soon as the hands permit, regardless of his current gait, halt and rein back included. In the words of General L'Hotte, "the horse must bound forward between the rider's legs like a cherry seed between index finger and thumb"; and to round out this image, let us add with Major de Salins that "the action of the legs must be irresistible, the legs limited in their power only by the maximum speed of which the horse they activate is capable."

This capital importance of the forward movement does not render the role of the legs more significant than that of the hands. They complement each other, and to give greater importance to one or the other would be as senseless as to give preponderant importance to an automobile's steering wheel, accelerator, or brake.

## Introduction to the Departure at the Canter

Up to now you have been content to make your two legs act at the same place, with equal intensity, keeping your reins even and taut, or to press the horse forward at the trot till he "fell" into the canter through loss of balance. You have left it to the horse to choose the lead on which he was going to canter.

Because, unlike the trot, the canter is a non-symmetric gait, the horse, at his own or his rider's will, can canter on the near or off lead; and so, depending on whether he is at a left or right canter, the sequence of the feet touching the ground is different.

*The left canter:* First beat off hind; second beat off diagonal; third beat near fore; 1 time of suspension where all four legs are in the air. *The right canter:* First beat near hind; second beat near diagonal; third beat off fore; 1 time of suspension where all four legs are in the air.

A horse cantering on the near lead gives us the impression that his near lateral biped passes in front of the off lateral; when cantering on the off lead, the opposite impression is produced. In order to avoid needless repetitions, we shall consider only the canter on the near lead, it being understood that by exchanging the words "near" and "off," "left" and "right," the same remarks and conclusion apply to the right canter. I am giving you the two most widely used, classic manners of striking off into the canter on a predetermined lead.

To strike off into the left canter weigh on the right buttock in order to lighten the near lateral and, on the contrary, delay the off lateral by burdening it. Slightly advance the left heel and make it act by small attacks. This left heel action draws the near hind under the horse's body, which prompts the left canter through the increase of impulsion. This manner is the most correct and academic, the horse remaining straight, capital point in all good horsemanship. It, however, can address none but the horse schooled to these aids. The second manner, easier to understand, may be applied to horses less advanced in their dressage, but has the drawback of traversing them. Weigh on the right buttock to burden the off lateral, tighten the right rein (direct rein of opposition) to delay the off lateral. The right leg, slightly retracted, shifts the haunches to the left and thereby aids all limbs in the departure on the near lead. Finally, the left leg at the girth will impart the impulsion for the strike-off.

Although this second manner is more easily understood by the horse, it is harder for you to bring each of your hands and legs into action at different moments, though in very close succession.

In both instances, the rider must be careful to place the head in the direction of the canter, i.e., to draw the horse's muzzle slightly to the left when cantering on the near lead, leaving the neck strictly straight. It is achieved by slightly raising the lower fingers by an outward twist of the wrist.

Since even General Decarpentry says, in *Equitation Académique,* "the problem of the departures at the canter has received, ever since Xenophon, such varied solutions that it makes us think that it is not simple," I have deliberately discarded anything not obviously indispensable to the young horseman's education in this respect.*

### The Half-Turn on the Forehand

In this movement, which is also called the half-pirouette in reverse, the horse's hind legs describe a half circle around the forelegs one of which serves as a pivot, while the other is describing its own half circle around its counterpart. For a half right turn on the forehand, the off fore serves as a pivot. This movement, if well done, must be carried out on the spot, without the slightest retrograde motion by the horse. He "mobilizes" the foreleg serv-

*For more information about the canter, see Instruction.

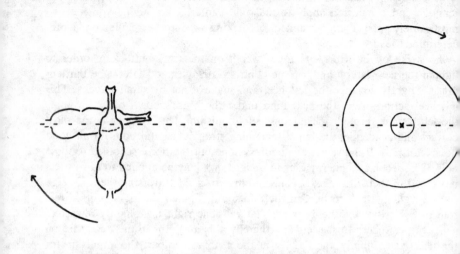

**Half-turn on the forehand.**

ing as a pivot by raising it at every step and touching down again in the same place. The hind leg on the pivot leg's side must cross in front of its counterpart.

The aids applied for the half right turn on the forehand are as follows. The left counter-rein keeps the forehand in place, places the head to the left. The right leg acts in a backward motion to drive the hindquarters to the left. The seat accented to the left aids the leftward shift of the hindquarters. The left leg at the girth maintains the impulsion.

## The Half-Turn on the Haunches

In this movement, also called the half-pirouette, the horse's forelegs describe a half circle around the hind legs one of which serves as a pivot, while the other is describing its own half circle around its counterpart. This figure is therefore the exact reverse of the preceding one but requires the same chief quality: impulsion. The horse should not at any moment back and must mobilize the hind leg which serves as a pivot at every step, raising and setting it down again at the same spot.

The aids applied for the half right turn on the haunches are as follows. The right rein places the head to the right. The left counter-rein drives the forehand to the right. The left leg is retracted and acts to hold the hindquarters in place. The right leg at the girth maintains the impulsion.

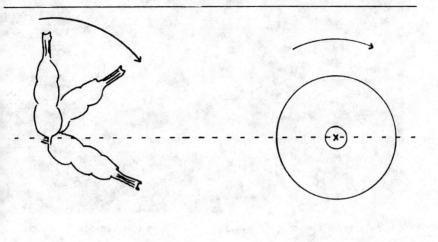

**Half-turn on the haunches.**

### The Rein Back

The rein back is a two-beat movement produced by successive contact of the diagonal bipeds with the ground.

If you want to rein back easily, do not pause too long between the moment when the horse ceases to advance and when you demand the rein back. Later you will be able to do it, but not yet.

So first request a shortening of the walk, closing your fingers alternately over the reins. When he has complied, demand the halt, closing the fingers of both hands simultaneously; but rather than yielding when he halts, repeat the alternate hand action, increasing the tension of the reins. If it does not work, do not give in to the temptation to pull, even "a little." The desired result would not be attained, far from it; the horse would respond to your traction by a reverse opposition, leaning on his hind legs as on buttresses. It is best to press him forward once more and to make your request anew. Your seat can aid the rein back by following smoothly and "permitting" the movement it feels while the horse is performing the retrograde motion. Do not remain "wedged" in the saddle by weighing down on it, make your seat supple and light.

**Saluting the king of Spain over a two-meter jump (early twentieth century).**

### Jumping

You can take your first true jumping lessons only after a series of exercises have given you the good reflexes needed in this kind of sport and have developed your seat and fixity.

At the moment of the jump, the horse, aside from having to reckon with the obstacle, is at the mercy of two enemies: your hands and the weight of your body. Hence you must become master of your hands in any situation and develop a seat which keeps you from swimming back and forth between your horse's head and tail.

You are already somewhat familiar with the sitting trot without stirrups, which increases the suppleness of your loins. At this gait you will now clear poles on ground level at different distances. Since for the moment they are on the track, no management problem will trouble you, and the role of your hands will be essentially passive (*i.e.,* the horse's mouth must be unaware of them). You leave your reins sufficiently long not to chuck him in the mouth while going over the pole. At that moment you lean farther back from the waist up, keeping your legs in place, which helps your loins absorb the shock. Very soon you will be doing the same while rotating the inside arm, which you follow around with your eyes. Thus the surprise effect is a little greater and the movement of the loins and upper body a reflex.

During this period you begin to practice the posting trot without stirrups. The position, including the raised toe, is the same as at the ordinary posting trot. If you want no fatigue, do not attempt forcibly to rise on your knees but wait for the horse's reaction to lift you up by itself, which will happen if your legs are placed right (in contact with the horse's body) and the position of your body aids this rise by a correct inclination from the waist up. If you do not go any higher than is strictly necessary to avoid the shock, the work assigned to your knees will be easier. This exercise lets you find surely and quickly the horseman's position at the posting trot; and you will not be caught helpless if later, in rounding a course, you should happen to lose a stirrup a few meters before the obstacle without time to pick it up.

At your instructor's demand you then pass these poles on ground level, now at a trot, now at a canter, now leaning forward, now back, always without stirrups.

These exercises will improve your seat and fixity, and presently, more pliantly joined to your horse's movements, you are going to take up the problem of your hands. In order to give you a comfortable time margin for the work of your hands, we have placed only two poles on ground level, in the middle of each of the long sides. This time your reins are "adjusted" in the outside hand, the other holding the pommel so no seat problem will arise. Leaning back, clear the poles at a trot and at a canter.

What happens at the moment of the jump? The horse extends his neck forward and downward. The rider, through the retreat of his upper body, retracts his hands; and if his fingers fail to relax, he pulls on the horse's mouth. Hence you must let your reins slide between your fingers at his demand. Having cleared the pole, pick up your reins and repeat the same movement over the next. Complete this exercise by letting go of the reins entirely at the instructor's cue, and pick them up once you have passed the pole. From now on you may let go of the pommel; you have sufficient self-reliance. Needless to say, the hands must remain low during this work.

Now the pole is placed in the center of the school. If you have followed this slow progression, your seat and fixity enable you to use your hands and legs to good effect in guiding your horse without cramping him. If your head is held high, if you know where you want to go, and if you look in that direction, you will eleminate nearly all management problems. For the present, and for a long time to come, you should jump the obstacle through its middle. So before you take the turn down the center line, turn your head, look at the pole, and leave the track at the right place for a straight approach to the middle of the pole. If you sense that your horse is reluctant and wavering it is up to your legs, not your hands, to make him take contact on a taut rein. Do not believe that you are doing right in letting him run at his own speed if it is not that of your choice; it is a disobedience no less serious than the refusal to move forward at the prompting of your legs. If you realize that he is going to run out and cannot straighten him out any more, stop him (if necessary, brusquely), but do not allow him to pass across the line of the obstacle; and if he was about to run out lefthanded, lead him back by a right turn, and vice versa.

You must be able to take your horse straight toward the middle of the obstacle at the pace and speed indicated by your instructor. So it is useless to go any farther until this goal, which constitutes the basis of all jumping technique, regardless of its level, has been reached.

The entire value of a rider on the obstacle course resides in the tact and science he applies in guiding his horse. This, later on, comprises the *sense of pace,* the *sense of balance,* the *sense of approach.* So apply yourself from the very first to solving the elementary problems of management which are the true problems of jumping. Do not focus your attention on ever higher jumps. The muscular effort in negotiating an obstacle is furnished by the horse, and it is only normal for you to take him there as correctly as possible within your capacities and thereby to permit him to make the best possible use of his own. All those who have made a name for themselves in competitive jumping are agreed that it is on the flat that you prepare the future jumper; and this is equally true for horse and rider.

Let us return to the poles we have left on the ground and repeat the same exercises in the same sequence and with the same procedures, but raising the pole to 40 cm.

When you jump correctly without stirrups at the trot, at the canter, on the track, in the center of the school, leaning forward or back, assuring impulsion and direction, then you may take your stirrups, sure that you will be able to become, if not an artist, at least a good craftsman, that is, an efficient and regular rider, which is not such a very trifling thing at that.

**Position of the rider on the course.**

Your position will be slightly changed.

— Keep a  foothold on your stirrups. No longer in permanent contact with the saddle, the joints of your ankles, knees and pelvis, remaining supple, are playing the part of shock absorbers.

— In order to go unconditionally with your horse, your loins must be allowed to play, so keep them supple, though sustained.

— The upper body at ease, leaning slightly forward.

— The shoulders relaxed.

— The head held high will let you look at the obstacle to come.

— The elbows bent and slightly spread.

— The hands low and in front of the withers.

— Since you are poised on your feet, your legs must be somewhat farther back than in the school position, thereby allowing your upper body to remain forward.

— The legs and thighs in contact with the horse and saddle.

— The stirrup leathers have been shortened to allow your knee joints more play, yet not so much that your legs become ineffective.

Such is the model position AT THE MOMENT OF THE JUMP which may be divided into three phases, *take-off* (rise), *suspension, landing* (descent).

| *A View of the Horse* | *A View of the Rider* |
| --- | --- |

### During the Take-off

| | |
| --- | --- |
| the forelegs leave the ground and bend at the knee joints. The shoulders rise. The neck and head extend and lower slightly. The hind legs in turn leave the ground; their release triggers the rise of the hindquarters and furnishes the propulsive force for the entire body to clear the obstacle. | for the weight of your body not to encumber your mount, you lean the upper body forward close to the horse. You advance your seat and place your hands on his neck. Your legs are at their place and locked. In this position, do not rise too high in the saddle. |

### During the Suspension

| | |
| --- | --- |
| the horse is on a horizontal plane, in full tension, over the obstacle. | your position is the same. |

### During the Landing

| | |
| --- | --- |
| the horse basculates; the forelegs stretch toward the ground, the shoulders descend, while the hindquarters are rising. At the end of this phase, after the forelegs have once more made contact with the ground, the hind legs in turn are set down close behind so as to resume the canter. | do not straighten up prematurely, wait for the horse to finish his jump. If you do not stir, the force of inertia will by itself make you straighten up. |

**Take-off. David Barker on Franco. (Photo** Irish Times**)**

**Suspension. Col. Danloux, ex-Equerry in Chief, Cadre Noir, Saumur. (Photo Blanchaud)**

Summing up, this is what happens. During the take-off, leaning forward, you are in advance of your horse. During the suspension he catches up with you, and you are together. During the landing he descends faster than you, and you are left behind. By the force of inertia, your upper body straightens up. So much for a succinct explanation of the different phases of the jump; additional explanations would take us beyond the scope of this book and complicate your task rather than clarify it.

When you are ready for your first horse show, let it be an easy one and your horse an old hand. Study the course thoroughly on paper and, when the time comes, on the grounds. Reconnoiter the places where you should turn for a straight approach to the jump.

Do not forget to limber up your horse, which does not mean that you should jump the pole a dozen times. This limbering up is supposed to set him on his legs and to warm up his muscles. So work calmly at the three gaits and after ten or fifteen minutes jump the pole two or three times. If your turn has not yet come, walk him on a long rein. Then enter the arena at a trot, go and salute the judges, adjust your reins and start your horse into the canter on a circle, a right volte if the first turn of the course is to the right.

**Landing. Frank Chapot on San Lucas. (Photo** Irish Times)

The hurdle at the starting line is usually not very dangerous; so, without neglecting it, do not lose time there. As soon as you have jumped one obstacle, look at the next. If you do not canter too fast, you will be better able to turn short and, above all, to keep control of your horse. Understand that it happens with horsemen as with drivers; one keeps absolute control of a car at a hundred miles per hour, while another driving the same car, loses it at sixty. If the cars are not the same, the gap between the two performances can become even wider. If you want to keep control of the direction, you must uninterruptedly remain master of your horse's speed.

This brings us to two essential points: the legs and the hands. Use your legs energetically, mainly during the last few strides before the obstacle, yet without letting them hustle the horse; use your hands with authority, yet without brutality, if you sense that he is trying to disengage from the bit.

These are the only problems you will have to cope with for the present; you must solve them as best you can if you intend to advance to a higher level. Whenever you need maximum effectiveness in your hands and legs, sit down in the saddle; your seat pushing forward reinforces your legs, your shoulders and the weight of your body reinforce the effectiveness of your hands.

Do not become a slave to a model position which is but a kind of compromise allowing the rider to be of least encumbrance to his mount without losing the maximum effectiveness of his aids. Do not worry about your horse's ability to go over, or the possibility that he might commit a fault, if, taken aback by a take-off somewhat distant from the jump, you are still sitting in the saddle. Just make sure your fingers allow the reins to slide. At the turn of the century, horsemen jumped leaning back, and their mounts did not therefore knock down the obstacles. Some of them jumped two meters and more. Only this position is not rational in that it imposes an additional effort and fatigue on the horse and is hardly functional for the rider. Let us say that you should know how to adapt your position to the situation.

### The Road Ahead

By the time you are able to ride according to the rules I have given you, a whole panorama opens up before you, its principal vista the education of the young horse, the subject of the first part of our book. Someday you will wish to own a horse and, honest horseman, you will want to take him into the arena such as you have "made" him, not as someone else, more of a horseman than you, has "fixed him up" for you. Even if your ambition does not aim beyond the hour in the school, a morning's hacking, or riding to hounds, you still won't be wasting your time if you now go back and read the preceding sections. Instruction will give you a better understanding of your teacher; Dressage, a better understanding of your horse—of why he acts as he does and why you must act as you must.

# IV. Hippology

Horse.—A neighing quadruped, used in war, and draught and carriage.
                                        —DR. SAMUEL JOHNSON, *Dictionary*

## Introduction

Before you exclaim, "anything but that," give me a chance to say why you should not skip the coming pages. Their subject may seem to many a pupil somewhat dry, if not downright unattractive; and one is tempted to dispose of it with the words of Dr. Johnson's which grace the title page. In fact, the same authority disposed of the matter of feed with the definition, "OATS: A grain which in England is generally given to horses, but in Scotland supports the people", and calmly answered a dinner partner's shocked question why he had defined the pastern as "the knee of the horse" with, "ignorance, Madam, pure ignorance".

But one should not dismiss this subject so lightly, since once you mount, the horse's body becomes, or should become, part of your own; and if you delight in the image of the legendary Centaur, you should be willing to accept the mechanics which prompted it. So, if you want to work in the school, ride across country, compete over the fences, then, Centaur, *nosce te ipsum!*

I should, all the same, hate to stretch your patience and good will to the breaking point and have therefore trimmed down our subject to the very essentials, leaving it to those interested in a more scientific study to pass on to more technical and comprehensive works. The few notions gathered here, however, represent a minimum of a rider's required knowledge for better comprehension, use and care of his mount, before experience and practice proceed to turn him into a horseman.

## The Skeleton

The skeleton of the horse has 193 bones. The central part of the spinal column in combination with the ribs underlies the barrel. Its front part is

**Untitled painting by J. L. Agasse. (Collection Dr. A. Schaefer, Zollikon, Switzer-
land. Courtesy L'Année Hippique)**

formed by the cervical vertebrae, where the head is attached, while its back part is made up of the sacral and caudal vertebrae. Finally there are the limbs.

We shall successively discuss:
— the head;
— the spinal column;
— the ribs;
— the forelegs;
— the hind legs.

## THE HEAD

Its upper part is formed by the skull, seat of the brain, which in turn is made up of the occipital (poll), the parietal (the apex of the head), the frontal bone, and the two temporals framing the skull on both sides. On the inside we have the sphenoid (the vault of the skull) and the ethmoid which delimits its lower part and walls it off from the face.

The face, which is the lower part of the head, is much larger than the skull. Among its numerous bones there are the upper and lower jaws; the palatines forming the roof of the palate; the vomer; the maxillae and pre-maxillae; the lacrimal and zygomatic bones.

## THE SPINAL COLUMN

The spinal column is made up of 7 cervical vertebrae the first two, atlas and axis; 18 dorsal vertebrae, to which are attached the 18 pairs of ribs; 5 lumbar vertebrae, 5 sacral vertebrae, which are ankylosed; and 12 to 18 caudal vertebrae which are also ankylosed, and atrophied.

The spinal column, which is the keystone of the entire skeleton, is very resistant to loads and hauls, thanks to the way the vertebrae are placed, interlocking, held up by strong individual and common ligaments which render the whole rather supple.

The upper thorax is formed by the 18 dorsal vertebrae, its sides by the 18 pairs of ribs. Its bottom is the sternum, which is a flat, paddle-shaped bone, its hind end called, xiphisternum, to which the 8 sternal ribs are attached. The remaining 10 are the asternal (or false) ribs, the lower ends of which are ankylosed.

## THE FORELEGS

The forelegs, from top to bottom, are composed of the scapulum (shoulder), the humerus (arm), the olecranon (elbow), the radius and ulna (forearm), the carpia (knee), the metacarpia (cannon), the great sesamoids (at the cannon-pastern joint), the first phalanx (pastern), the second phalanx (coronet), the third phalanx and small sesamoid (foot).

The scapulum is a large, flat bone articulated with the humerus by the scapulo-humeral joint. Since the horse lacks a collar bone, the scapulum is not attached to the spinal column but kept in place by various muscles. The humerus is a long bone, widening at both ends, the upper end articulated with the scapulum by the scapulo-humeral joint and the lower, with the radius and ulna by the humero-radio-cubital joint. The radius and ulna are ankylosed. The first and most important of the two is articulated with the humerus at the top and with the carpus by the knee joint at the bottom. The ulna, attached to the hind face of the humerus, has a tuberosity, called olecranon. The 7 or 8 carpia are placed in two tiers. The metacarpia include 3 bones: the principal metacarpal bone, and 2 rudimentary metacarpia, the latter ankylosed with the principal one and shaped like a stiletto, point down. The 3 metacarpia are articulated with the carpus, but only the principal metacarpal bone is articulated with the first phalanx by the fetlock joint.

The phalangeal region comprises the first phalanx, that is, the pastern bone, and the 2 great sesamoids; the second phalanx, that is, the coronary bone; the third phalanx, that is, the pedal bone (also called, foot or coffin bone). The third phalanx and the small sesamoid (navicular bone) are lodged inside the hoof. The joints between first and second and second and third phalanx are of insignificant size.

## THE HIND LEGS

The hind legs comprise, from top to bottom, the pelvis (croup), the femur (thigh), the patella (stifle joint), the tibia and the fibula (gaskin), the tarsals (hock), the metatarsals (shannon), the great sesamoids (at the shannon-pastern joint), the 1st phalanx (pastern), the second phalanx (coronet), the third phalanx + small sesamoid (foot).

The pelvis is formed by the fusion of three bones: the ilium, the ischium, the pubis. The outer tip of the ilium forms the point of the hip, while the opposite end (inner tip) marks the top of the croup. The ischium, by way of the pubis, is the downward and backward extension of the ilium; its hindmost part forms the point of the buttock. Unlike the scapulum, the pelvis is directly jointed to the spinal column.

The femur is a long bone, having on top a rounded head which fits into a cavity of the pelvis (coxo-femural joint). The lower part ends in two extremities; the upper one, hollowed out, is the joint with the patella, the lower one is articulated with the tibia (femur-tibial joint). The tibia, also long, is the leg's principal bone. The fibula is much thinner and only about two-thirds as long as the tibia to which it is coupled; its head fits into the lower part of the head of the tibia. The patella is a short bone attached to the tibia by strong ligaments.

The tarsals are 6 or 7, placed like the carpia in two tiers. In the upper tier we find the two most important bones: the os calcis in back (point of the hock) and the astralagus in front. The metatarsals and the phalangeal region present the same characteristics as the metacarpals and the phalangeal region of the forelegs.

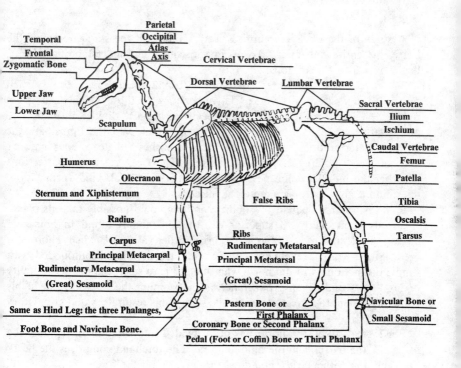

## The Muscles

Since a study of the muscles is of scant interest in the limited framework of this hippological part, let us just recall a few generalities.

There are 2 categories of muscles: muscles with striate red fibers contracted at will, and muscles with plain fibers contracted by reflex. They are attached to the bones, either directly by means of muscular fibers, or by means of tendons. Most can use either end for mobility, which permits one and the same muscle to engender movements in different directions. The movements are:

| extension | = | back to front |
|-----------|---|---------------|
| flexion | = | front to back |
| abduction | = | inside out |
| adduction | = | outside in |
| circumduction | = | rotation around self |

## The Outside

A study of the outside comprises, rather than just the static points of the horse, his entire dynamics. To avoid subsequent misunderstandings, let us begin by a list of definitions.

The *beauties* are the horse's qualities. Absolute beauties are those which remain valid whatever his work; relative beauties are those which suit a given purpose. The *defects,* the opposite of beauties, are also divided into absolute and relative. The *blemishes,* a term usually applied to the limbs, are the different deteriorations, divided into hard blemishes (of an osseous nature) and soft (of a tendinous, synovial nature). The *vices* are the imperfections of either the moral (viciousness, restiveness), or physical, kind (crib biting, intermittant lameness)—innate or acquired.

*Blood* is a horse's patent of nobility; nothing could possibly take its place. It affords great energy, a superior constitution, and is found in horses of oriental stock and their different strains and derivatives, English Thoroughbred, Anglo-Arab, Trakehner. *Quality* although popularly confounded with simple distinction, is to the horse what temper is to steel, the intrinsic quality of his tissues and organs. *Substance* is the stamina the horse shows in his work, dependent to a great extent on the state of his respiratory and circulatory organs.

For logical study, the horse has been divided into three main *regions:* the forehand, the barrel, and the hindquarters. The forehand comprises the head, the neck, the withers, the shoulders, the breast, and the forelegs. The barrel comprises the back, the loins, the chest, the belly, the brisket, the flanks, and the ribs. The hindquarters comprise the croup, the tail, and the hindlegs.

## THE FOREHAND

The head at the top is limited by the poll with the ears and the forelock, the hair falling from it onto the forehead. In front, we have successively the forehead, the face, and the muzzle. On the sides, are the parotid glands, the temples, the eyes and their lids, the eyebrows, the eyepits (the hollows above the eyes). Farther down are the cheeks and the nostrils. Behind, starting at the top, are the throat, the jaw with the chin groove, the underlip, and the chin. Below are mouth and lips.

The neck is adorned by a mane. On each side there is a longitudinal swelling formed by the cervical vertebrae with a depression underneath, called jugular fossa, where the jugular vein passes. The withers right behind the neck, is formed by the protuberances of the first dorsal vertebrae and serves as a hold to many muscles. It should be high and extend well back. The shoulder, the bone of which is the scapulum, points down and forward, its top ending at the withers, its front at the neck, its back at the flanks, its bottom at the point of the shoulder where the arm begins. It should be long and sloping. The breast is the front limit of the thorax and should therefore be rather broad.

The forearm, formed by radius and ulna, should be straight, long and well muscled. At the lower third of it there is a small horny protuberance, called the chestnut. It is considered to be an atrophied toe (the first). The knee, formed by the carpia, is a complex joint. It should be oriented vertically, barely convex in front and bony on the sides. The cannon, lying between the knee and the fetlock, has two different parts: the essentially osseous front, and the back which is formed by the tendons. It should be broad and clean. The suspensory ligament and the two flexor tendons (perforans and perforatus) should be lean, firm, straight and well-defined, smooth and devoid of swelling to the touch.

The fetlock at the articulation of the metacarpus or metatarsus with the phalangeal region, should be broad, thick and neat. The ergot, a horny protuberance like the chestnut, surrounded by long hair, called the feather, sits on its lower part and is considered to be the second atrophied toe; the other three are fused into a single bone, the pedal (foot or coffin) bone. The pastern, formed by the first phalanx, should in volume be proportionate to that of the cannon, and rather long and sloping. The coronet separating pastern and hoof, is formed by the second phalanx. The hoof will be studied in a special section dealing with the foot and shoe.

## THE BARREL

The dorsal vertebrae are at the base of the back. The back lies between withers and loins. It should be short, just about horizontal, slightly higher near the withers than in back, well muscled and well coupled with the loins which are its continuation. It is the transmission shaft of the hindquarters' propulsive forces. The loins, formed by the lumbar vertebrae, should also be short, broad and well muscled. The chest is delimited by the dorsal vertebrae, the 18 pairs of ribs and the sternum. It should be high, broad and deep. The brisket lies behind the elbow and is usually marked by a sternal depression. The ribs is the part formed by the last 12 ribs (the first 6 are under the shoulder). The flank lies between the point of the hip and the last rib. The belly is the lower part of the abdomen.

## THE HINDQUARTERS

The croup, the base of which is the pelvis, stretches from the end of the loins to the root of the tail. On the sides are the haunches (or hips), their points formed by the front tips of the ilium. The croup should be long, slightly sloping, and well muscled.

The thigh, formed by the femur, is not very clearly separated from the croup under which it lies. Below, it extends to the top of the stifle joint (that of the patella, where the gaskin begins). Its hind part is called the buttocks; these are, at the top, limited by the points of the buttocks which are formed by the hind tips of the ischia, and, below, end slightly beneath the level of the stifle joint.

The gaskin, formed by the tibia and fibula, extends from the stifle joint to the hock. It should be long, broad and well muscled.

The hock is the joint which, in the hind leg, is the counterpart of the knee in the fore, formed by the tarsal bones which are arranged in two tiers. The upper tier is articulated with the tibia, as well as with the lower tier which, in turn, is articulated with the head of the shannon bone. The role of the hock is very, if not most, important for locomotion. High up in the back we find the point of the hock, formed by the os calcis. The shannon, fetlock, pastern and coronet have the same characteristics as their counterparts on the foreleg.

## BEAUTIES AND DEFECTS

The study of the beauties and defects of each of these regions would take us too far afield, to no practical avail for the rider of two or three years' experience. We shall thus only mention the most common and most easily recognizable and recommend that for the rest you look up the canons of the good saddle horse under Dressage, Training.

If the head is long, and thus heavy, mainly if the neck is long and horizontal, the horse will weigh heavily in your hand, making management more difficult and the forehand topheavy. If it is roman-nosed, that is, convex in front, the horse is said to be ram-headed. If, on the contrary, it is concave, the horse is called dish-faced. Neither is a sign of class.

The head is said to be well set on when the parotid region is well hollowed out, permitting easy head carriage. It should be in harmony with the neck and body, its forehead and face broad, the nostrils wide open to facilitate breathing at the lively gaits, the jaws short and well defined. The eyes must be expressive, yet gentle—the sign of a lively character devoid of viciousness. Delicate, short ears, well set on, lend distinction to the whole. With a horse in eating position, the head should be at about a straight angle with the neck; when this angle is more open, the head approaching the horizontal,

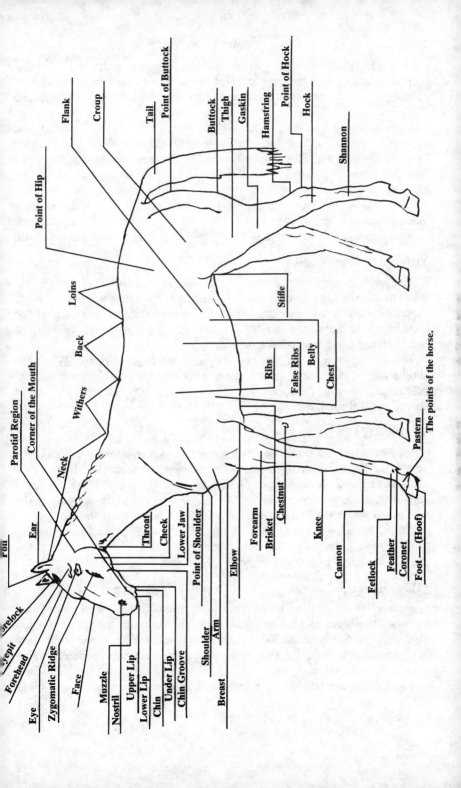

The points of the horse.

the horse is liable to star-gaze; in the opposite he is overbent.

The neck is of like importance, since the horse's balance is largely dependent on it and its management easier or harder according to its length and direction.

It should be carried high, at an angle of about 45°. Its muscles should be firm, its length at least equal to that of the head. It is considered to be carried low (horizontal) when it stretches forward at the same height as the top line (the line formed by the upper part of the back, loins and croup). When, on the contrary, it is carried excessively high with a concave crest, the horse—usually a star-gazer—is called ewe-necked. Be that as it may, it makes management difficult and delicate, giving the rider the impression that the neck is independent from the rest of the body over which he has but scant control.

## THE BACK AND BELLY

The horse is sway-backed when his top line is excessively concave, bringing with it an overly convex cow-belly. The opposite defect is a convex back, called camel-back or roach-back; and the opposite of the cow-belly is the greyhound- or herring-gutted belly which gradually narrows, following a nearly straight line from sternum to stifle joint.

The croup when sloping excessively, is called a goose-rump. When the middle line of the croup causes a marked jut and the two sides are sloping, it is called sharp; in the opposite case, it is called a double croup, a relative beauty for a draft horse.

## MEASUREMENTS

Measurements are taken with a horse-standard (or measuring stick); the unit in the English-speaking world being the hand (4 inches). The height is taken from the top of the withers in a perpendicular line to the ground, the animal standing plumb on his four limbs. His length is determined by the distance between the point of the shoulder and the point of the buttock.

Except for a polo pony, which is always a "pony," regardless of height, and the Arab horse, which is never a pony, no matter how small, an animal not standing over 14 hands 2 inches is called a pony.

## THE TEETH

Since a horse's age can be determined by examining his teeth, we should know a little about them. The adult horse has 40 teeth: 12 incisors, 4 canine teeth (or tushes), and 24 molars. Mares, not having canine teeth, only have 36, though there are (normally barren) mares with atrophied canine teeth.

The incisors are laid out in a half circle in the front of the mouth (6 in

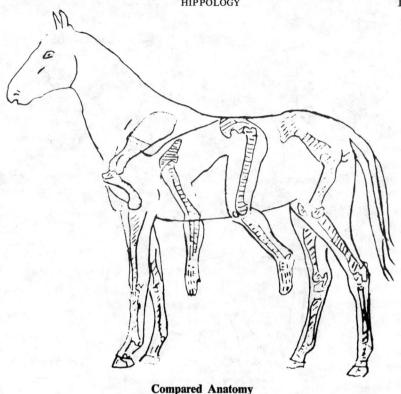

**Compared Anatomy**

the upper, 6 in the lower jaw). The 4 in the middle (2 above, 2 below) are called central incisors; following are the 4 lateral or intermediate incisors; and then the 4 corner incisors or corners. The canine teeth are at a short interval behind the incisors. Behind the canine teeth, preceding the molars, there is a rather wide toothless space, called the bars. Since the molars are no help in determining age, we shall ignore them, except for saying that there are 6 on each side of the upper and lower jaws, a total of 24.

The incisors are classified as milk and permanent teeth. When first the incisors start to come out of the jaw, only the front edge is visible which therefore wears out more quickly. At the center of the table surface is the cup, a small indentation surrounded by ivory which, in turn, is surrounded by enamel. When wear has made this indentation disappear, the tooth is said to be razed. Besides, the shape of the table surface evolves with age and passes successively from oval and longish to round, later triangular.

Ram-headed.                               Dish-faced.

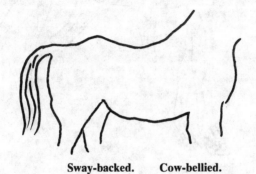

Sway-backed.        Cow-bellied.

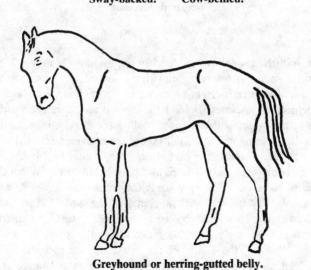

Greyhound or herring-gutted belly.

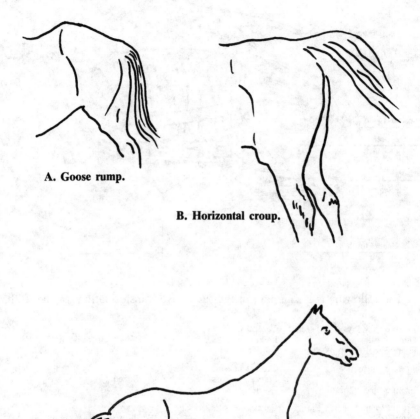

A. Goose rump.

B. Horizontal croup.

C. Medium sloping croup (normal), good top line.

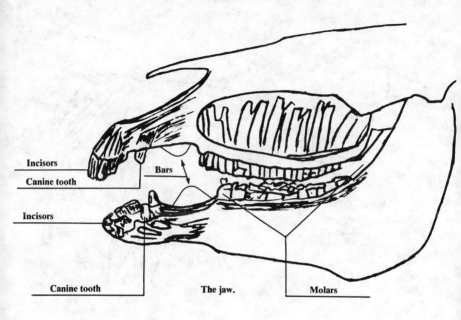

Incisors

Canine tooth

Bars

Incisors

Canine tooth          The jaw.          Molars

The following is a summary of the successive transformations of the teeth.

| | | |
|---|---|---|
| From 6 to 8 days | Central incisors | |
| One month | Lateral incisors | Milk teeth come out. |
| From 6 to 10 months | Corner incisors | |
| | | |
| At 10 months | Central incisors | |
| At 1 year | Lateral incisors | Razed. |
| From 16 to 20 months | Corner incisors | |
| | | |
| From 2½ to 3 years | Central incisors | |
| From 3½ to 4 years | Lateral incisors | Permanent teeth come out. |
| From 4½ to 5 years | Corner incisors | |
| | | |
| From 5 to 6 years | Central incisors | |
| From 6 to 7 years | Lateral incisors | Razed — horse is called |
| From 7 to 8 years | Corner incisors | smooth-mouthed. |
| | | |
| 9 years | Central incisors | |
| 10 years | Lateral incisors | Rounded. |
| 11 years | Corner incisors | |
| | | |
| 12 to 13 years | All teeth | Rounded. |
| | | |
| 14 years | Central incisors | |
| 15 years | Lateral incisors | Turning triangular. |
| 16 years | Corner incisors | |

At the age of 4, the canine teeth come out as permanent, adult teeth.
The slant of the teeth also is an indicator of age. With the passing of the years, they lengthen and tend to become horizontal.

**4 years**

**19 years**

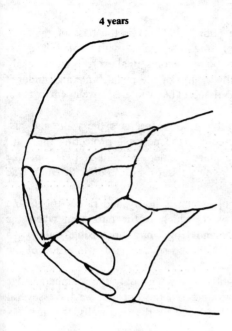
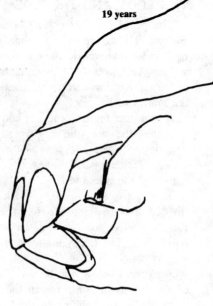

**Lower Teeth**

**Lower teeth**

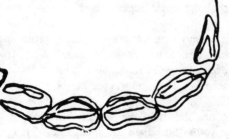

**Telling age.**

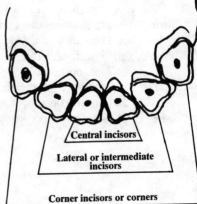

Central incisors

Lateral or intermediate
incisors

Corner incisors or corners

# THE FOOT AND ITS SHOE

The pedal (foot or coffin) bone (third phalanx) is the base of the foot. Behind it is the navicular bone or small sesamoid with which it is articulated, and over it, the coronary bone (second phalanx). As shock absorbers, cartilages are placed laterally on top of the pedal bone and under it a plantar cushion formed of elastic tissue. The whole is enveloped in flesh, the matrix of the hoof.

At the top there is the coronary band which secretes the wall; and just over this, the perioplic ring which secretes the periople protecting the wall. The fleshy leaves (flaky tissue) are placed under the wall at the front like small interlocking laminae. The spongy tissues are under the foot, the matrix of the sole and frog.

The foot is enveloped by the hoof, which is horny and rather tough and divided into two main parts: the wall, which is the part seen when the foot is on the ground, and the sole and frog which are visible only when it is lifted. The horny matter of the wall and sole is hard, while that of the frog is supple.

Seen from below, the hoof is slightly hollow and only the peripheral edge of the sole is in contact with the ground. On the outside, we have several parts of the wall: the toe is the front, framed by the side walls; the quarters follow, and then the heels.

The sole covers the lower surface of the foot, except for the hind part where the frog wedges in like a V, the two upper tips of its buttresses forming the heels. The frog is raised in relation to the sole and provided with three furrows: one median and two lateral. It should be noted that the forefeet are rounder than the hind, and that the outer edge of each foot is rounder than the inner.

The good foot is distinguished by smooth horn and a regular, rather long form. It must prolong the pastern, following the same angle. Seen from below, the heels must be wide open, the sole reasonably hollow, the frog supple, full, intact, and free of seepage. The importance of the foot is obvious. "No foot, no horse."

The different parts of the shoe are shown in the sketch; but there is no sense in elaborating on this, since young horsemen are incapable of judging whether or not a horse is correctly shod.

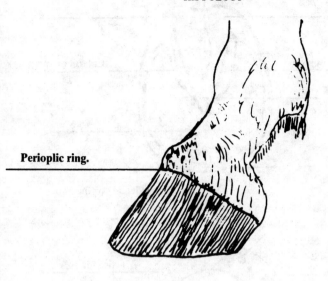

Perioplic ring.

The foot.

The outside of the hoof.

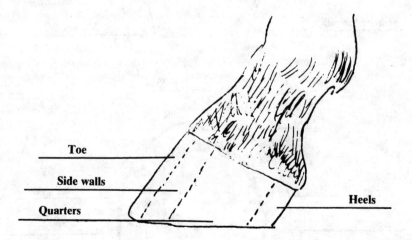

Toe

Side walls

Quarters

Heels

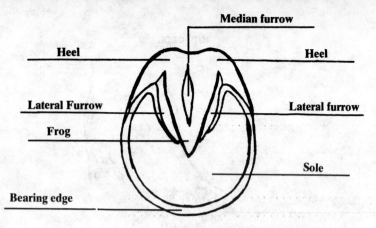

Median furrow

Heel         Heel

Lateral Furrow        Lateral furrow

Frog

Sole

Bearing edge

The underside of the hoof.

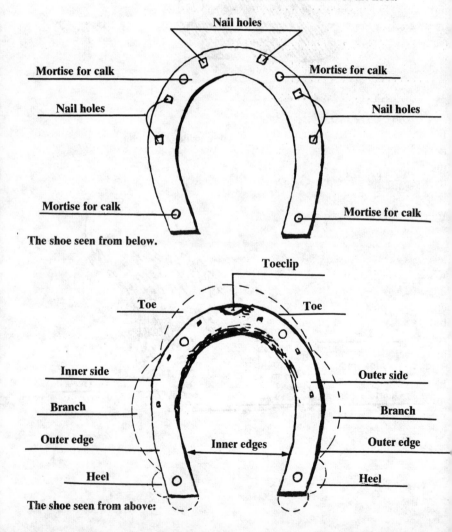

Nail holes

Mortise for calk       Mortise for calk

Nail holes            Nail holes

Mortise for calk       Mortise for calk

The shoe seen from below.

Toeclip

Toe         Toe

Inner side          Outer side

Branch             Branch

Outer edge     Inner edges     Outer edge

Heel           Heel

The shoe seen from above:

**The nail.**

## COATS AND COLORS

A horse's color is determined by the combination of body hair and mane and tail. Though, strictly speaking, there are five categories, we must brace ourselves for controversy. The fact that custom (notably on the young continents) has added not only national but regional variations to this basic spectrum did not seem at first an overwhelming difficulty. I meant to set down the basic spectrum and add for you some national and regional subdivisions. But rather than sub-divisions, most of them turned out to be often overlapping popular expressions. Whenever I questioned horsemen from different regions of one and the same country, they either called a horse's color by two different names or gave the same name to two horses of different color, while a third upheld that the name did not even rightly exist.

Teeth on edge, we would naturally end up with our heads over *Webster's International,* only to run into entries such as, I quote, "Sorrel a) a light bright chestnut horse often with white mane and tail b) a dark red roan horse." These few words, by inconclusively proving everyone wrong, including Noah Webster, saved the friendship of four men; but I am still shaken by the experience, most of all by its bewildering dénouement. Nevertheless, I shall try to break down the spectrum for you as best I can, so you will be able to recognize colors and talk about them with a minimum of verbal footnotes.

Some juggling has been necessary in adapting the five categories, as I learned them at my mother's knee, to your particular needs. The American word "roan" for instance, stands for two French words, *aubère* and *rouan.* The definition of the *aubère* is two colors (chestnut and white) mixed in coat and mane and tail; that of the *rouan,* three colors (white, chestnut and black) mixed in coat, mane and tail, though it is customary to call a horse *rouan* if only two colors (white and chestnut) are mixed in his coat, but mane and tail are of a third.

In my original classification, then, the *aubère* (equivalent to the strawberry roan) is listed under Category III which comprises the horses of two mixed colors of coat; but for your practical use I have lifted the strawberry roan *(aubère)* from this third category, where he rightly belongs, to establish one exclusively devoted to the horses called roan in this country.

On both sides of the ocean, nearly all colors are sub-divided into many more shades than I have mentioned; but to recite each and every one would truly be "hair-splitting," without, for all that, enabling you to distinguish among them "on a real live horse."

### Category I—Coat, Mane and Tail of the Same Color

*White.* A rare color with shades such as, milky, porcelain, creamy white, etc.

*Chestnut.* All shades from tan to dark brown, called variously and respectively, true, yellow, golden, liver chestnut, etc.

*Black.* A rare color with shades such as, coal, dull black, etc.

*Cream-colored or buckskin* (U.S.). Different shades of beige, light to dark.

### Category II—Coat of solid color; Mane, Tail and Lower Limbs Black

*Bay.* Shades such as brown, red, plum-colored, dark bay ,etc.

*Dun.* Different shades of beige, in addition to black mane, tail and lower limbs, dorsal stripe, sometimes shoulder stripe.

*Mouse-colored.* Greyish-brown shades of differing intensity.

### Category III—Two Colors Mixed in Coat, Mane and Tail

*Grey.* White and dark (black or brown) body hair, mixed in differing proportions and/or patterns, called variously and respectively, light, ordinary, dark, speckled, dapple grey, etc.

*Wolf-colored.* The individual hairs have two colors: yellow at the root, brown at the end.

### Category IV—Two or Three Colors Mixed in Coat, or in Coat, Mane and Tail

*Roan.* Variously and respectively called, strawberry, blue, red, chestnut, bay roan, etc.

### Category V—A Combination of Two Coats

*Piebald.* Large fields of white hair among black. The white, by its predominance, should be considered to be the basic color, as is the case with the *Skewbald.* Which is composed of large fields of white among brown hair.

The *palomino* is a color breed, a light chestnut with an almost white mane and tail.

## THE MARKINGS

There are certain markings, peculiar to various parts of the horse, which

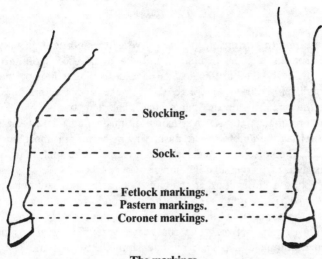

The markings.

are important parts of his description and indentification. These are as follows: On the forehead spots and stars formed of white hair; on the face bands of white hair more or less covering the whole face or sides of it, known as stripes if narrow, as blazes if broad. On the nose, on the muzzle or around the lips or nostrils, appear spots of discolored pinkish-white skin known as snips. If the iris of the horse's eye is almost white, it is known as a wall eye. Markings on the limbs are: coronet markings, white hair immediately above the coronet; pastern markings, white hair covering the area from below the fetlock downward; fetlock markings, white hair from the fetlock down; a sock, white hair extending about halfway up the cannon or shannon; a stocking, white hair extending to the knee or hock region. A horse having no hairs of a color other than the basic is called whole-colored. A dark band going from the base of the mane to the root of the tail is called a dorsal stripe or list. A dark band passing over the withers from one shoulder to the other is known as a shoulder stripe.

Here, as with the colors in general, you will have many a merry fight with people who call the shoulder stripe a dorsal stripe, and the dorsal stripe or list an eel stripe, and others who call the eel stripe a dorsal band and differentiate it from the withers stripe which others, however, call the transverse stripe . . . So if ever anyone raises an eyebrow at what you are calling anything, just shrug your shoulder stripe and trot off.

## The Gaits

There are *natural, artificial,* and *defective* gaits. The natural gaits are the walk, the trot, the canter, reversing, and the jump, used spontaneously by the horse at liberty. The artificial gaits have been taught him by man. They may be stylized natural gaits, like the passage and the piaffe, or fancy gaits, like the Spanish step or Spanish trot. The defective gaits are a consequence of prolonged fatigue, overtaxing or mismanagement, unless taught by man, such as the amble or the paso, which the animal mechanism, however, rejects. The horse also executes certain leaps on the spot, many of which have been stylized in the school jumps.

Before taking a closer look at the gaits, let us recall a few definitions.

The *hoofprint* is the impression left on the ground by the touch of the foot. The *beat* is the sound made by the foot on touching the ground. The *time* is the length of time between two successive beats. The *stride* is the space covered in a complete step and, by extension, the step itself. The *track* is the succession of hoofprints. A limb is said to be *in the air* when it is not in contact with the ground. A limb is said to be *on the ground* when, being on the ground, it partially or totally supports the weight of the body. The position "on the ground," however, is in truth preceded and followed by two moments of transition. After the foot has been "in the air," there is a moment when, placing it "on the ground," the horse is not yet leaning on it; then, with the foot still "on the ground," he is not leaning on it any more, ready to raise it to be "in the air."

A horse's walk is *ordinary* when the hind foot covers the hoofprint of the corresponding fore. He is *short stepping* when the hind foot remains behind the hoofprint of the corresponding fore. He is *long striding* when his hind foot goes beyond the hoofprint of the corresponding fore.

Let us recall the definition of the six bipeds:

> Fore biped — the two forelegs
> Hind biped — the two hind legs
> Near lateral biped — near fore and hind
> Off lateral biped — off fore and hind
> Near diagonal biped — near fore and off hind
> Off diagonal biped — off fore and near hind

## THE WALK

The walk is a natural, diagonal, marching, four-beat gait, with the following succesion of feet, when started by the left fore: First beat—left fore, second beat—right hind, third beat—right fore, fourth beat—left hind. A single foot is in the air, the other three are on the ground; but only one of

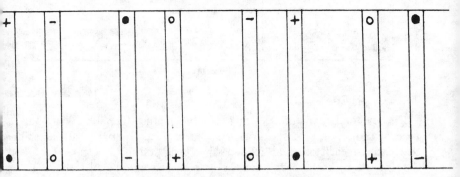

**The walk started by the near fore.**

**+ about to bear down.      — about to rise.      ● on the ground.      o in the air.**

the three is leaning on it, the other two, respectively, are about to rise and to bear down.

The sketch below shows the succession of the four feet in one complete stride. The regulation speed of the walk is 110 m per minute (1 m = 39.37 in); that is, 6½ km per hour (1 km = 0.62137 mi). The average lies between 6 and 7 km per hour.

**The trot.**

## THE TROT

The trot is, as you will recall, a natural, jogging, two-beat gait on alternate diagonals, the two beats separated by a time of projection or suspension. A normal stride of the trot comprises, for example: first beat—left diagonal on the ground, right diagonal in the air; one time of suspension—both diagonals in the air; second beat—right diagonal on the ground, left diagonal in the air; one time of suspension—both diagonals in the air.

The regulation speed of the trot is 240 m per minute; that is, 14.400 km per hour. The average lies between 12 and 16 km, at times up to 18 km per hour.

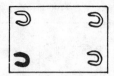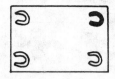

**The canter.**

## THE CANTER

The canter is a natural jogging and basculating three-beat gait, plus a time of projection or suspension. As you will recall, at the left canter the feet succeed each other as follows: first beat—off hind; second beat—off diagonal; third beat—near fore; one time of suspension—all feet are in the air.

The ordinary canter, then, is, in effect, a three-beat gait, or may at least be considered as such, although, actually, the two feet constituting the diagonal only rarely touch down together at the second beat. But the time separating the two is insignificant, and the expression, four-beat canter, is used for a defective gait where the break-up of the diagonal is complete.

The regulation speed of the canter is 340 m per minute; that is, 20.400 km per hour. The average may reach from 450 to 500 m per minute; that is, 27 to 30 km per hour. The duration of this canter depends, of course, on the condition of the horse and the kind of going. It may last as long as half an hour if the horse is in fine condition and the going is good.

## REVERSING

Reversing is a natural retrograde gait on alternate diagonals. Although natural, the horse at liberty only rarely executes it, except when he cannot turn on the spot.

## THE JUMP

In the ascending phase of the jump, the horse uses the forefoot which is on the ground in raising his forehand. Once this rear of sorts has raised the forehand and thrown the weight back onto the hindquarters, he tucks up his knees and retracts his neck. Then the hind legs spring off and the neck stretches and curves.

In the suspended phase, the horse is on a horizontal plane over the obstacle, taut from head to tail.

In the descending phase, the horse basculates; the hindquarters are higher than the forehand, aiding the passing of the hind legs over the obstacle; the forelegs stretch, the neck rises. The horse lands on a single forefoot, the second following close behind; the hind legs, in turn, touch the ground. It should be noted that it is generally on the second fore to hit the ground that the horse restarts into the canter after the jump.

The jump usually inserts itself in the canter; but the horse can jump from the trot (an excellent exercise to raise his forehand), from the walk, even from the halt. Let me emphasize, however, that these three "exercises" are only just that, requiring, as they do, tremendous effort of the horse and a great deal of savoir-faire and tact of the trainer.

## ARTIFICIAL GAITS

Among the artificial gaits we shall only mention the passage and piaffe, both originating in the trot. The *passage* is a more shortened, more elevated trot of a slower cadence with a longer time of suspension than the ordinary trot, the horse covering less ground. The *piaffe* is the passage on the spot.

## DEFECTIVE GAITS

Among the most common of the defective gaits, we shall mention the *amble,* a two-beat gait on alternate laterals; and the *rack* or *broken amble,* a four-beat gait obtained by the disassociation of the lateral beats. Another is the *fox-trot,* a disunited trot resulting from the disassociation of the diagonal beats; when not artificially induced, a sign of wear on the part of an over-taxed horse. The *sobre-pass* takes from the trot and from the canter and is the gait of the ruined horse who, barely advancing any more, canters at the front and trots at the back, or vice versa. The *disunited canter* is performed by the horse executing the left canter in front and the right canter behind, or vice versa.

## LEAPS

Horses are able to perform leaps on the spot, as they are doing when rearing, kicking or bucking.

*Rearing* is the raising of the forehand and barrel above the hindquarters; one of the most dangerous defenses of the horse who is liable to overturn if rearing high, either through loss of balance or because the hocks, being weak, give way under the weight of the mass. This natural jump has given us the following school jumps: The *levade,* the *pesade,* the *courbette.*

When *kicking,* in contrast to rearing, the horse leans on his forefeet and lifts his hindquarters with a brusque release of the hind legs. The school jump developed from this is the *croupade.* The combination of the courbette with the croupade results in the *capriole,* where the demand for the courbette is followed, as the forehand comes back down, by the demand for the croupade. Thus the horse has none of his feet left on the ground and the forelegs slightly bent at the knees, the hind legs completely stretched out backward. It is the most beautiful of all school jumps.

Finally, *bucking,* when the horse, rounding his back, rises from the ground with all four feet at once, has been developed into the *ballotade,* another of the school jumps.

While the Spanische Reitschule of Vienna continues to use all these school jumps, only the courbette, the croupade and the capriole are now practiced at the Ecole de Cavalerie of Saumur.

## *Formation of the Legs*

By the formation of the legs is meant the direction of the legs at a halt and in action. For proper evaluation, the horse should be examined from front, back, and profile.

### THE FORELEGS

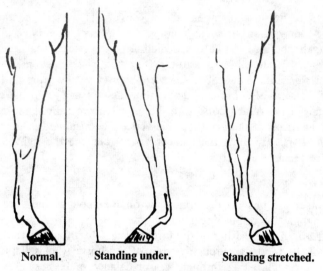

| Normal. | Standing under. | Standing stretched. |

**The formation of the forelegs.    Side view.**

*Side view.* The formation of a foreleg is correct when a plumb line falling from the point of the shoulder ends somewhat in front of the toe. When it slants backward, it is said to be set too far under the horse, and the horse is said to be standing under. In the opposite condition, it is said to be in camping position, and the horse is said to be standing stretched.

The horse is over at the knees or buck-kneed when the knee advances;

**Calf-kneed.**

**)ver at the knees or buck-kneed.**

**Cocked ankles.**

calf-kneed in the opposite condition. When the fetlocks advance, one says that he has cocked ankles. When the pasterns do not slope sufficiently, they are called high, low in the opposite case.

The slant of the fetlock is usually in direct relation to the length of the pastern, and a short pastern is also high, as a long pastern is also low.

**High and short pastern.**

**Low and long pastern.**

*Front view*. The formation of the forelegs is correct when they just about follow the direction of a plumb line which, in falling from the point of the shoulder to the ground, would evenly divide the knee, the cannon, the fetlock, the pastern and the hoof. If the legs fall outside of the plumb line, the horse is too wide at the chest. In the opposite condition, he is narrow at the chest. If the legs are turned out (the elbows turned in), the horse is splay-footed;

**The formation of the forelegs. Too wide at the chest.**

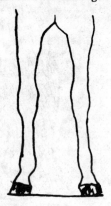

**The formation of the forelegs. Narrow at the ch**

in the opposite condition (with elbows turned out), he is called pigeon-toed. If the knees fall outside of the plumb line, the horse is bow-legged: in the opposite condition, he is knock-kneed. A horse may be splay-footed or pigeon-toed without it affecting the legs.

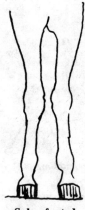

**Splay-footed.**

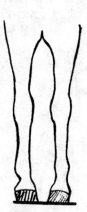

**Pigeon-toed.**

## THE HIND LEGS

*Side View.* The formation of the hind legs is good when a plumb line, in falling from the point of the buttock, touches the hock, goes by the shannon,

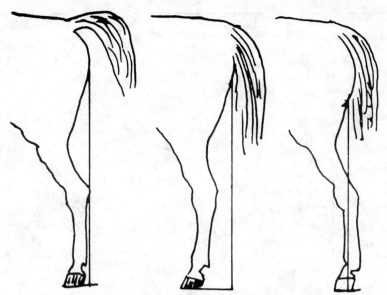

**Normal.**     **Standing under behind.**     **Standing stretched behind.**

**The formation of the hind legs. Side view.**

almost touching it, and ends slightly behind the heel. The horse is standing stretched behind when the legs pass behind this line; in the opposite condition, he is standing under behind.

As on the forelegs, there are cocked ankles, short, long, high or low pasterns.

*Hind View.* The formation of the hind leg is good when a plumb line, in falling from the point of the buttock, passes over the point of the hock. From the hock to the ground, the leg must continue along the same plumb line.

**Formation of the hind legs. Hind view.**     **Formation of the hind legs. Hind view.**
**Too wide at the hocks and pigeon-toed.**     **Too narrow at the hocks and splay-footed.**

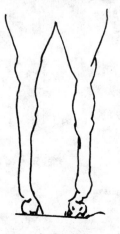 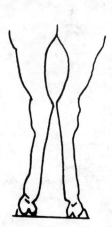

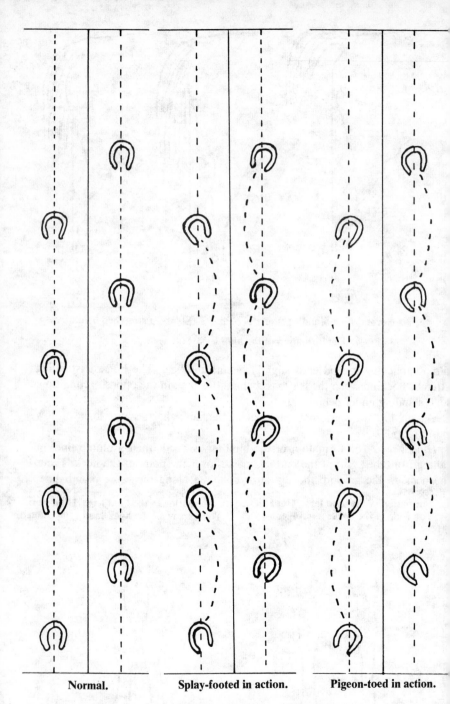

**Normal.**   **Splay-footed in action.**   **Pigeon-toed in action.**

**The formation in action.**

The horse is too wide at the hocks when the legs are too widely set apart, too narrow at the hocks when the legs are not sufficiently set apart.

The hind legs of a horse who is splay-footed behind are turned out, their hocks thus more than normally drawn together, and the horse is called cow-hocked. When he is pigeon-toed behind, he is called bandy-legged.

## THE FORMATION IN ACTION

A side, front, and hind view is required for judgment. Correct formation causes us to say that the horse moves straight and true. Seen from behind, the hind legs hide the corresponding forelegs; seen from the front, the forelegs hide the corresponding hind legs.

The horse *dishes* or *paddles* when, splay-footed in action, his foot in lifting approaches the supporting foot and moves away from it when coming down. He is *pin-toed* when, pigeon-toed in action, his foot in lifting, on the contrary, moves away from the supporting foot and approaches it when ready to touch down. He *crosses* or *plaits* when he places his feet on the same alignmen in front of each other. He *interferes* whenever the rising foot strikes the supporting one. He *brushes* when he interferes to the point of *speedy cutting,* leaving an injury on the affected limb. He *cross-fires* when he hits one of the forefeet with the opposite hind. He *forges or overreaches* when the toe of the hind shoe strikes the front shoe; forging referring to the noise produced. He *stumbles* when he strikes the ground with the toe.

## *Breeds*

It may be said that there does not exist, nowadays, a noble breed without an admixture of Arab blood, whether by crossbreeding with pure-bred Arabs or with the English Thoroughbred stallion in whom the Arabian blood is also flowing. At the turn of the seventeenth and eighteenth centuries three Arabian stallions—Byerley Turk, Darley Arabian and Godolphin Arabian—were imported to England where they were crossbred with Arabian and native mares, becoming the foundation sires of all English Thoroughbreds, who have been constantly upgraded through careful selective breeding and special feeding and training conditions.

Very soon the public powers and individual breeders became aware of their potential for improving other breeds, even though they did not require of their sires the same excellence as in producing Thoroughbreds. They were looking for the full-made, well-balanced type, clean-legged and harmonious in conformation, while in the latter everything was sacrificed to speed. The individual value of the sire, his performance on the racetrack, mattered most. English Thoroughbreds have been used for upgrading the native breeds in Europe and the United States and have transmitted to them the noble Arab blood of their oriental ancestry.

Horse Breeder in the Pasture, c. **1800. (Kupferstichkabinett, State Art Collections, Kassel. Retzlaff Archive)**

**Hyperion, English Thoroughbred. (Photo W. W. Rouch & Co. Ltd.)**

Some famous breeds carry an accurately known percentage of Arabian blood, such as the Trakehner in Germany and the Anglo-Arab in France. The former is 50 per cent English Thoroughbred, 25 per cent Arab, 25 per cent native, while the Anglo-Arab is a result of careful crossbreeding of English Thoroughbreds and pure-bred Arabs. The product of this cross-breeding is an "Anglo-Arab Thoroughbred." Certain Anglo-Arab Thoroughbred sires have serviced native mares of southwestern France (the "Navarrine Race") who had themselves an oriental strain and produced the part-bred Anglo-Arab. Today, as for all great breeds, there exists a Stud Book for this type which has been fixed. The minimum percentage of Arab strain required, which appears on the horse's record, is 25 per cent.

## THE ENGLISH THOROUGHBRED

The Thoroughbred, proudly considered by the British as "of a perfection

**Kilbarry, famous English jumper. (Photo W. W. Rouch & Co. Ltd.)**

hitherto unknown in the world," has an expressive head; a long, light, well-set-on neck; a well-defined, lean withers extending far back; high back and loins; a powerful croup; an ogival, high and deep chest; a long, sloping shoulder; a long forearm and thigh; strong limbs; broad, thick joints; clean tendons; fine hair and silky mane and tail.

## JUMPERS

There is no special breed of jumpers. Part-breeds and Thoroughbreds alike have provided a long list of champions.

## THE HUNTER

The hunter is the result of crossbreeding part-bred mares with full-made Thoroughbred or Hunter sires. Easy of action, robust and energetic, rather

**Gold Dust, English champion hunter. (Photo W. W. Rouch & Co. Ltd.)**

full-made, with powerful hindquarters, a good jumper, flowing at the extended canter, he is the ideal mount for the hunt.

## THE HACK

There is no such breed as the Hack, only a saddle horse deserving of the name; that is, of a perfect type of this category. If nowadays the name stands only for pleasure and show, at the turn of the century it meant the all-purpose horse, from the gentleman's Thoroughbred to the farmer's cob.

## THE ENGLISH THOROUGHBRED BRED IN FRANCE

Officially imported to France as late as 1833, the Thoroughbred's principal breeding countries are the Paris region, Normandy and the southwest. It bears very favorable comparison with the British products.

Blue Link, British hack champion. (Photo W. W. Rouch & Co. Ltd.)

An English Thoroughbred bred in France. (Courtesy the French Department of Agriculture, Division of National Studs)

**Palais Gallien, Thoroughbred bred in France. (Author's collection)**

## ARABIAN THOROUGHBRED BRED IN FRANCE

Arabia is the home par excellence of the most beautiful, most precious of all equine races. Through migration, imports, conquests, this breed has spread to the four corners of the world. Outside of Arabia, it exists more or less unalloyed in Syria, Iran and Mesopotamia. There are five strains—called *"El Hams"*, meaning, "the five"—at the origin of the Arab horses of noble

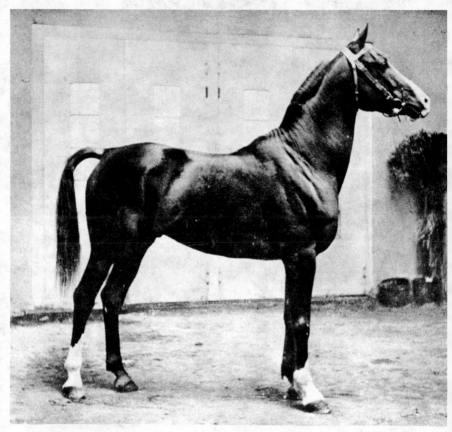

**Arabian Thoroughbred bred in France. (Courtesy the French Department of Agriculture, Division of National Studs)**

blood which, legend says, descend from the five mares on which Mohammed and his companions fled Mecca on the night of the hegira:

Kehilan
Seglami
Abeyan
Ajuz
Maneghi

These good little Arab horses (standing 14 to 14.3 h) sober, well-muscled, of great refinement, are outstanding for their stamina, their generosity, their frugality, over and above any larger horse (15 to 16 h).

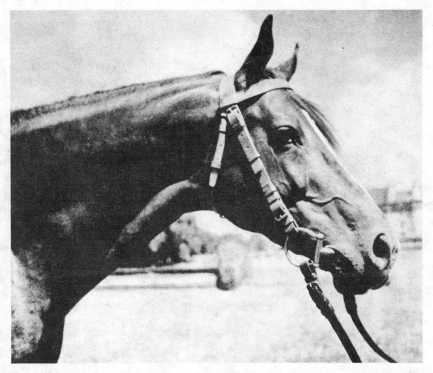

**Head of an Anglo-Arab.**

## THE PURE-BRED ANGLO-ARAB

Standing barely over 16 h, he has a broad forehead; expressive eyes; rather long, mobile ears; withers extending well back; shoulder sloping; arm well-muscled; back short and well-sustained; chest deep; hocks low; good joints; sound feet.

His oriental heritage endows him with intelligence, endurance, natural balance, sobriety, a capacity for heavy weight-carrying in proportion to his size. He is the perfect type of all-purpose saddle horse. After a brilliant military career, he is now a jumper, a combined training and dressage horse and has been shining with equal *éclat* in all three disciplines since the end of the war.

When fox-hunting was launched in southwestern France, the Anglo-Arab revealed himself as a remarkable hunter, due to his proverbial adroitness and endurance.

**Pure-bred Anglo-Arab. (Courtesy the French Department of Agriculture, Division of National Studs)**

## THE ANGLO-NORMAN

The Anglo-Norman averages from 15½ to 16½ h. He is of strong build, with a long, muscled neck, a well-placed withers, a long croup and a good top line. He is the product of crossbreeding of native mares and Thorough-bred stallions, with an admixture of Hunters. Even nowadays we find, beside saddle horses, excellent carriage horses among this breed.

## FRENCH TROTTERS

Normandy is also the home of the French trotter. Through crossbreeding Norman race horses and Thoroughbreds and a few Norfolk and American

**The Anglo-Norman. (Courtesy of the French Department of Agriculture, Division of National Studs)**

trotters, the type has now been fixed and boasts many a champion, among others the famous Jamin.

## THE LIPIZZANER OF THE SPANISH SCHOOL OF VIENNA

This breed originates with the Spanish horses which were imported to Austria under Charles VI. The five sires, Majestoso, Conversano, Napolitano, Pluto, Favori, founded five families which have been maintained perfectly distinct from one another, first at the Stud of Lipizza, later at Piber. Their perfect resemblance to their foundation sires gives an idea of their careful breeding. Standing close to the ground, well ribbed-up, with good legs, a high and slightly arched neck, they combine strength and suppleness, gentle-

**French trotter. (Courtesy of the French Department of Agriculture, Division of National Studs)**

ness and grace, peerless in the work of the manège. The world owes it to them and their riders that the full prestige of this unique repository of equestrian art has remained intact in all its glory.

## THE TRAKEHNER

This horse takes his name from the Trakehnen Stud Frederick William I, King of Prussia, founded in 1732. He is an elegant horse, well-muscled, full-made, of great stamina and gentleness. His breed alone accounted for 60 per cent of all German remounts before World War I, which shows how greatly developed it had become. It produces excellent saddle horses of great distinction, good action and fine stamina.

**The Lipizzaner. (Courtesy Col. Podhajsky)**

**The Trakehner. (Photo Werner Menzendorf)**

**The Hanoverian Horse. (Photo Tiedemann)**

## THE HANOVERANIAN HORSE

The Hanoveranian, useful under the saddle and in harness, goes back in his present form to the nineteenth century. Closely related to the Holstein, he owes everything to the Celle Stud which has constantly graded him up over the years by strong admixtures of English blood. He is, however, of a softer breed than the Trakehner.

## THE HOLSTEIN

The Holstein has been developed in this north German region which for climatic reasons is ideally suited to horse breeding. It is Germany's oldest breed and one of its best. The Dukes of Holstein began, as early as the fourteenth century, to breed a type which resulted from crossbreeding with Spanish horses (oriental blood). The present strain goes back to the nineteenth century, has nothing in common with the earlier, and has received a con-

**Holstein, Winzer. (Author's collection)**

**The Holstein. (Photo Werner Menzendorf)**

**The Westphalian. (Photo Vogelberg-Münster)**

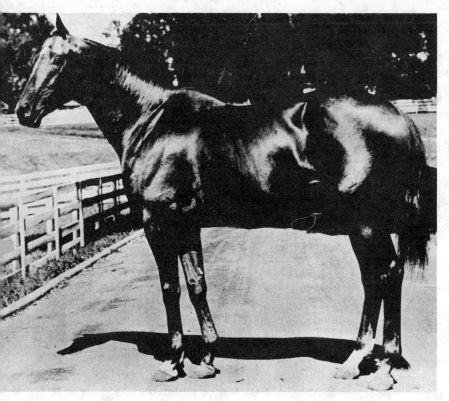

**English Thoroughbred bred in America, the Kentucky Derby winner Swaps. (U.S.D.A. photograph. Courtesy Mr. I. P. Earle)**

siderable admixture of English blood. It produces strong, sturdy-legged horses with good endurance. One of the many German jumpers of Holstein breed is the famous Meteor.

## THE WESTPHALIAN

This is a breed very similar to the Hanoveranian.

## ENGLISH THOROUGHBRED BRED IN THE UNITED STATES OF AMERICA

Selim and Othello were the first English Thoroughbreds to be imported to the United States in 1750. The American Thoroughbred is strong, powerful, and very resistant and has played a predominant role in the development of the American trotter.

**The Standardbred, Star's Pride, world's champion trotting stallion. (U.S.D.A. photograph. Courtesy Mr. I. P. Earle)**

## THE STANDARDBRED

This breed has been created entirely and exclusively in the United States by crossbreeding Thoroughbreds, Morgans and Amblers. Though he resembles the Thoroughbred, he is less refined, has a somewhat larger head, heavier limbs and greater endurance. The English Thoroughbred, Messenger, is the foundation sire. He was imported to the United States in 1788, and one of his descendants, the famous Rysdyk's Hambletonian 10, was foaled in this country in 1849. About 90 per cent of all present-day Standardbreds go back to him in the male line.

## THE MORGAN

His foundation sire was the stallion Justin Morgan who was foaled in 1793 in Vermont and lived to the ripe old age of 28 (1821). He stood but 14 h, was sturdy and energetic and transmitted his prepotent traits to the entire race which then became most useful in crossbreeding trotters and saddle horses alike. The Morgan is extremely good-tempered and obedient, long-lived and resistant. He stands 14 to 16 h.

**The Morgan, Bay State Wardissa, grand champion mare. (U.S.D.A. photograph. Courtesy Mr. I. P. Earle)**

## THE QUARTER HORSE

His foundation sire was the English Thoroughbred Janus who was foaled in 1756. His descendants reach extraordinary speeds over a quarter of a mile; hence their name. Crossbreeding of their Thoroughbred ancestors with the native mares has produced the cattleman's round-up horse. He stands about 14 h.

## PALOMINO

The term does not designate a race, but a color-breed. He looks somewhat like an Arab, but is larger, less refined, has a heavier head. He originally comes from Spanish Colonial Mexico, which explains his resemblance to the Arab. His color may be any of several golden shades, his eyes and skin must be black, his mane and tail flaxen, almost white. Only on the face and legs are white markings admissible. He stands 14.2 to 16 h.

The Quarter Horse, Poco Bueno, leading sire of breed champions. (U.S.D.A. photograph. Courtesy Mr. I. P. Earle)

Palomino, Top Hat, champion and sire of champions. (U.S.D.A. photograph. Courtesy Mr. I. P. Earle)

**The Cleveland Bay. (Courtesy Mr. Alexander Mackay-Smith, Editor,** The Chronicle of the Horse**)**

## THE CLEVELAND BAY

Originally the product of crossbreeding Thoroughbred stallions and native mares of the Cleveland District (England), the type is now also bred in the United States. Once a work horse, he is today a carriage horse, full-made, elegant, large, swift and resistant.

## Blemishes and Unsoundnesses

## THE HARD AND SOFT BLEMISHES

We shall discuss only the *hard and soft blemishes* which affect the limbs and are the most common and thus most useful to the young horseman's acquaintance. At the end of the section we shall describe the principal diseases of the foot and of the horse in general.

The hard blemishes (those affecting the bones) are: *splint, ringbone, sidebone, bone-spavin* or *shoe-boil, curb, false curb.*

The soft blemishes (of synovial, cystous or tendinous origin) are: *windgall; thoroughpin; hygromata.*

*Splints* occur on the cannon or shannon bone, generally on the inside face, due to blows, or, with very young horses, to premature and excessive work. There may only be one, or there may be two, one inside and one out, at the same height, or several lined up vertically.

While developing, they often cause lameness which disappears when they are fully formed. For treatment, the affected part is rubbed with a mercury ointment (blistering) or daubed with an iodine compound. The best treatment is obviously preventive: leather leggings or exercise and stable bandages, no overtaxing of the horse.

*Ringbones* are, like splints, bone tumors. Located either on the upper or lower pastern, they are most frequent and dangerous on the lower, right by the coronet. *Sidebones* are cartilaginous and caused by an excessive ossification of the cartilages of the foot. Both ring and sidebones are generally due to blows. Their treatment is practically the same as that of the splints (blistering).

*Bone-spavins* are situated on the inner and lower face of the hock. As are all hard blemishes which affect the hock, except for the curb, they are caused by ligamentary strain. Their seriousness depends largely on their place; the farther to the front or top, the more serious they are, because they increasingly handicap the normal flexing of the hock. They almost always cause a lameness when, upon leaving the stables, the muscles are cold, but which disappears with warming up. The handicap of the hock in flexing causes an alteration in the way of going.

*Curbs* are located on the inner and upper face of the hock, caused almost always by a traumatism, sometimes by a ligamentary strain, and do not handicap the locomotive system. *False curbs* sit on the outer, lower hind face of the hock and are as serious as the bone-spavins.

*Windgalls* and *Thoroughpins* are synovial tumors. They may be articular or tendinous. Windgalls are located on the fetlock (front and back). They are articular (the more serious condition) when they sit between the suspensory ligament and the cannon bone, tendinous when between the suspensory ligament and the flexor tendons. They may be found on a single side or on both at once, may be acute, hot, and cause lameness, or chronic, cold, and not cause lameness. Treatment consists of hosing down, wet bandages (water or astringents), all the way to tapping and firing. The best is to forestall them by limiting one's demands, hosing down the legs after work and using exercise and stable bandages.

**Articular windgall (soft blemish).**

**Tendinous windgall (soft blemish).**

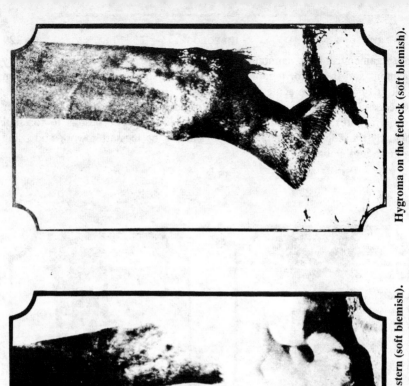

Hygroma on the fetlock (soft blemish).

Windgall on the pastern (soft blemish).

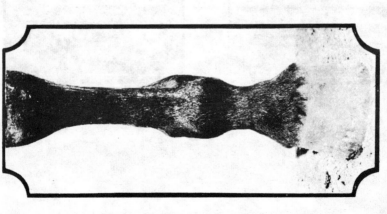

Windgall showing on both sides (soft blemish).

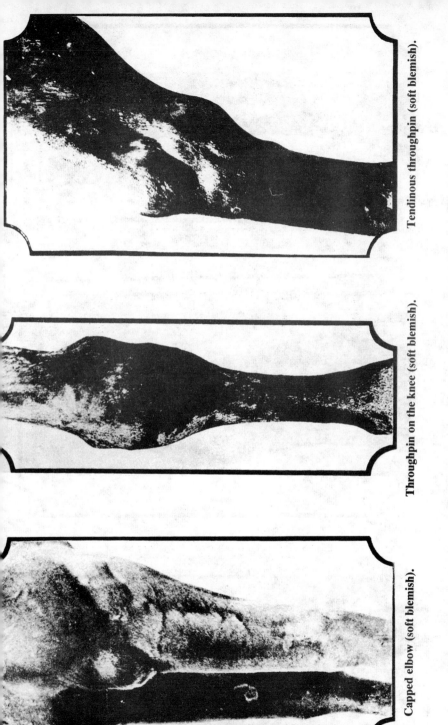

Capped elbow (soft blemish).

Throughpin on the knee (soft blemish).

Tendinous throughpin (soft blemish).

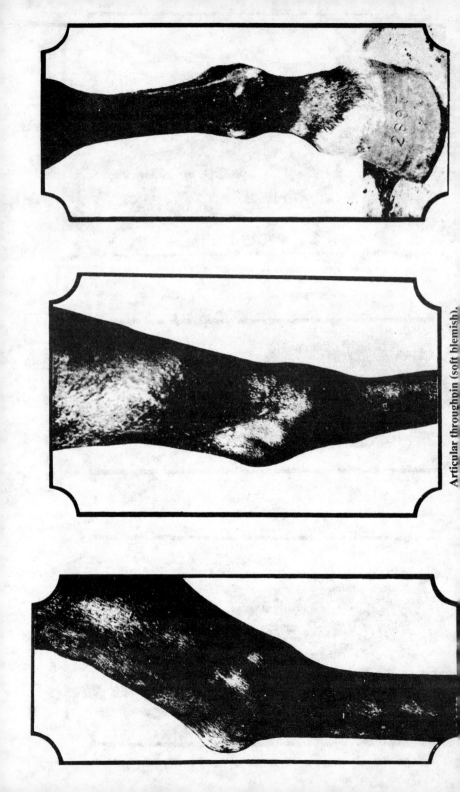

Articular throughpin (soft blemish).

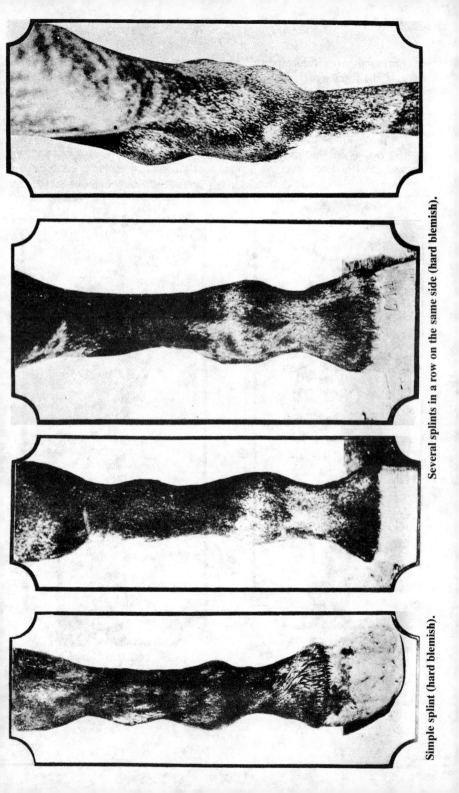

Several splints in a row on the same side (hard blemish).

Simple splint (hard blemish).

*Thoroughpins* are located on the hock and, more rarely, the knee. In the case of the foreleg they are tendinous when in the back of the knee, articular when on its outer surface. In the case of the hind legs they are tendinous when either in the hollow of the hock, inner face or both inner and outer faces, at the hamstring, or at the hock's inner lower face; articular when either in the hollow of the hock, inside or out, like the tendinous thoroughpin, but farther down and to the front. They are treated like windgalls.

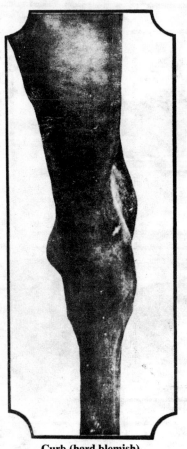

**Curb (hard blemish).**

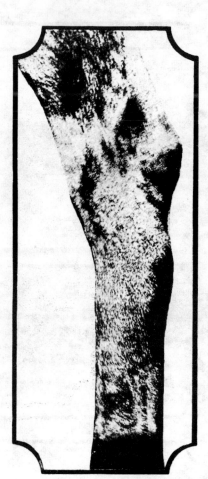

**False curb (hard blemish).**

*Hygromata,* depending on their location, are called capped elbow or capped hock. Both are usually due to rubbing or knocking against a hard body. The former may indicate deficient bedding, the latter almost certainly that the horse kicks inside his box. Treatment consists of dabbing on an ointment for absorption.

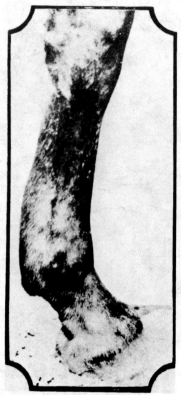

**Tendon sprain.**

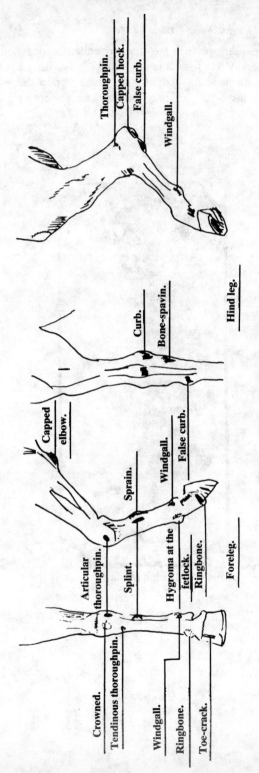

The seats of the blemishes (outside).

Thoroughpin.
Capped hock.
False curb.
Windgall.

Hind leg.

Curb.
Bone-spavin.

Capped elbow.

Sprain.
Windgall.
False curb.

Articular thoroughpin.
Splint.
Hygroma at the fetlock.
Ringbone.

Foreleg.

Crowned.
Tendinous thoroughpin.
Windgall.
Ringbone.
Toe-crack.

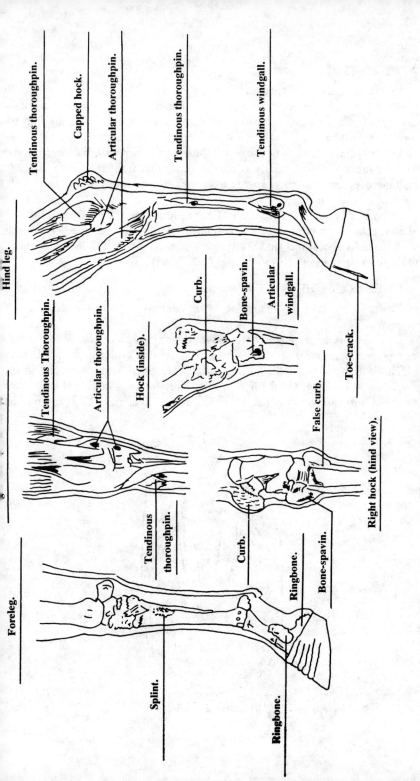

Hind leg.

Tendinous thoroughpin.

Capped hock.

Articular thoroughpin.

Tendinous thoroughpin.

Tendinous windgall.

Foreleg.

Tendinous Thoroughpin.

Articular thoroughpin.

Hock (inside).

Curb.

Bone-spavin.

Articular windgall.

Toe-crack.

Tendinous thoroughpin.

Curb.

Ringbone.

Bone-spavin.

False curb.

Right hock (hind view).

Splint.

Ringbone.

The seats of the blemishes (inside).

## ACCIDENTS

*Rope burns* are self-explanatory, and the chapter on tack tells us how to prevent them. If the accident occurs, cut the rope or free the horse immediately, no matter how, so as to limit the consequences. These may be insignificant or serious; if you are not sure which, call the veterinarian.

The preventive treatment for *cracked heels* is to dry well, but not rub, the folds of the joints, particularly at the pasterns, after hosing down or working on humid ground. If the harm is done, wash with soapy water and apply vaseline or glycerin.

*Sprains* are a violent distension of the tendon due to a sudden effort; or else, regular overtaxing which eventually unsettles the tendons. Heat will soon make its appearance and, if overwork continues, will also lead to sprains. Only the veterinarian can treat these (line-firing).

## AILMENTS OF THE FOOT

The principal ones are *sandcrack, corn, contracted heels, thrush,* and *nail in the foot.*

*Sandcrack* is a vertical split through the thickness of the hoof, called, depending on its location, a toe-crack, quarter-crack or bar-crack. It may pinch the flesh and make the horse stumble. Treatment requires special shoes.

*Corn* is bruised flesh at the heels (particularly of the forefeet, almost never the hind). It may be dry, wet, or suppurating. Treatment also requires the services of a farrier.

**Contracted heels.**

*Contracted heels* is the narrowing of the hoof, mainly at the heels. It is characterized by an ever more hollow sole, an atrophied frog. If severe, it may cause lameness and overheating of the foot. The wall should be rasped down at the heel and a special shoe applied.

*Thrush* is characterized by a purulent discharge caused by a suppuration which is liable to cause detachment of the frog. It is treated by applying wads soaked in a copper or tar solution.

*Nail in the foot* is a wound occasioned by a sharp or pointed object which injures the underside of the foot (sole, frog, heels). It is likely to cause immediate lameness. The object must be picked out and the wound well washed. If the injury is not perfectly superficial, call the veterinarian, and always keep the nail for his inspection.

## THE PRINCIPAL DISEASES OF THE HORSE

*Flatulent colic.* In veterinary science this word means intestinal pain. It may be caused by diet or overwork, though some horses are colic-prone; they are problem animals. Usually it is just a matter of an obstructive calculus preventing the expulsion of excrement and winds. But sometimes it is an *intestinal impaction or obstruction* which is caused by a twist of the bowel, bringing about the death of the horse because the intestine does not let excrement pass any more.

A horse who has the colic stamps, scratches, incessantly looks at his flank, lies down, rolls, stands up again. His belly is bloated. If your horse should show these symptoms, it is best to call the veterinarian who will administer a morphine or pilocarpine shot. While waiting for the veterinarian, remove whatever there is left of his feed, rub him down vigorously and massage his flanks. Walk him and put a blanket on him. If he is in a stall, you had better place him in a loose box with thick bedding. You may administer a three-quart enema of lukewarm soapy water.

*Sunstroke.* Place the horse in the shade in a well ventilated spot, perform a slight bloodletting (at the tip of the ear), sprinkle cold water on his head and body.

The *general symptoms of the sick horse* are that he does not feel like eating, his eyes are sad, he seems restless. A temperature of over 100.5°F confirms these symptoms.

*Other diseases of the horse* are: tetanus, glanders and farcy, anthrax, bronchitis, pneumonia, pleurisy, staggers or megrim, periodic ophtalmia, roaring and whistling.

Diagnosis and treatment of these diseases lie, however, within the sole competence of a veterinarian, and their description is of no use to the young rider. The foregoing list is meant to acquaint him with their names, no more,

Procedure for Giving Medication in a Princely Stables, **early nineteenth cent**
**(Kupferstichkabinett, State Art Collections, Kassel. Retzlaff Archive)**

while another serious part of this subject and which concerns him
directly is

*The back injuries caused by the saddle.* Most of the time there are not
but several causes for these: the panels of the saddle are not sufficiently pad
any more and their leather is stiffened from lack of care; poor groom
and the subsequent friction of saddle against dust-and-sweat-soiled
eventually leads to injury; beginning riders, through lack of seat, slide b
and forth, shifting the saddle which ceases to fit the horse's back corre
a pad is used which is not clean and supple (maybe brushed and beate
take off the dust, but not washed to rid it of the dried sweat which has m
it hard and lumpy). Some injuries are of the horse's own doing in that he

a bad back, hard to saddle, or an extremely delicate skin. Such horses mean everlasting trouble to a riding school.

Cleanliness is thus necessary in order to avoid injuries—cleanliness of horse and tack. Obviously the saddle should be chosen so it fits the horse perfectly: the panels must bear on the entire length in contact with the back and the pommel be roomy enough not to bother the withers where injuries are far more serious than on the back. During the hot season, the back must be sponged after work to take off the sweat and refresh the tissues. If the horse is very hot, yet the season does not permit a good wash with water, he should be rubbed down vigorously with a wisp changed as often as necessary so as to finish the operation with a dry one.

At the first sign of injury, the horse should be taken off work. If this cannot be done, he must not be given to beginners and double care should be taken of the wound before and after work. It is also a good idea to change his saddle, for no two used saddles bear down on the same back in exactly the same way; and when it is taken off, the back, and particularly the wound, should be cleaned and treated. On a sound horse, ridden by a horseman with a good degree of fixity who rides light on a good saddle, a wound on the back, provided it is not too deep, is very likely to heal. If quite superficial, charcoal powder is an excellent remedy, if applied after the wound has been cleaned when saddling and unsaddling, so that the wound is constantly covered with the powder.

The panels of the saddle, to stay supple, must be washed and treated as soon as it is taken off with glycerin soap or Brecknell. If you can afford to sacrifice a pad, cut into it a hole corresponding to the location of the wound to keep it free and out of contact despite the rider's pressure on the saddle. For this solution to be effective, the pad must be of thick felt and well fastened to the saddle so it will not slip and slide.

During the hot time of the year, patches of small pimples appear on the back. If they are not cared for from the first, a wound develops. Though they are caused by the blood and have nothing to do with the tack, its rubbing on the affected part will lead to a wound. Refreshing feed should be given for a while and oats cut down or out. If necessary, administer a laxative. The horse should be taken out of work for a few days, the pimples soaped and rinsed with a bicarbonate and water solution.

Another of the saddle horse's injury-prone regions is on and around the brisket. The only way to heal these wounds is, at the first sign, to take the horse out of work and to change the girth which is either too broad or too narrow. Leather girths are superior to others in that they can be had in a greater variety of models, can be well and easily washed after work and suppled, if necessary, by intensive applications of glycerin soap.

Stables at the Rest Quarters, **by Philip Wouvermans. (Rijksmuseum, Amsterdam)**

## *Care of the Horse*

The daily grooming not only cleans but invigorates the whole body by stimulating skin and circulation. Do it outdoors as often as your time permits, and keep your curry comb away from the bony parts: head, haunches, shoulders, limbs. Here you should use the dandy brush which takes off every last bit of dust all over the body and also cleans and disentangles mane and tail. Follow this up with the body brush over the entire horse and finish with a dry rag, following the direction of the hair of the coat. The damp sponge cleans eyes, nostrils and other openings; the hoof pick picks the feet, after which they are washed and greased.

After the day's work, hose down the legs, once more pick the hoofs, pass the dandy brush over the back which you tap well to bring back circulation after hours under the saddle. If ever you want special brilliance of the coat, use your hands in finishing up, always in the direction of the hair; they will take with them the last and least of dust particles. The blanket in winter and

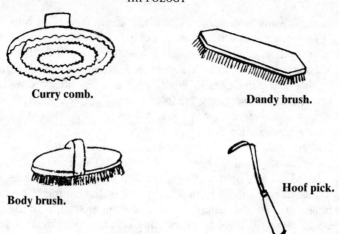

**Curry comb.**

**Dandy brush.**

**Body brush.**

**Hoof pick.**

the sheet in the summer will protect it from dust, make it shiny and generally easier to keep well groomed.

When the mane and tail have been brushed out strand by strand with the dandy brush, you use the water brush.

If the tail is muddy or soiled with dung, dip it into a pail full of water and rub the hair together. Shake out the water and finish drying with a rag. From time to time, mane and tail should be washed out with soap. Never comb them; you would pull out the hair in irregular bunches and end up with a "rat tail." But the mane needs occasional shortening and thinning, accomplished by pulling out a few hairs at a time, those longest and nethermost. The same is done beneath and on either side of the tail to make it look tidy. If your horse's mane is clipped, the clippers must be used once a week.

Clipping makes grooming easier and keeps the horse from perspiring too much during work in the winter. When, as it should be, the winter coat is left under the saddle and on the legs, we speak of a hunting clip. If you clip before the first frosts, you will have to repeat it once or twice during the winter.

Another part of the care of your horse is baths. Meant for refreshment, they should be given during the warm season, for a quarter of an hour at a time, preferably in a running brook with a sandy bottom, immersing the whole body, or just the legs.

## The Bedding

Bedding consists of straw, peat, sawdust or wood shavings, of bracken or heather. Straw is best, particularly wheat straw. You need 6 to 10 pounds a day per horse; and although it is not necessary to remake the bedding entirely every day, it must be done at least once a fortnight, once a week being a good average. The soiled straw and droppings are withdrawn every day, leaving the damp straw. Whatever has been lifted is replaced with fresh straw. Once a week, the stalls and boxes are completely mucked out, the floor washed, before new straw is put in. All this should be done with doors and windows wide open.

The litter must be sufficiently abundant for the horse to lie down and stretch comfortably and without risk of injury. The exact quantity depends on the size of the box or stall. Boxes should be 12 by 9 feet; stalls should be 10 by 6 feet. There should be nothing on the walls that might hurt the horse. The manger may be of concrete, wood, cast-iron, enamel, with rounded edges and easy to clean. If there is not running water in every box or stall, a pail should be fastened onto the wall, not by a nail but a metal hoop, like a sort of collar, from which the pail can easily be lifted and replaced. This avoids exposing the horse to injury on a nail.

The hay can be placed on top of the litter; and if the horse is in the bad habit of scratching and thereby wasting the hay, his ration must be given him in several small portions. Racks are not recommended; there is no sense in accustoming the horse to raising his head and hollowing out the withers by taking his feed from above, when it is often hard enough during training to make him lower his head and all one's efforts are bent on developing the withers by giving the right direction to the neck muscles. Besides, even the cleanest hay is somewhat dusty, and there is no need for him to shake the dust down into his eyes.

The partitions may be swinging bails or stationary. The latter are more expensive but superior, provided they are high enough and reach back sufficiently. They should be covered by door-matting. Thus equipped, they are the only kind of partition to offer efficient protection against kicks. The swinging bails are attached to the manger by a hook and hung, behind, either from the ceiling or by a chain from a pole. This chain must have a hook for easy opening regardless of the pressure exerted on the bail, in case, for instance, the horse gets his leg caught over it.

**Hook used in hanging swinging bails.**

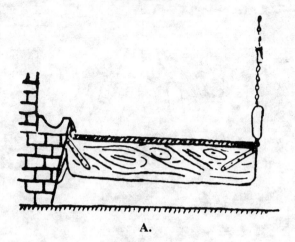

**A.**

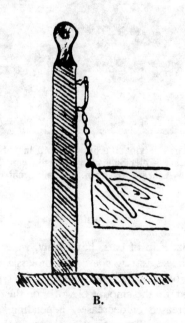

**B.**

A. Swinging bail hung from the ceiling.
B. Swinging bail hung by a chain from a pole.

Horse Races and Popular Merrymaking at Augsburg in 1509. **From a manuscript belonging to the lansquenet leader Sebastian Schertlin von Burtenbach (Augsburg, c. 1570-1577). (University Library Erlangen. Retzlaff Archive)**

## Feeding

A horse's feed is made up of oats, hay, straw, water, and foodstuffs containing sugar and molasses (straw chaff with molasses and straw chaff with molasses and crushed oats). The rations depend on type and conformation and breed, on one hand, on the amount of work, on the other.

Oat rations are increased or decreased, depending on whether the work is light, or hard and long. The rations indicated below are average, and experience alone will make a good horsemaster who finds the right dosage for each horse, at rest or at work.

Oats          6 to 12 pounds per day

| Hay   | 8 to 12 pounds per day           |
|-------|----------------------------------|
| Straw | Enough to assure good bedding    |

The rations are usually equally divided into two or three daily feeds. An Arab proverb says that "the morning's oats go into the droppings; the evening's into the croup."

If you want to allow for three-hour intervals between feedings and work, the exact hours depend, of course, on the working schedule. A few oats should be given to the horse in the morning so he will not go out on an empty stomach. A medium horse working morning and afternoon, for instance, should be fed as follows:

| 6:00 A.M.   | 2 pounds of oats                       |
|-------------|----------------------------------------|
| 8:00 A.M.   | Start work                             |
| 12:00 noon  | 4 pounds of oats and ½ ration hay      |
| 3:00 P.M.   | Restart work                           |
| 6:00 P.M.   | 6 pounds of oats and ½ ration hay      |

Horses consume in 24 hours an average of 5 (sometimes up to 8) gallons of water. A bucket of water is best left permanently in the box or stall; but if the horse must be watered at the trough, this should be done at least two or three times a day, preferably after eating a little hay so he will not ingurgitate on an empty stomach, but never after eating oats.

Do not give very cold water to a hot horse. In winter, you had better let the water warm up in the buckets inside the stables. When watering him after work, do not let him bolt the water at one long draught without catching his breath. Raise his head and make him open his mouth by lightly pressing your fingers on the lower bars.

Whatever foodstuffs you give, they must be of good quality. *Oats* must be heavy, without odor or dust. They may profitably be given crushed, mainly to horses with poor chewing habits (in whose droppings you find grains).

*Hay* is a complete food, sufficient nourishment for a horse at rest, or almost at rest. It should be dry, nonfermented, not over one year old, but not freshly cut either (wait two or three months) and not contain any foreign bodies or dust. *Wheat straw* is the best of straws; it should be golden yellow, shiny and sweet smelling.

*Water* must be clean, clear and non-polluted.

*Carrots* which may be given as a supplementary ration of 4 to 6 pounds per day, singly or mixed with bran, are an excellent food; tonic, refreshing, laxative.

*Mash* should be given from time to time to avoid heating of the bowels; some kinds are good remedies for reluctant eaters. Some are made with barley (about 1 pound) and bran (2 to 3 pounds) mixed in a pail, wetted down with water and possibly an admixture of carrots and crushed oats. Some, a little harder to prepare, contain linseed, barley meal, oats, bran and straw chaff, all of it wetted down with warm water.

## *Tack*

All leather, steel and cloth objects clothing the horse in the stables or at work are included in the concept of tack (an abbreviation of tackle).

For work, this includes: saddle, bridle, pad, breast-plate (or breast-piece), racing (or newmarket) girth, standing and running martingale, leggings, knee-caps, exercise bandages.

In the stables, tack includes: halter (or head collar), halter ropes, sheets, blankets and rugs, roller, stable bandages.

### THE SADDLE

The *tree* is the frame of the saddle. The *pommel* is the raised front part, the front *arch* of the tree. The *seat* is the leather part between the pommel and the cantle. The *skirts* are small pieces of leather protecting the rider's thighs from the stirrup bars. The *stirrup* bars are metal pieces on the tree beneath the skirts, which hold the stirrup leathers and have spring safety catches. While they keep the stirrup leathers from slipping out backward, they also open to release them in an emergency. The *flaps,* leather pieces protecting the rider's thighs and knees against the girth, constitute the sides of the saddle.

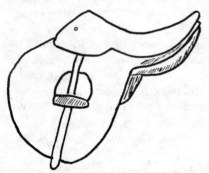

Saddle with stirrup.

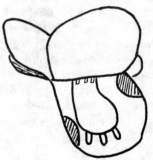

Saddle with raised flap.

The saddle seen from underneath, the part which is in contact with the horse, is made up of: the *panels* going from the pommel to the cantle with a free passage down the middle so as not to bear down on the spinal column. The *sweat flaps,* somewhat smaller than the flaps, protect the horse from the

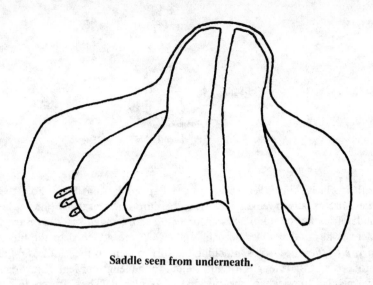

**Saddle seen from underneath.**

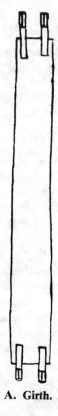

**A. Girth.**

**B. Girth.**

**Eye.**

**Branch.**

**Tread.**

**Stirrup.**

girth buckles. The *billets,* between the flaps and sweat flaps, hold the girth. There are usually three on each side, the third an emergency billet. The *girth,* made of leather or webbing, sometimes plaited, keps the saddle on the horse's back. It has two buckles on each end which are attached to the billets. The *stirrup leathers* are straps attaching the stirrup irons to the saddle, D's punched into a part of their length for adjustment to the length of leg. The *stirrup irons* are metal fittings where the rider's foot is placed. They are composed of a *tread* from which branches rise in an arch to meet at the eye, through which the stirrup leather is threaded.

## THE BRIDLE

This may be a *snaffle bridle* or *double bridle.* The *headpiece* or *headstall* forms the top, resting on the poll. The *browband* lies on the forehead; it has a loop on either end through which pass the straps of the headpiece. The *cheekstraps* run down the sides to the *snaffle rings* and are buckled onto them. The straps of the *noseband,* running beside them, have an adjustment buckle to hold the noseband at the desired height. It is butt (bridle leather is called, butt) passing along the lower edge of the face and keeps the horse from opening his mouth too wide. It is more than anything an ornament, unless composed of three pieces, joined by two small rings and a buckle and placed between the lower edge of the mouth and the snaffle rings. In this case, it really keeps the horse from opening his mouth and reinforces the action of the snaffle. This is called a *drop noseband,* and is used only in combination with the snaffle bit (without a curb!). Finally there is the *snaffle bit* or *bridoon* which will be dealt with when we get to the various bits.

When the bridle is complete, there are two additional cheekstraps for the curb bit and the bit itself with its curb chain. It is the snaffle used in this combination, not by itself, which is called the *bridoon.*

A *pad* is often placed under the saddle—shaped like it and attached to it by straps at the billets—made of felt or lambskin. It has advantages and disadvantages; at any rate, it must be kept impeccably clean and supple, devoid of any foreign body which might injure the horse's back.

Snaffle bridle. Side view.

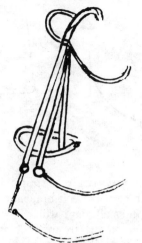

Double bridle. Side view.

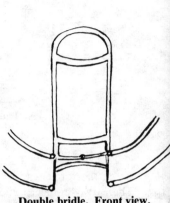

Double bridle. Front view.

A. Drop noseband.

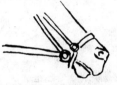

B. Drop noseband.

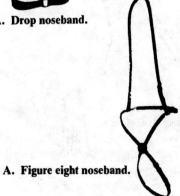

A. Figure eight noseband.

B. Figure eight noseband.

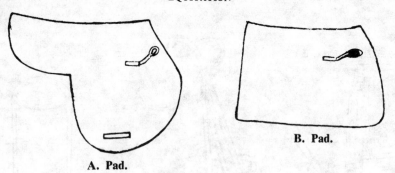

**B. Pad.**

**A. Pad.**

The *breast-plate* (or *breast-piece*) is a strap passing from the girth between the forelegs to the breast where it branches out by means of a ring. These two branches end in small rings which in turn are linked by a flat little piece of butt on the neck, slightly in front of the withers. From each of these rings, there goes a small strap to the saddle where they are attached by a ring under each-skirt. Its purpose is, officially, to keep the saddle from sliding back; unofficially, to permit the inexperienced rider to hold on to the strap over the neck if need be, without jobbing his horse in the mouth.

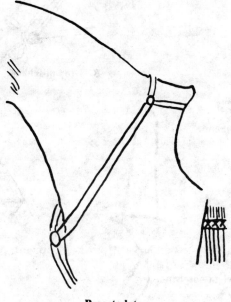

**Breast plate.**

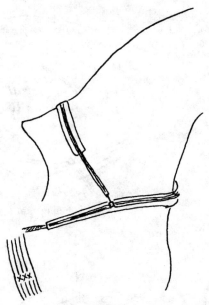

**Racing or Newmarket girth.**

If in jumping you are afraid the saddle might slip backward, the *racing* or *Newmarket girth* is a better device. It is a flat, rather broad leather, usually lined with lambskin. The two ends are attached to the billets. A rather narrow piece of butt, attached on each side of the racing girth and pasing over the base of the neck, keeps it at the desired place.

*Martingales* are meant to keep the horse from exaggeratedly raising his head. The *standing martingale* is a strap from noseband to girth, passing through a leather collar; a buckle makes it adjustable. It rather aggravates the vice it is supposed to cure; the horse leans on this device in order to escape its action, working the neck muscles in the opposite direction—upward; so it is a very bad training gear, good only for the horseman who unexpectedly must ride a star-gazer.

The *running martingale* is far superior. It is a strap starting at the girth, passing over the breast, where by a ring it branches out. These branches, in turn, each end in a ring through which the reins slide. Its length is adjustable by a buckle at the bottom; and the fit is correct if, at a halt, with a normal position of the head, reins taut, the reins tauten the martingale. It reinforces the action of the snaffle, leaves the role of the hands intact, is not a purely mechanical means of constraint like the standing martingale.

**A.  Standing martingale.**

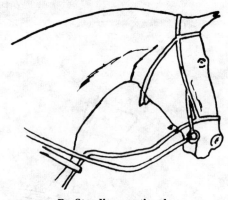

**B.  Standing martingale.**

**A.  Running martingale.**

**B.  Running martingale.**

The leather *leggings,* lined with foam rubber, protect cannons, shannons and fetlocks from the blows the horse may give himself during work. The *exercise bandages* support tissues and tendons and thereby avoid tendon strain. They also successfully prevent windgalls. A layer of cotton wool is usually placed between them and the leg. Like stable bandages, they are most useful, but must be put on right. Of slightly elastic cloth, they should be tight enough to do the job and not slip but not so tight as to bother and squeeze the tendons, which would render the remedy worse than the evil. The strings tying them up must lie flat, their knots on the outside of the leg; never in front, much less behind on the tendon.

**Leather legging.**

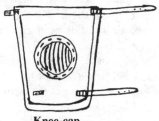

**Knee-cap.**

**Head collar.**

*The stable bandages* are of thicker material (wool, cotton stockinette, flannel). They also are useful over occasional applications of cotton wool soaked in water or astringent lotion. All bandages must remain absolutely supple, and the greatest care must be taken lest some foreign body get rolled between them and the leg. All horses should use stable bandages which, though they must not be too tight, are less delicate to put on than are the exercise bandages, because they need not be adjusted quite so perfectly. Even when a little too loose, they are less liable to slip, since the horse is not moving; and the consequences, should it happen, would be less serious. In short, you cannot afford to make a mistake with the exercise bandages (one way or another), while the main thing with the stable bandages is not to tighten them too much. If they slip, you tighten them a little more next time, till they stay in place. You may use stable bandages without exercise bandages, but not vice versa.

The *knee-caps* protect the knee. They are made of sturdy cloth, reinforced with leather and used in schooling over the fences at liberty and during transfers by rail or van.

The *cavesson*, the *lunge*, the *roller*, the *long reins* and the *chambon* have been discussed in "Training."

The *halter* (or *head collar*) should be of leather and well adjusted to avoid injury of the head and keep the horse from getting loose. He may be haltered in his stall by a chain, by a rope, or by a leather line. Although the first device is certainly the most solid and lasting, it rattles every time the horse moves his head and, in an emergency, cannot be severed as easily as rope or leather. It should be used only with horses who might bite through their line and then take a turn around the stables at night, causing serious kicking accidents. The chain also requires a slanting iron bar firmly affixed to the wall where it can slide, so as to avoid rope burn. For the same reason it is better to use a *log-headcollar* with rope or leather: two lines, one on each side of the halter and which are kept stretched by a block of wood at the end, beyond the attachment ring.

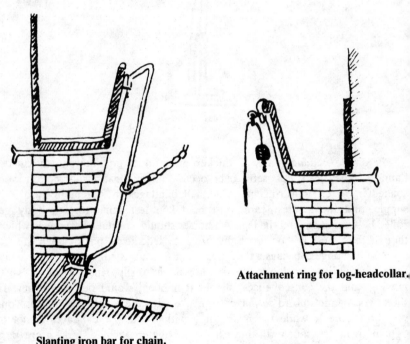

**Attachment ring for log-headcollar.**

**Slanting iron bar for chain.**

*Muzzles* of different types exist for horses who eat too much straw. They are needed only in boxes, for in a stall you can just pull the straw back a bit. Another item is the *bib,* a leather fitting for the head-collar of horses who bite and tear their clothing (bandages and blankets).

We shall discuss neither blankets, nor rollers; there is nothing in particular to say about them, and the best way to acquaint yourself with all these objects is, anyway, to do some "browsing" in a friendly saddler's shop.

## THE BITS

Their great number is complicated by a mass of different combinations. We shall be content to enumerate the most current which can be utilized by most riders and with all horses.

There are two main categories: snaffle bits, and curb bits. Others are part one, part the other, such as the *Pelham* and *Goyoaga* (or Spanish jumping bit).

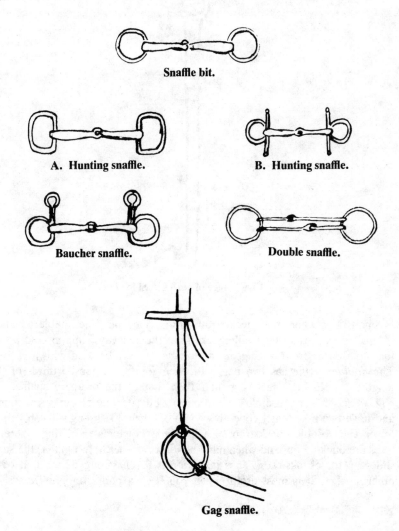

**Snaffle bit.**

**A.  Hunting snaffle.**          **B.  Hunting snaffle.**

**Baucher snaffle.**          **Double snaffle.**

**Gag snaffle.**

The snaffle bit has a rather thin mouthpiece, jointed in the middle, with a ring on each end where the reins and the cheekpieces connecting it with the bridle are buckled on. There are double-jointed snaffle bits, good for use with a port-mouthed curb bit. The *hunting snaffle* is different only in that the mouthpiece is somewhat thicker and the rings on each side a little larger. Some have a vertical bar for more efficient action in turning, others have smaller bars ending in flattened rings. The mouthpiece of the *Baucher snaffle* is like that of an ordinary snaffle but there are two little upper cheeks ending

**Cheekpiece of curb bit. Side view.**

in small rings where the cheek straps are buckled on. The double advantage of this snaffle is that the small cheeks limit the sideways slipping and prevent the mouthpiece from resting on the tongue. It may be used with a curb bit. The *double snaffle* has two bars with their joints at opposite thirds of their length; its relaxing effect is greater than that of the ordinary snaffle. The *gag snaffle* has an ordinary mouthpiece, but its lateral rings are thicker and have two holes each (one above and one below) through which pass the lower ends of the cheekstraps. Each cheekstrap ends in a ring where the reins are buckled on, and when hand action causes them to tighten, the snaffle slides up the cheekstraps. Thus its action is much stronger than that of the other snaffles. It is most useful when you have a puller on your hands, but one must be experienced enough to use it safely. Since it makes free contact with the bit difficult, its effect may be attenuated by the addition of reins on the snaffle rings. While you are using only these, the snaffle bit acts like any other snaffle, and the gag reins will not perform unless the ordinary ones become ineffectual. The *curb bit,* unlike the snaffle acts on the bars, not on the corners of the lips. Acting by the lever system, its effect on the mouth is proportionately stronger than the action  of the horseman's hand on the rein. It is made up of a *bar* (the mouthpiece) and two *cheeks* which, one third down, are attached to the bar. At the top they end in rings for the cheekstrap buckles by which the bit is attached to the bridle. At their lower ends there are rings to receive the reins. At the top of each cheek's lower third there is a D for the lip strap.

The *curb chain* is an integral part of the curb bit, acting as its fulcrum. It is hooked onto the bit. When upon rein action the latter comes to swing, the curb chain bears down into a depression, called the curb-chain groove. If well adjusted, with the cheeks at a 30 degree angle, the curb chain touches this part without twisting or riding up. The *lipstrap* keeps the horse from seizing the cheeks of the bit with lips or teeth. It is a narrow strap, its ends attached to D's on the cheeks and passing through an extra ring in the center of the curb chain.

The bridle should be adjusted so the inclination of the cheeks of the bit may attain 45 degrees, no more. The greater the difference in the length of the lower cheek and that part of the upper cheek where the curb chain is hooked on, the more powerful is the curb.

**L'Hotte bit (arched).**

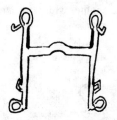

**Port-mouthed curb bit.**

The *bar* may be straight, arched (half-moon bit), port-mouthed. The choice depends on the thickness of the tongue (see Schooling). The *L'Hotte bit,* an arched bit, is the most universal and generally adaptable to every horse's mouth. The *swinging* or *Weymouth bit,* where the mouthpiece, rather than immobile in relation to the cheeks, slides up and down them for about half an inch, is used to incite the horse to "champ the bit." It may or may not be port-mouthed. I have spoken of its advantages and disadvantages in "Schooling."

There are variations to all these bits, but let us close our list with mention of the *reversible bit* which may be used with or without a bridoon. It is a crooked bit, powerful and gentle at once. Since the lower parts of the cheeks recede, the horse cannot grasp them and the use of a lipstrap becomes super-

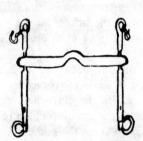

**Port-mouthed, swinging or Weymouth bit.**

**Reversible bit.**

flous. The Pelhams have the same general shape as the curb bits. They have a bar mouthpiece or are made up of two hinged pieces, have two branches with rings at the lower ends where the bridle is buckled on. Each branch has a ring at the level of the mouthpiece. The Pelham also has a curb chain, so that the reins attached to the upper rings (at mouthpiece level) make it act like a snaffle, while the reins on the lower rings make it act like a curb bit.

**Hinged Pelham**

**Non-hinged Pelham.**

When the mouthpiece is made up of two pieces, like a snaffle, the Pelham has the same advantages as a snaffle bit, but less power than an ordinary curb bit; if a bar mouthpiece, it has the same power as a curb bit, but not the relaxing effect of an ordinary snaffle bit. Moreover, lightness is less easily obtained, since the horse only carries one mouthpiece. It is a hybrid bit, not suitable for work or training, but useful in the open for certain horses when the rider's hand is not very adroit. Its usefulness is null in horse shows where the rider would be encumbered by its four reins, without enjoying its advantages. Some solve the problem by buckling a single rein onto a strap with one end attached to the upper, the other to the lower, ring. Thus the rein acts simultaneously as a snaffle and curb rein, without the rider being able to regulate anything whatsoever, except the tension of the rein.

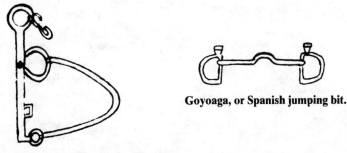

**Goyoaga, or Spanish jumping bit.**

**Pelham (special arrangement).**

Let us limit our study to these models, which are in universal use by horse-men practicing classic equitation, and leave aside all those peculiar to a single region and, if not unknown, at least not used elsewhere in the world.

## Conclusion

You will agree with me that there has been little in the foregoing that we could have dispensed with. On the contrary, there are several details, even subjects, I have not touched but which will come up from day to day as you begin to be in contact with horses. Those are, however, of such a nature that they cannot be properly understood on paper. I know your instructor will initiate you into them by demonstrations and practice sessions.

One such matter is the delicate one of saddling and bridling. Its subtlety has been hinted at by the comparison of that most smiled at yet most beloved of literature's horsemen, Don Quixote, who asserted that " 'tis an office of more trust to shave a man's beard than to saddle a horse."

# V. The Lighter Side

La Cavalière. **Marie Elizabeth Wrede. (From the author's collection)**

When all the world is young, lad,
And all the trees are green;
And every goose a swan, lad,
And every lass a queen;
Then hey for boot and horse, lad,
And round the world away:
Young blood must have its course, lad,
And every dog his day.
—CHARLES KINGSLEY

## Introduction

It is perhaps not fair to enter into this part, which is so enticingly called "The Lighter Side" with pages and pages of what at times may come to weigh most heavily on your shoulders—the organization and running of your establishment. Yet none of the distractions and successes will come to you unless the infrastructure is there to support them.

So let us step together onto our new premises which will eventually be or not be what we make or fail to make of them. It would be most functional to assume that our establishment is small to medium size, with just the necessary amount of serviceable horses, two or three grooms, a secretary and, at its head, you, a young instructor. Until you can persuade them to mend their ways, crack horsemen will tend toward the great schools or clubs where the locality's "grand masters" are officiating. So most of your customers, or members if you have a club, are probably in the beginner to intermediate class; and until they have become sufficiently impressed with you to bring their friends, their number will remain about as average as the rest.

I am using this example of a school or club run by you, because working under the supervision of a more experienced riding master or manager, you would learn from him, in the normal course of your working days, a great deal of what I am going to tell you, and, if he is a dynamic teacher, would be moulded by him in his image without any conscious effort on his part.

## *At the Head of a School*

A few rules never change, regardless of the size or nature of your establishment. The machine will function no better and no worse than how you set it up on its tripod: the *office* which plans and organizes and the *stables* and *riding hall* where plans are carried out and organization is implemented.

## THE OFFICE

The office should not be far from the ring where you give your lessons, so you can drop in, if necessary, even in the middle of a class, although such interruptions should be held to a minimum. Few are the telephone calls which cannot wait one hour; and, in principle, a caller should be told you are in class and be asked to leave a message. You should be called out of class only at the caller's most convincing insistence; and it is up to your secretary to convey that this policy springs from your preoccupation with your class, not from a reluctance to disturb your nibs.

Not only in the school but in the office also, one tends to talk too much. Keep a firm rein on runaway discourse. If the telephone rings, do not sit down to answer it. The time seems shorter when seated and one becomes long-winded, while a few pleasant words suffice in arranging an appointment or changing one already made. Information such as hours and rates is easily given in a very few sentences; the fewer they are, the more leisurely and politely you can convey them. If more detail is required, invite the person to come to see you; and when I say "invite" I mean just that, not something like, "You'll have to come to the office for that; we can't give this kind of information over the 'phone."

When they do come to see you, do not enter into all kinds of detail which would only muddle up what is clear and simple. Everything is in the tone of your voice, the unhurriedness of your gestures and the attentiveness of your listening, while you answer questions in a very few sentences which explain everything there is to say. If the person is gregarious, do not give him the impression that whatever he is saying is either of no importance, or that you know beforehand what he is going to say. Take the time to answer the first few questions, which usually are most relevant, and then proceed to close the conversation by indicating that all others will explain themselves during and after the first few lessons when you shall, moreover, be in a far better position to comment. You excuse yourself because you must not leave your class alone any longer and invite your visitor to watch its progress from the gallery.

In one word, remain as efficient in your work outside as inside the ring, without ever ceasing to be polite and cheerful. You are the soul of a great body composed of pupils, parents, friends, visiting horsemen, horses, grooms —people you like to see and people you would rather not see. Your attitude and ways are echoed in their behavior. If the moment you cross the threshold of your school or club, you are one hundred per cent the riding master till the moment you leave it, it will facilitate your work and improve the atmosphere of your establishment.

You do not want to turn your office into a public market place. It is up to your savoir-faire to make the world at large understand that no one may enter there without an invitation, except to transact business, such as appointments, checking of subscription cards, pertinent information. Else you will soon find a pair of mud-caked spurs where your telephone register should be and someone's hunt cap squarely on "November 26" of your appointment book; and when the telephone rings you will either not be able to hear who is on the other end on account of the din of conversation around you, or a polite silence will make every one of your telephone conversations a matter of public record.

This reminds me that you should as far as possible avoid using your caller's name if at the time of the call you have someone in your office. It is a rule doctors, lawyers, all professionals should, but do not always obey. The telephone call is equivalent to a letter—it is addressed to you; and since it does not come in an envelope, you should at least cover the signature. It would have saved Mrs. X, who had told Dr. Y's secretary that she must break the following day's 10 A.M. dental appointment on account of a bad fever, a great deal of embarrassment if Dr. Y had not heard you say, "that will be fine, Mrs. X, tomorrow Sprinter for you for the 10 o'clock hack."

Since you insist on comfort and privacy in your office, you should offer others a lounge outside of the locker rooms, where they can gather before class and discuss their lesson after dismounting, where they can wait up to an hour or so in comfort for the rain to stop before riding out or going home, where they can warm up in the winter and cool off in the summer. A clubhouse-type room, preferably with a bar, is, of course, best; but since, anyway, the gallery is the favorite gathering place, your ideal arrangement would be for one of your lounge's glassed-in long sides to face the ring. From there horsemen and visitors can watch, away from the dust, having a drink, if they wish, free to talk without disturbing you and your class.

## THE STABLES

The number of grooms depends on the number of horses. With good organization, one man can well take care of ten horses; but you need one serious, experienced head groom on whom you can count; for the conditio of your horses will depend on him. Manager and riding master at once, yo are too busy to supervise the grooms, "to be after them" all day long an tell them what to do. You must be able to rely on the head groom to super vise their work so you only have to take a turn through the stables once o twice a day to know what is going on, and in the evening to brief him fo the following day.

You keep track of the horses' work in a register where an entry is mad each time a horse has been out (if you lack the time, the head groom wi keep it for you in the tack room) which lets you check at any time an at a glance the work of each particular horse and helps you double-chec your appointment book: the number of pupil hours must equal that o horse hours.

Not all horses can work the same length of time. The number of hour is not determined solely by the nature and condition of the horse, but b the kind of work demanded of him and the way he is ridden. The average day' work is four hours, some horses can do five, but all depends on the kin of work. So your main care should be given to its rational organization.

## THE RIDING HALL

In organizing our schedule, we distinguish among *lessons, classes, an courses.*

*Lessons* are private or semi-private, occasionally there may be three partici pants; but they are always sessions arranged by special appointment. A couple of hours should be reserved for them. Lessons are good or bad, ac cording to whether you use them or abuse them. They are of true interes above all to accomplished horsemen riding their own or, anyway, rather highl schooled horses; or else for jumping lessons for riders already somewha versed in this specialty.

In all other cases, the greatest circumspection is in order, because thes lessons often only help you skirt, without actually conquering, the difficult which should be surmounted. You may use them with persons who are s insecure that at first they just drift without advancing in the classes or courses Two or three lessons, six at the most, should suffice to "help them across. Private lessons may be useful also for an occasional adult taking up ridin again after a long interruption; and just a few lessons should suffice there, too

Summing up, counter to general belief, private lessons, at least on continual basis, can only benefit horsemen of rather superior ability; for an other they must remain strictly temporary, spanning a very short period durin which pupil and teacher overcome a well determined difficulty.

*Classes* are established sessions, not tailored to a group of individuals, bu of a certain type and level; and the individual riders are then placed into one or the other in accordance with their type and level. Homegeneity of horsemanship is, of course, the prime criterion; but once your riders have been "sorted out" this way, there begins the sorting process as to personality. And when all this has been neatly and logically laid out on paper, you realize that Miss X, who is working, can only ride on Friday evenings, and Dr. Y's only chance to slip away comes on Wednesday mornings at 8, while Mrs. Z is free to ride any day, but not before 10 or 11 A.M., so as not to interfere with her social life or sleep. The problem is, of course, not always quite so unsolvable; and if you keep your schedule flexible, you usually can arrange very compatible groups.

Where children and adolescents are concerned, the age factor encroaches upon that of horsemanship, and school and homework encroaches upon both.

*Courses* are especially convenient for students because they (a) are divided into terms of quarters in accordance with the school year and take place on days and at hours chosen so as not to interfere with school activities and (b) are graded to permit each group to work together toward a certain goal and to "graduate" together to the following "grade."

In countries where the incentive of examinations given by the national Federation of Equestrian Sports does not exist, you might want to institute annual tests (equestrian theory and practice and the rudiments of hippology) by which pupils pass from one grade to the next. Registration in such courses should be subject to a deadline and each term or quarter payable in advance; because their progression and progress would be fatally disrupted by the drifting in and out which is only normal in lessons and classes. These courses are well suited to absorb the scouts working for a horsemanship badge; because for those who "graduate" from your courses, obtaining a scout badge should be a mere formality.

Though there is no fixed age to begin to ride, there are norms for learning to ride which cannot be ignored. While occasionally very young children (eight, nine, ten years old) are truly gifted and know how to use certain horses better than some adult riders, it is equally true that those same children are incapable of using horses those same adults are able to handle. For in saying that the problems of horsemanship are not problems of physical force, we are speaking of adults. This fact has been proved to me over and over during my life as a teacher.

In sum, you may let a seven year old child begin to ride if he or she so desires. But you will have to wait till the age of thirteen or fourteen to teach him or her to use his aids with any degree of effectiveness. On the other hand, a fourteen-year-old having begun very young will obviously be, and most likely stay, ahead of his contemporaries for quite some time, if the latter are, at fourteen, riding their first horses. The examples of children younger than fourteen winning in horse shows and dressage tests by no means demolish or overturn our thesis; for their merit is restricted to a very precise feel for the horse which they thus do not encumber and which, blessed with a gentle nature and fine schooling, the work of an accomplished horseman, takes over the rather more active part of the operation: the overcoming of the difficulties.

## Public Relations

At a dinner honoring Marshal Foch in Denver, someone remarked that French politeness was nothing but wind; and the Marshal, who was noted for his brilliant gift of repartee, replied that there was nothing but wind in a tire either, which yet wonderfully eased the jolts along the road.

This statement gives expression to the entire basis of public relations, their functioning and their ideal results. An organization runs on courtesy; not stilted ceremony, but on a simple savoir-faire which Emerson described unaffectedly when he said: "There is always a best way of doing everything , if it be to boil an egg. Manners are the happy ways of doing things."

Beware of the brand of artificial courtesy which is but momentary obsequiousness toward a customer. The whole atmosphere of your school must breathe a courtesy so all-enveloping that whoever enters will find it necessary and easy to adjust to it, or stay away; for, to speak once more with Emerson, "fine manners need the support of fine manners in others."

So if you wish polite intercourse between your staff and yourself on one side and the outside world on the other, these must be borne on a firm and elastic cushion of courtesy between your staff and yourself. To make this possible, you need, in hiring, even in an organization as small as yours, the flair of a personnel officer. I should say mainly in an organization as small as yours, because on account of its smallness there is no way of isolating the able but loutish stablehand. This problem of finding grooms who have a gentle hand with horses and riders alike is a very real one. The gentleman's groom is as extinct, outside of England, as is the "gentleman's gentleman," and while such a degree of polish is not expected nowadays of stable personnel, civility is of the essence.

I do not want you to bristle now with democratic protest, because this is not a matter of class distinctions. If you require your pupils to take off their hats when greeting you or anyone else on your premises, failure to require the same of your grooms would be nothing but rather undemocratic condescension. If you are supposed to bear down with the whole weight of your authority on any pupil who speaks roughly to one of your staff, this same authority should inexorably come to bear upon the groom who replies curtly to one of your riders. You may remember, and adopt for the guidance of all, the lines from Shaw's Pygmalion: "The great secret, Eliza, is not having bad manners or good manners or any other particular sort of manners, but having the same manner for all human souls: in short, behaving as if you were in Heaven, where there are no third-class carriages, and one soul is as good as another."

After having thus considered the courtesy of others, let us make a quick survey of the rules governing our own conduct; and the best way to do this is to remember our experiences when we were pupils, when teachers and stable managers were "the others." Just as I think I have kept the promise I made when I was a child to remember the foibles of my elders and not to fall into the same, I remember very clearly my annoyance at the various peculiarities and mannerisms of certain individuals in riding schools I then frequented.

My greatest resentment was reserved for the riding master who was invariably late. Even then I understood that, if my lesson was to take place right after the end of a hack in the park, there was no assurance that something unexpected (a spill, a runaway horse, or simply a beginner with stitches in his side) might not make the whole company somewhat tardy. But I resented it if it happened habitually and, on the occasions when I myself formed part of the group, I realized that often those delays were due to an unnecessarily late departure or to the riding master's chance meeting with an acquaintance on horseback or in his automobile, on account of which everything came to a stop for about ten minutes.

All this is not only inconsiderate of others, but bad policy for yourself. The nervousness resulting from such a halt can only cause accidents, and habitual tardiness naturally sets back your whole schedule and you close your doors "after another long, hard day."

There is little advice one can offer about this; punctuality is a natural gift and/or training. Let me just give you one tip as an example. If one morning you have a group for hacking at 10 A.M. and simultaneously a class in the school which you entrust to an assistant, always distribute first the horses which stay in the hall, get everyone into their saddles and start off the class for your assistant. When you see that everything is running smoothly, take care of your other group. A five or ten minute cut into a two-hour hack is of no significance; five or ten minutes taken from an hour of instruction is too much.

When giving the lesson yourself, "stay" with your pupils sixty minutes out of an hour. I am not speaking here of the fact that you should not physically leave the ring, which I have mentioned before, but that your presence should not, half of the time, become little more than symbolic. We have all known the riding master who was joined in the middle of the hall by a friendly horseman and promptly became engrossed in animated conversation about horseflesh from which he emerged but occasionally with a quick, "come on now, Miss X, a little lively, you're putting your horse to sleep!" only to duck under again till once more he surfaced with "At a walk, long reins, rest, press your horses forward at a walk . . ." and, lighting a cigarette, picked up where he had left off with his visitor till . . . when? This is the other, even darker side of the coin, in contrast with the young, insecure teacher who practically smothers the pupils in his perpetual grip.

As to your attitude toward the individual pupil, as distinct from that toward the class as a whole, there are two special types whose handling is of the most delicate: The one "who does not have it in him" and, even more delicate, the one who is "formidable". The first should constantly be encouraged, not by flattery, but by recognition of whatever progress he may be making. And yet, it is much less a question of words than of attitude on your part which will encourage or discourage him. The pupil who is left to follow like Sancho Panza the more gifted riders in his course, with nothing more than an occasional, "lower your hands," when everyone else is being corrected and even gently scolded at times, will be well aware of the futility of the reassurance you may give him in your office.

But your real problem of self-control is the pupil who arouses your admiration. It is only human and to your credit that you should feel an enthusiastic affection for the extremely gifted student who "has the sacred fire," who hangs on your lips and carries out your directions with a near-perfection way beyond anything that might be expected of him; or for the little tot, barely higher than a cauliflower topped by a hunt cap, who has the kind of blessed hand under which any horse will go, who is not afraid of anyhing and always has a ready smile, even when sitting, somewhat startled, in the sawdust. Because not only are you in danger of giving them a "private lesson," as if on an island in the midst of the indifferent ocean that is for you the class around him or her and you, which is greatly resented by the others, but your submissive, grateful disciple will soon be in a state where it would take a long series of exercises to make him "relax at the jaw," and your brave little trooper will before long tell everybody that the only reason they may be better in the saddle is the greater length of their legs. Since I have fallen into the habit of quoting all kinds of literary lights, let me dip once into obscurity and quote myself in saying that, as I remarked concerning the vices and ill-manners of horses, it is easier to prevent an ill than to cure it.

If, however, there were but pupils, horses and grooms to contend with, the life of the riding master would be easy indeed. But there are parents. Mothers of young children who not only tell you at the start of the lesson that they don't want Billy "to ride that beige horse," but who help you with the lesson from their observation point in the gallery. While only polite firmness, with an accent on firmness, can help you there, I want you to be a little understanding concerning a certain initial distrust you may fancy in the manner of mothers when first they bring their children to you. If they know nothing of horses, these appear terrifying and bigger than life to them; if they are horsewomen themselves, they know how powerful a horse is. If they entrust you with their children all the same, it is because they believe in your ability. Their reticence is, most of the time, rather a reserve made up of reservations. They do not believe that they know better than you; they do not distrust you, they just do not trust you fully as yet. And why should they? Do you blindly trust each doctor or dentist or teacher to whom you take your own child for the first time?

So make allowances. But if ever you should have excessive trouble of this kind, lose a customer or member rather than prolong the suffering for everyone involved.

Another problem is the rider who, although "motherless," complicates your existence, on the contrary, through rank or age or both. The young teacher's special spook is the former cavalry officer who wants to take a few lessons to see "if the old bones still have some horsemanship in them." And yet, if it is the real article, there is no reason for you to shrink from this assignment. If he actually is a "horseman" (not the case with all retired cavalry officers, even those who love to reminisce over their exploits during the times "when the cavalry still had nothing but soft noses"), and if you are, too, you can learn a great deal from each other.

There also are the exceedingly middle-aged ladies who want to benefit from all the indulgence their age affords them, without it ever becoming apparent. The worst you could possibly do—not only for the functioning of your class, but for her self-esteem—is to tell her twenty-year-old neighbor to hurry up and jump that higher pole and ask her if she, too, feels like doing so, or to tell her neighbor, "not bad" and to exclaim at her similar performance, " Fine . . . bravo!" On the whole, I must here trust your courtliness which you cannot acquire in the riding school but have or have not brought with you from your drawing room.

Apart from these personal in-and-out-of-the-stirrup relations, there exists, in your profession, as it does in any other, a simple code of ethics. If, for example, you were entrusted with boarders, there is the possibility of the owner paying the full board, with the understanding that no one except he will ride the horse, or else of the owner paying part or none of the board, with the understanding that the horse is to be ridden a specified number of hours and, possibly, only by horsemen of certain characteristics. Once you accept a boarder and the conditions accompanying the transaction, keep your word, even at the height of the holiday rush and when several of your horses have suddenly gone lame; even if there is among your pupils one who "would ride the horse better than his owner"; even if the horse has not been exercised for days "and it is only for his own good"; even if you could ride him yourself during that New Year's morning hack and thus free your own mount and give him to a pupil. You have made a bargain, and bargains are made to be kept. And if your self-respect does not decide this matter for you, remember that it is a small world and that there is at least a 50-50 chance that the owner will find out about it. As far as the New Year's morning ride is concerned, it is so easy to inquire beforehand with one of your owners whether—in a pinch—he would authorize you to ride his horse. You will know to which one you should turn in order to avoid a refusal.

There should actually be no need to mention the matter of the sale of a horse. The stories of the "horse deal" are too well known, and you are not a "horse dealer" but a gentleman who owns horses and occasionally sells or trades one. Most of your selling will, anyway, be of horses you train for a pupil or customer and it will be in your interest to choose a good one which will set off your training abilities. As to the price you ask, be sure it reflects the true value of the animal; for "too smart a deal" is made once or twice, never three times.

Although I am cautioning you most emphatically against greed in selling to your necessarily gullible pupils, which would truly mean taking unfair advantage of their ignorance, I want you to be realistic when buying a horse, not to expect your seller to apply with you the same unalloyed ethics he would, or should, apply when selling a horse to Miss X. Among horsemen the price you pay and the value you receive are a measure of your worth as a horseman. I could, I think, evaluate and price a horseman by looking at his horses. So buying and selling among peers becomes part of the sport, like horse shows or racing—a taking of one's measure between competitors.

Another problem which sometimes poses itself to your conscience is the pupil of one of your colleagues who shows up in your office, wishing to register for, let us say, your special dressage or jumping class, although she intends to continue her regular lessons at her school. This is perfectly all right as long as you are sure that she has informed her teacher of this arrangement; and it then is only a matter of your own tact not to counter too obviously in your own lessons the teaching she is receiving from him. Beware of the cutting remark, the involuntary slight to another's work.

And this brings us to a point which concerns you not only as a teacher, but as a horseman. It is only natural for you to feel sure, most of the time, that you know more than another of your own class; and do not pretend that you do not feel that way. But so does he; and your modesty lies in the fact that you wonder whose feeling is correct. Keep this philosophical doubt toward yourself and others. Do not sneer at their "gods," and do not hero worship the master who has formed you, like a starry-eyed ex-cadet. Keep your perspective.

Another weakness of many horsemen of which you should steer clear is the horsy type of humor, the off-color wisecrack, no matter how descriptive, descriptive sometimes to the point where it would seem functional in teaching. Every horseman knows those, and you may be sure that the few you do not know will be taught you by your "old bones" ex-cavalry officer during the private lessons when he tells you what the sergeant said to the recruit and what his own glorified superior officer ("the old so-and-so, what a character!") once hollered at him. They are fine stories, fine in the atmosphere where they happened or are supposed to have happend, fine to tell your colleagues over a drink or even to chuckle over by yourself while watching a similar situation during your own course. But do not speak out. You are not in the army, you do not have recruits on the track. And if, best of all, one such crack, a really good one of your own invention, were to occur to you, as hard as it may be to swallow a *bon mot,* it is the one instance where you will have less of a hangover if you down it than if you don't.

You may feel like telling me that you know enough about the code of manners of the horseman's world not to derail; for its is not esoteric, but common, almost proverbial, knowledge that a horseman ought to be a gentleman, that you have been bred, if not born, in this environment; but since I have the annoying quirk of quoting, let me indulge in it once more and for the last time with a quotation from *Hamlet:*

> But to my mind, though I am native here
> And to the manner born — it is a custom
> More honoured in the breach than the observance.

## An Afterthought

In my grandfather's library you would find many books on the horse and its uses, some of them devoted to side-saddle riding; but mostly works on general equitation, all of which have a few chapters, like an afterthought, on the subject of the side saddle.

From what one can read between the lines, after so many years, it seems

**Side saddle, eighteenth century. (From the Hermès Museum, Paris)**

not so much neglect causing those pages to be so few, as rather a vague gesture of "I couldn't tell you" on the part of the riding masters, usually in the form of praise for the feminine intuition and physique which allowed the *"monte en amazone,"* for the frail ladies, young and elderly, following the hounds, over the fences through fields and woods, along with their men, and as saddle-fast and hard-riding and straight, on their strangely oblique perches, as any.

This came to mind as I sat down to write this little "afterthought" for my feminine readers whom I have so far addressed, without distinction, along with their male colleagues; for in our day they are as saddle-fast and hard-riding and straight, astride in the English saddle, as any.

It came to mind because, setting out to talk to my modern day amazon, who sometimes finds herself teaching rather than being taught, about the special situation this creates for her, I have the same feeling of "I couldn't really tell you," this temptation to remark, "just exactly how, I cannot say, except for the result I'd like to see. It's a devil of a position to be in, and I trust your feminine intuition to carry you through with effectiveness and grace."

And truly the parallels impose themselves; the most convincing, most essential that, in one situation as in the other, your finesse and sense of balance must compensate for the strength and means of action which have been denied you.

No matter how you strut and holler, no one will take you for a man, not even a very small and ridiculous one. So if you want to be respected by your pupils and obeyed by your grooms, taken seriously by other horsemen and accepted in society, do not shout in the ring like a drill sergeant (it will never be a bellow, but somewhere between a squeak and a squawk); do not walk around spraddle-legged, with a cigarette dangling from your lower lip—men will not just for that treat you as an "equal," though you may be almost sure they will not give you the consideration due a woman but look upon you as the very small, ridiculous man you are striving to emulate.

And then when you are treated as such, you will not even have the "smallest, most ridiculous" man's possibilities of demanding redress. Because, my friend you are a woman, and you look glorious in your riding breeches, and the feet of your boots are wondrously small compared to mine, and, no matter how short you crop your hair, there is a curl creeping out somewhere from under your hunt cap; and now do stop, will you, stomping about the school like a Dickensian coachman when you are mad, and do not punch me in the ribs when I tell you a joke . . . The times are past when Hollywood conveyed to us that Rosalind Russell was a businesswoman by making her masquerade in horn-rimmed glasses; besides she never stuck to them all through the film.

Be comfortable; with or without curls, handsome, or kind of ugly, or just plain homely, anything but grotesque. If then you ever find yourself in difficulty, your dignity and the respect it commands (and, let us face it, precisely the fact that you are a woman) will make your lack of force of no import. In this, your tact acts like the equestrian tact in the side saddle; your emotional balance works for you in class as physical balance used to compensate for the strangely oblique seat in the saddle of old.

I know, it is hard to command and not to shrill when one is blessed with a woman's voice . . . I couldn't really tell you, I only know the result I should like to see. . . .

## Etiquette — An Introduction for Young Riders

> For manners are not idle, but the fruit
> Of loyal nature and of noble mind.
> —ALFRED LORD TENNYSON

Though the word "chivalrous" has survived as part of our everyday speech, chivalry, in medieval terms, was a way of life. Its etymology goes back to the French, *chevalerie*, as the derivation "cavalier" ("a gallant, courteous gentleman") goes back to the Italian, *cavaliere*. Both have their first origin in the Latin *caballus*, a horse. The horseman was meant to be "the embodiment of courage, fairness, high spirits and courtesy"; the gentle knight. We usually find the word "gentle" attached to those other attributes.

The ideal knight was, in effect a gentle man—a gentleman on whom the dictionary until very recently imposed the double condition of being "of noble birth," as well as "chivalrous, kind, patient, not loud or disturbing . . ."; that is, being of the character befitting a person of good birth." Defining a nobleman as a gentleman placed upon his shoulders the obligation to be chivalrous.

If today we do not require a gentleman to be a nobleman, we require the more emphatically a nobleman to be a gentleman; and although we shun the pathos of medieval romanticism, the assocation of the ideas of chivalry (the ways of a horseman) and good breeding has survived.

The aptest expression of our modern day attitude is probably the muted statement (which I have quoted previously on technical grounds) by which the British exhort their young "to keep their elbows close to their bodies at table, in conversation and on horseback." It expresses, in effect, the Englishman's striving for good manners, which essentially means but the striving to be inconspicuous. His casual reference to a horseman's bearing in connection with a lesson in manners is quite adequate in a country where the pleasures of horsemanship are as much part of a person's life as those of table and conversation. You, however, are entering a new world where you may expect variations from the standards of your daily environment; and yet, what are good manners anywhere but a form of consideration for the rights and comforts of others—not outmoded mannerisms but, if played straight by everyone, a set of rules for making life together safer and more pleasant.

So why not simply watch and emulate the riders with whom you will, from now on, be associating? Alas, by its very nature, the true horseman's perfection lies precisely in that he is neither heard nor seen; and so he is often overshadowed by the counterfeit horseman holding the center of the stage. You are in danger of innocently patterning yourself after the image of a character in boots and spurs who uses swear words, gestures, and a tone of voice which—to give him the benefit of the doubt—he would be the first to find shocking in his drawing room.

You will also watch Messrs. X and Y agreeing on the excellence of everything, from their methods to their mounts, and tread underfoot those of absent Mr. Z, only to repeat the game with Z in the absence of X or Y. They are not—no matter how well they may ride—sportsmen; they are, at most, showmen. True horsemen are courteous even when in high spirits and have the courage to be fair. They are not afraid to acknowledge the merits of their companions, are self-assured enough to play them up and, when the occasion calls for it, to be charitable.

The elementary guidelines of equestrian etiquette remain valid up to the summit of horsemanship, just as the elementary guidelines of equestrian technique remain valid after you reach the point where you may call yourself a horseman or a horsewoman.

Be punctual. If you are late, you interrupt the sequence of the lesson. If, exceptionally, you cannot help it, pause at the door and ask for permission to enter (as you always should, if there be just one rider in the hall), so as not to frighten the horses on the track. If early, do not march into the previous class, do not post yourself beside the instructor to tell him of your latest parking ticket. Rather go up to the gallery and watch in silence. The less you speak, the more you see, the more you see, the more you learn. And, above all, do not voice your criticism of those on the track to your neighbor; it is not nice, and she may be your target's mother. If your own kid sister is in the saddle, do not help your teacher with her instruction.

When your turn comes to mount, do not protest when you are given a leg-up. The health of your horse's back is more important than your vanity. Beside, there is the risk of your vanity being greater than your grace or verve in mounting. Once in the saddle, do not enthrone yourself there waiting for your teacher to adjust your stirrups. If you are having difficulties, he will do it for you; and then swing your leg up and forward immediately. Nothing is more unpleasant for him, and for you, than the grappling for the buckle under your thigh.

Your instructor's intent is for your hour on horseback to constitute a full sixty minutes of profit for you. Even riding a horse at a walk, letting him and yourself rest, is a matter for learning. Thus the occasional rest periods form part of your lesson and are not to be filled with conversation among pupils. Whatever you want to discuss should be attended to before or after class. Any explanation given to one of the group addresses itself to all; for all, at one time or another, commit the same faults. Obedience to orders must be accurate and immediate. A second's delay may entail the fall or the kick that your own uncorrected error has caused. When you are tired, raise your hand, do not slow down, stop, or leave the ranks at your own initiative. You are but a part of the clockwork of your group and have no right to interfere with its functioning. When you are in trouble, your instructor realizes it even before you do; and for a long time to come only he can get you out of it, for he alone controls your horse. So do not cry out or gesticulate; not only will you irritate your horse all the more, but also those of your fellow-riders.

Once you have successfully passed this, "Sir, I can't stop him!" phase, you will have to familiarize yourself with a few "traffic rules" reigning inside the school. Once more I remind you of the need to request permission before entering. The rider using a slower gait than that practiced on the track, not only takes the inner track, but turns in the opposite direction. Different countries differ as to which rider has priority in the manège, when both are at the same gait, the one on the left, or the one on the right, hand. But whatever the hand, the livelier gait has priority over the slower.

After dismounting, hold your horse's reins and pull up the stirrups so they will not frighten him in tapping against his flanks; but do not insist on taking him back into his stall yourself. It holds up things, may be dangerous for you, and more likely than not your horse will not be haltered properly. Do not feed him sugar before unbridling; it makes the bit sticky and hard to clean for the groom.

All horsemen like to stick around and talk and watch. By all means, do, and know that your instructor will only be too happy to answer your questions during moments of leisure. The more you ask, the more you will learn; not only from teachers and other riders, but from some of the grooms, namely concerning the main object of your interest: the horse without whom you could not be a rider.

Speaking of grooms, always have a smile for them, say good day after they greet you. If the service is not included in the charge, do not fail to tip, and do not forget them on your Christmas list. If you have known them for some time, take an interest in their families, their troubles with the tax collector, their rheumatisms. But do not shake hands, much less become chummy or engage in horseplay; they would not appreciate it. The old-time, often stylized, groom belongs to an almost extinct breed and you cannot bring him back by auto-suggestion.

No matter who you are with in the stables, do not make a great deal of noise, do not try to be "the center of the stage." The riding hall belongs to the horses; they are its *raison d'être,* its cause, and its aim. If you adjust to their world, you are allowed to become a part of it; if you do not, you will forever be a slightly ridiculous intruder.

## *Dress*

Have you seen the girl in blue jodhpurs, the tight sleeveless V-neck sweater, moccasins on her nylon-stockinged feet, on her head a ski cap with a horseshoe pin over the forehead? Her shoulder-length hair flowing from under it like a mane, her black-rimmed eyes glittering under bright blue lids, her lips crimson.

Your answer is, "It surely was not me," and it certainly was not. But if you analyze this caricature, can you cross your heart and hope to die that nothing, but nothing, of it has ever been seen on you? Have you not ever, even for a moment, pinned this pretty horseshoe pin on your sweater and, on second thought, put it back on the dresser? Long live second thoughts!

The question of what to wear for riding is answered so quickly; the enumeration of what not to is so long. There is only one classic, inconspicuous color for your breeches: beige. Black, even tobacco, and above all green or blue, are taboo. They should be large enough in hips and seat for comfort and camouflage and, in the case of jodhpurs, tight enough from the knee down not to look like ill-shaped slacks.

Your coat should be a riding coat, not a converted suit jacket, of black cloth or tweed of a subdued color. It should not be pinch-waisted, but fall straight from the shoulders, and long enough to cover all curves. By all means wear a coat; no matter how slender, a girl's hips and what goes with them are not made to be seen astride on horseback. If, however, you cannot afford a truly first-class coat, a good sweater over a firm foundation is preferable to a bad coat (such as left-over suit jackets, leather coats, windbreakers). In a heavy, very loose, very plain, long-sleeved sweater (black, brown, beige, or grey), high around the neck and well covering your hips, you will look better and be just as warm.

Do not tell me you cannot afford jodhpur boots. Every pair of your many shoes—and they do not last as long—costs as much.

For a head-covering use a man's felt or straw hat, but preferably the simple hunt cap. Pick it small enough so you will not have to hold on to it; and leave derbies, top hats and the like for special occasions, such as show riding. The same goes for the stock where you are allowed a narrow gold pin in the shape of a riding crop, unadorned by horseshoes or stones, genuine or fake. It is there to serve a purpose, to pin down your stock, that is all. Do not ride without gloves any more than you would go to town without them; tan (leather on the inside, knit on the outside), not white.

Have your hair under control. If it is long, turn it down and in and wear a net. The net is invisible even from close up, the flying locks are shocking even from far away. If your skin is handsome, wear no makeup; if you need it, let it be discreet.

Keep your paraphernalia in your pockets; but if you must carry a pocket book, choose a sort of small briefcase. Take off your spurs when not riding and never walk out into the street with them on. They are a working tool, not an ornament, and wearing them when not in action is the sure sign of a Sunday rider.

Last but not least: use a light, fresh cologne over a heavy layer of deodorant. Marie-Chantal, the heroine of French "shaggy-snob" stories, when reproached by an old lady for not ever having obtained anything by the sweat of her brow, replied haughtily, "in our family one does not perspire, Madam." But if, on horseback, you are never hot, then you never work; and there is nothing more offensive to the boy who is giving you a leg-up or holding your reins while you slip out of the saddle, nothing more embarrassing to the girl with whom you are discussing your ride in the stable yard, than the evident lack of deodorant combined with the presence of a sultry perfume. How often have I felt tempted, when picking out a gift, to buy instead of the horsy book or the lovely equestrian engraving, a cologne and deodorant set. But I will not, and no one ever will; because people are polite, they do not wish to embarrass you. So be polite yourself and do not embarrass them.

**Jeannie and David in Paris.**

As it goes for the young ladies, so it does for the young men. Just as you choose tidy and functional dress for school or office, use suitable clothes for the manège: jodhpurs, not blue jeans or slacks; a tie; and, if you cannot afford a coat, a good sweater. Cover your head, preferably with a hunt cap, not because it is flattering but because it protects your head in case of a spill. So keep it on at all times, except when you are in a room other than the riding hall or the stables or when you greet someone, be it your elders or your peers, in which cases it must come off as inexorably as it must otherwise stay on. If the occasion for a salute presents itself on horseback, let me remind you to place your reins in your left hand and to uncover yourself with the right, a left-handed salute being almost more discourteous than none at all.

## Going to Horse Shows

The first book you should order for your school library is the manual of regulations published by your country's equestrian federation (in the case of the United States, the Rule Book of the A.H.S.A.). Whether or not your school or club is ready and able to join, a number of your pupils will want to enter horse shows individually or in small groups; and once there, they are the exhibits for your organization.

It is ineluctably your responsibility to train them for it, to get them and their horses there in good time and condition, and to see to it that all entry requirements are met. Do not expect them to look after this; they will too often make mistakes, forget or misunderstand something vital, and it will become common knowledge that "there is always something wrong with their entries"—"their" meaning your club or school.

Since you will find in the manual everything you need to know concerning local rules, I am only giving you a little advice concerning the very day of the event and of universal application.

Horses usually travel by van. If the trip is long, there is decidedly an advantage in arriving on the eve of the show and letting them get over the fatigue of travel; otherwise, two hours in advance is sufficient—the time to unload them, walk them about, saddle and limber them up. In this case, they should eat two or three hours before departure, two hours a minimum.

For the transfer you need a blanket for each horse, knee-caps, bandages, a good leather head collar with two halter ropes. If the horses have never been placed in a van before, rehearse them several times during the preceding days. I have never yet known a horse which could not be got into a van, but I have seen some cause a great deal of trouble in the process. It is a question of tact, patience, gentleness, firmness, never force.

Take a complete grooming kit with you, as well as calks. Once on the grounds, you shall see whether or not calking is necessary. In some places it is indispensable; during the season, all your horses' shoes should have mortises. If the event continues into the night, take feed bags along, adequate rations of oats, and (preferably cloth) pails. An extra pair of reins and stirrup leathers are a good idea.

Upon arrival, find out where space has been reserved for you in the stables, unload your horses and dispose of the entry formalities. Stay with your riders, supervise them while they limber up their mounts, and have them pass the trial bar.

In pacing the course, it is a matter of psychology not to exaggerate its difficulties, while emphasizing them properly. With horse-show beginners or semi-beginners, a great share of the success or failure falls to you. Two riders may have diametrically opposed reactions to a reputedly difficult obstacle; one feels that if nearly all are having trouble there, he most certainly will, while another thinks he can do better and blames the frequent failures on a fixed idea. You must know your riders no less than your horses and send them onto the course with explanations so clear and precise they will stay put in their minds from starting to finish line.

## Touring

When touring on horseback you do not intend to set distance or speed records. You are using riding school horses, and your riders, though advanced, are learners. The averages I am going to recommend are those adopted by the French cavalry. The German cavalry, with horses different in qualities as well as faults, used very similar norms, which proves that one cannot, without falling into fancy, stray from them to any considerable degree. They represent the experience of lengthy warfare between the two countries, were evolved in peace and tested in war.

My own tours with pupils over distances of 125 to 135 miles, experimenting with different averages, have confirmed the soundness of the military norms in their application to civilian purposes. So do not prepare your tour on the basis of what has been done just a few times or by a single horseman. Leading a troop of eight or twelve riders of little or no experience, without undue fatigue, is a far cry from what a single rider in good training can do with a horse hand-picked and trained for trekking.

Success depends no less on preparation than on execution; the more careful the former, the easier the latter. The daily schedule should cover from 19 to 22 miles, so that you do not have to travel after noon. A day of complete rest should interrupt midway any tour of over four days' duration.

Make a careful preliminary survey on the map, then by car. Avoid the main highways; have a close look at the shoulders of the roads, for where they are good you can provide for long trots, where they are bad you will have to walk, and so your schedule will depend on the state of the roads along your itinerary. Make sure that there is a farrier along your route, preferably at midway; the shoeing problem is capital and requires your closest attention.

Stables are a problem nowadays; few inns which "lodge on foot and horseback" have survived, and you will have to find farms which might offer you, if not stables, a hangar or a barn; and where there are not partitions, you can manufacture them with bales of straw. The bivouac under the starry skies may be romantic when all goes well, but one of its many inconveniences is possible exposure to bad weather during the few hours of rest. It is not worth the risk.

The Friends Riding Out into the Wide World, **from a fifteenth-century tapestry.
University Museum, Marburg. Retzlaff Archive)**

Your average traveling speed is 5 to 5⅝ mph, divided between walk and trot, as follows:

| Trot | 1¼ mi | in 10 minutes | = 7½ mph |
|------|-------|---------------|----------|
| Walk | ⅝ mi  | in 10 minutes | = 3¾ mph |

The Average is 5⅝ mph.

If the going is good and the road without ups and downs, you can average 9 mph at a trot, that is, 264 yds. a minute, and this for 1⅞ miles at a time, although it is a maximum if you wish to keep your horses in good condition.

On steep inclines, dismount rather than riding up or down hill. Even where the road is level all the way, it is a good idea to lead the horses and let their backs rest while the riders stretch their legs. Place them by two's when you mount again; the horseman on the right mounts first, and then his neighbor, who can easily move over to hold the right stirrup leather for him without letting go of his own horse, returns to his place and mounts, while his neighbor to the right, already in the saddle, holds his right stirrup leather for him. These precautions will keep the saddles from turning, which otherwise would surely happen with tired riders and horses carrying packs.

In very warm weather, leave as early as possible and dismount before 11 o'clock. Before departure make a quick inspection of the horses (tack and pack). The first mile must be traveled at a walk, as well as the last two. Make a halt two hours after departure; and if it is very hot, let the horses drink as often as possible.

For best results, organize your pupils by pairs, if possible an experienced tour rider and a novice who are growing used to working together. Upon arrival at quarters, where date and hour have been known for some time past and reconfirmed a few days earlier, loosen the girths immediately but without unsaddling if you want to prevent saddle sores. One half of the riders hold the horses while the other half prepare the bedding and set up the bales of straw. Halter the horses up. The place you choose for each, important at any time, is, if you want to prevent kicking accidents, of the greatest significance here.

Unsaddle, rub them down and massage their backs to avoid trouble there. Feed and water them. Check their shoes; some may not last through the next day's march and must be replaced in the early afternoon. For such an emergency, or if a piece of tack should need repair, you have all afternoon before you; while, had you planned to travel in the afternoon, you would not have left yourself a margin to cope with it.

No matter how gentle your horses and how good the installations, you must post two stable guards at night. If there is the slightest incident, one can report to you immediately, while the other takes care of whatever is most urgent.

Just a word about your impedimenta. Although you may have at your disposal one or two cars which carry the paraphernalia of all riders and make it possible to find the bedding prepared upon arrival, this is not necessary. What you need, above all, are army saddles, designed to carry a pack. For a four to ten day tour you need not encumber yourselves with untold baggages, and the truly necessary is easy to carry. When preparing a tour with novices, you had better distribute a list which has been stripped down to the essentials; for you may be sure that each will add to it his own "indispensables."

Do not forget that the Lord makes rain. Army ponchoes I hold in highest esteem; they not only protect the rider perfectly, specifically thighs and knees, but the pack, and even the horse's loins. Wide, buttoned only sideways, they let the air through, which keeps you from getting wet with perspiration underneath; and their length when unbuttoned makes them most practical when sleeping in the straw at night. Practice soon overcomes their only discomfort, in mounting.

Though satisfied with my work in giving you the practical aids that can be learned by reading rather than riding, I am closing this chapter with a sense of frustration for not having conveyed to you, beyond the words "miles per hour," "good or bad going," "quarters" and "litter," "shoeing" and "pack," anything of the nature of touring. Although printer's ink can make you visualize the dangers of the highways I asked you to shun, it cannot at the same time make you envision the collector's joy and pride in discovering "still another" of the small forgotten roads one never sees from the highways, the spellbound ride through the brightness of a submerged world to which, in our time and day, one only accedes on horseback. At least on the "old continent" it is like this, and I should think there would be such corners left on the new as well.

## Preparing for a Show

The horse has been our companion since time immemorial, as he appears in antique images—by the chariots of our wars; in the pursuit of our games. In Greece, drawing the chariot of Apollo's sun, he was the sublimation of shackled lives; and, Pegasus carrying the Poet to victory, occasional escape. We meet him in representations of the earthly, yea earthy, pleasures of each day and age; as Art recorded them for us: from the polo games of the nebulously remote Persian past, by way of rude and stylized tournaments.

**Cover for program "Equestrian Days."** The Palace of Versailles During the Early
Reign of Louis XIV, at an epoch when the traditions of the French School were in
flower at the "Grande Ecurie." **(Courtesy Musée de Versailles)**

and falconry, hybrid of haughty solemnity and colorful trappings, into the
Renaissance. Art, in her flight from court to court in search of commissioned
portraits of mounted kings and vaulting fools and playing courtiers,
caught countless glimpses of merry hunts and country fairs and peasant
jousting and jotted them down good-humoredly without reward. She went
on to preserve for us the carrousels of the Spanische Hofreitschule in Vienna's
Hofburg and the golden spectacles at Versailles; the morning rides in the
Bois de Boulogne of mothers and children the way Renoir saw them on any
day in spring; the circus, from arduous rehearsal to triumphant salute, in
the Paris of Toulouse-Lautrec; afternoons at the racetrack; Jorock's country
and the lover's ride on a deserted beach somewhere up north. . . . Horse and
Rider, wherever there was a man, and a horse to carry him. It seems he
has borne on his supple back the burden of humanity, peasant and burgher,
up to the heights and down to the depths each could attain: beauty and war

# LES DRAGONS DE NOAILLES
## (1678 - 1766)

Cover for program "Spring Festival." Les Dragons de Noailles

**The salute of the carrousel of the Cadre Noir, Saumur. (Photo Blanchaud)**

rior, sovereign and clown, highwayman and saint; and though today he has ceased to be our associate in all we do and all that happens to us, our companionship continues in the pursuits which way back in his time and day his masters used to call so gracefully, *les Plaisirs et les Fêtes*.

These traditional spectacles, competitions, and games have found their modern home in the riding club and school, where they are as functional as the lessons in the ring and the rides across country. They teach young horsemen how to set themselves a goal and let them see, in the eyes of the spectators, the fruits of their efforts; they oblige them to ride with and against one another, to be good team mates and competitors, often to one and the same individual, and they break the monotony which threatens the life of a club or school, give it excitement and help to make it known.

From what we have seen in discussing a workday in our establishment, it is small, a relative newcomer in its locality, has a young instructor and an average number of average horses and riders; and with this at our disposal we are now preparing our first show.

Two factors engage our immediate attention: one essentially unchanging, such as publicity and material organization; another variable, such as the choice of performers, the assigning of individual mounts, the sequence of the programs, the date, and so forth.

Performers may have to be selected, but not participants; for everyone willing in a school or club is a participant, and a good thing it is, because you could not single-handedly organize such a show. The first thing, in fact, is to rally around you a few adult pupils, or parents of pupils, who are likely to help and stick with you. The latter is important, for a show is not conceived today and put on tomorrow; you should allow yourself three or four months of preparation and not have some of your collaborators "run out" somewhere before the finish line.

Be sure the date does not coincide with another spectacular or important event which might drain away a good part of your audience, or with a major examination period in the schools; and confer with the pillars of your school or club concerning their personal plans for business or pleasure trips.

Once your date is set, you inform your wider entourage, while word to the press should await the emergence of a more definite framework. Our outline will fit a private show that could be organized by any school or club in any country or community. Our considerations do not apply to the official horse show, the organizational rules and advice for which may be obtained from the national federations of your respective countries. What follows here is not a "horse show," but a *fête* in its fullest, and at once most restrictive, traditional sense.

For how many spectators should you provide? This is one of the hardest questions. If you expect too few, they will not keep a pleasant memory of "the crush where one could not even find a miserable seat." If you expect too many, and, for this reason, find yourself with a fair amount of vacant seats, your show will be an apparent "flop," which tends to chill the atmosphere. The ideal is for people "to have to squeeze a bit for everyone to get a seat."

The initial estimate of this numbers question should be made at the first meeting of a committee composed of you (who are shouldering the entire technical organization, as well as the coordination of the work of the committee members) and several teams of two, in charge, respectively, of

1. The installation of seats, microphones, loudspeakers, etc.
2. Preparation and servicing of the grounds.

**Jorrock's Country. "The zest of her ladyship knows no bounds, She's in at the death in spite of the hounds!" (Courtesy Lt. Col. W. E. Lyon)**

3. Receiving the spectators and organizing a team of children as ushers and program distributors.
4. Preparation of invitations, programs and other printed matter, as well as press relations before, during, and after the show.
5. Set-up and service of the bar.
6. An announcer and a general factotum who will make sure that horses and riders are ready for their entries on time.

Each team should have at least one "understudy" and assemble the staff it needs from among the rest of the members or pupils. They should co-ordinate their activities in frequent and regular meetings, so the bar people will not be counting on 200 spectators and the promotion department on 300, while the installations experts are trying to get hold of 150 seats. Since one of your responsibilities is to keep this from happening, you should busy yourself with everything and nothing in particular before, and

Travail de Répétition du Panneau, **by Toulouse-Lautrec. (Courtesy Musée Toulouse-Lautrec, Albi)**

be ubiquitous and therefore not stop anywhere during, the show.

We must be prepared for the worst. Suppose it rains. Whether our show takes place inside or outside the school, spectators and bar must remain dry. If in the open air, some awning arrangement must be provided to shelter the audience. Close to the stables, where the horses are protected, there must anyway be plenty of space, covered either permanently or by another awning, where the riders can mount without getting drenched and where it is easier than in the stables to check the tack. This spot should, like the stables, be well lighted if the show takes place at night.

If the entire event is held outside, you might set up your bar at one of the narrow sides of the riding hall. Obstacle elements, such as walls, fences, hedges, etc., make extremely decorative bars; then, all you need is a couple of posters on the wall behind it and a makeshift floor so the spectators who, remember, are not in boots, may come and go without carrying pounds of sawdust out in their shoes.

If your event takes place inside the school, your bar must be in a tent or under an awning so it can function unimpaired regardless of the weather. While the same *fête* with the same people does not have the same atmosphere with or without a bar, people do come for the show, not for the drinks and should not miss too much of the former to enjoy the latter; so keep your bar pretty close to the school. Provide a few tables and chairs, if there is room, and have sandwiches on hand for those who had no time for a regular meal and the lucky among the young whom excitement does not choke but makes ravenous.

So we shall suppose that we have set up our wall, converted into a bar, under a gaily striped and pennoned tent outside the covered school whose dimensions, alas, are a bare 22 by 16 yards. Its entrance, at the center of one of the long sides, has been framed by bleachers, over a length of 9 yards to each side, 4 rows deep, set up in tiers. Chairs are doubly inconvenient: their maximum capacity is equal only to their numbers and they obstruct the aisles when moved around. Bleachers are infinitely less comfortable but seat more people and cannot be pushed all over the place. A compromise would be to have two rows of bleachers and two of individual chairs tied, ten by ten, by a board along the back legs. A 4 ft. barrier should be erected in front of the first row, covered, if not very decorative, with bunting or camouflaged with hedges or potted shrubs such as are used for obstacles.

Let us suppose we have a small gallery which usually accomodates our workaday spectators. It holds about fifteen persons and overhangs the hall like a balcony. On one side we install our announcer and phonograph or tape recorder operator; the rest is given over to the gentlemen of the press who thus can come and go without having to perform a steeplechase across the rows of spectators.

Have your final installations and decorations ready three days ahead of time to let the horses get used to the flags and bunting, the noise of the chairs, the rustle of the crowd, the glare of spotlights . . . . Rehearse with music; normally lamblike horses turn into tigers at the first try-outs with music and props. Also remember that your horses will be more difficult outside than in the hall, and that it is better to use the outside school in the daytime and the riding hall at night. If you want to have a horse show, remember that at night it needs not only abundant, but perfect, lighting; else the shadows will cause so many refusals you will lose count of them.

If you devise a program within their capabilities, all students should be able to ride in your show. As with everything else, it is better to organize a

Ecuyère de Haute–Ecole. Le Salut, **by Toulouse-Lautrec. (Courtesy Musée Toulouse-Lautrec, Albi)**

simple, well done carrousel or game than one more complicated which, doubtlessly more spectacular if well performed, is above the level of your riders and horses. The program as a whole should accommodate everyone, from beginners (one year of riding) to accomplished horsemen. Among those of equal strength some will do better in a carrousel, others in a game. Keep one or two for solo numbers, if not more. If you envisage jumping, keep your courses short. A horse show is one thing, a *fête* something else.

## The Press

It is not the week, or even the month, before your show that you should be thinking of your press relations. By then, your school or club should have become a concept in your community and your show a result of this, not a means to make you known. In one word, your "image" should promote your show, not your show your image. By the time you organize your first event, the local news media should be acquainted with you and your work, and you should have sufficient knowledge of them, their special interests and approach to choose for each the right kind of material.

None of this should present major difficulties in a small community but takes some doing in the larger towns. In your efforts there, you should never forget that none of the newspapers or magazines will print a single line, a single picture for love of you, that whatever they publish is exclusively aimed at the interests of their readership. You, the earthquake in Japan, the Mona Lisa, are worthy of their consideration only in so far as either of you can be sold to their particular public. There is no sense in pretending that horsemanship is a noble art which can dispense with the public favor. Acquaint yourself with the editors and reporters, send in short items about your activities and keep a record of the reactions.

This does not mean that you should be slavishly submissive to the press just for the sake of breaking into print, no matter how. In your beginnings, some publications will take a wait-and-see attitude before dignifying you with their regular sports writer's attention. They may classify you somewhere between sports, entertainment, teenage interests and society and, the day they decide to do a story on you, send around a reporter who knows about as much of equitation as you do about higher mathematics. The results are often disastrous, the more so because by the time you behold them they have multiplied by the sum of the paper's circulation. The reporter's version of an interview which, in our own beginnings, we gave to a large circulation weekly, appeared in print as follows:

Children who have not advanced to the stage where they can control their horses completely at all times take most of their riding lessons around the stable's indoor riding pit where they learn to put their favorite horses through what is called, in horsy terminology, "high school stunts," such as Spanish step, rearing and group maneuvers. . . . But the biggest event comes when they progress sufficently to take their horses out for a canter, though some have to wait until they grow big enough to exercise more control over the horse with their legs. . . . One boy who started out as a beginner made such rapid progress that he's now past the instruction stage and comes to the stable to ride as a customer.

Avoid any term, phrase or allusion which might lead to such misunderstandings and keep some mimeographed material handy for the reporter who either confides to you that he just adores horses but knows nothing about riding, or else walks into the nearest stall to pat "the old man" on the nose, telling you that he loves horses and has ridden them since before he knew how to walk, on his grandfather's farm back in Georgia, Normandy, Westphalia. The locale will change, but the type is universal and will live on as long as there are horses.

On the other hand, I am quite sure that newspapermen have quite as much reason to complain of horsemen's amateurish handling of press matters as we have of their handling of ours. Your material may go to sports, society, or feature editors; send each only the kind that is of interest to him; let it be accurate not only in content but also in syntax, spelling and punctuation, delivered within, and even well in advance of, the publications' regular deadlines. Add one or more fair-sized glossy photo prints with the corresponding captions.

Distribute sufficient press passes and reserve generous space for a well-situated press box staffed by a "liaison officer" able to answer any question, make all the desired introductions, facilitate every move. You probably want to choose for this office one of the urbane and enthusiastic men or women who are every riding circle's most enjoyable assets, who are faithful to their hour in the school and their morning ride in the park, but neither care for, nor aspire to, participating in a carrousel or competing over the fences.

See to it that at horse show time the office is not invaded by participants, spectators, or anyone extraneous to the establishment; but its doors should be wide open to reporters and their typewriters. A team of two "secretaries" should be in permanent attendance, typing out and mimeographing a running report of the results. This is particularly important if we are a young club or school and may not rate a reporter's around-the-clock attendance; thus when he looks in or leaves in the middle of the show you at least are sure that he has all the news up to the moment. Your two "secretaries" should be recruited from among teenagers who, for one reason or another, are unable to ride in this year's event. They should have on hand all additional information material, including short relevant biographies of all participants.

Be sure to have a specialized photographer on the grounds and, to make it worth his while, to give his name and address on the program for those wanting to order prints. Do not rely exclusively on press photographers for your post-event releases; because photographing a horse and rider in action is specialized work. But do have your pictures taken in action, or at least on horseback. Horsemen and women, smart as they may be in the saddle, are more often than not disappointing on a bar stool and almost always grotesque when dancing in boots. If you want to illustrate the social atmosphere, give your spectators a break—there are usually a few chic young women in tweeds or linen, leaning against a white rail, watching a redcoat taking a fence.

After the event, along with the photographs of your choice and any information you may find newsworthy, send out realistic attendance figures to the press and an outline of things to come; announce a tour on horseback, a series of lectures, a registration notice for new courses, whatever is next on your list.

## Invitations

Your invitations should be sent out ten to fifteen days in advance. While they should always be engraved on fine paper to avoid the commercial look and their form remains essentially the same, if you intend this to be an announcement rather than a formal invitation, you may omit the name of the person(s) and simply phrase, ". . . requests the pleasure of your company . . ." In that case, you may also, if necessary, discreetly add your telephone number and concise driving directions in a lower corner.

SAINT GEORGE ACADEMY
requests the pleasure of the company of
Mr. and Mrs. ...............
at the

SPRING CARROUSEL
on Saturday, the twenty-second of May
at eight o'clock
1892 Linden Road

## Programs

This program has been fashioned for an evening in the covered school and may be shown on two successive evenings if you have more spectators than space.

SAINT GEORGE ACADEMY
Saturday and Sunday
May 1 and 2, 19....
SPRING CARROUSEL
first part

| | | |
|---|---|---|
| PARADE | Mr. | on |
| | Mrs. | on |
| | Mr. | on |
| | Miss | on |
| | Mr. | on |
| | Mrs. | on |
| | Mr. | on |
| | Miss | on |
| | Mr. | on |
| | Mrs. | on |
| | Mr. | on |
| | Miss | on |
| DRESSAGE SOLOS | Miss | on |
| | Mr. | on |
| MUSICAL CHAIRS | Miss | on |

|                              | Miss |      |
|                              | Miss |      |
|                              | Miss |      |
|                              | Mr.  |      |
|                              | Mr.  |      |
|                              | Mr.  |      |
|                              | Mr.  |      |

|                              |      |      |      |
| ---------------------------- | ---- | ---- | ---- |
|                              | Miss | on   |      |
|                              | Miss | on   |      |
|                              | Miss | on   |      |
|                              | Mr.  | on   |      |
|                              | Mr.  | on   |      |
|                              | Mr.  | on   |      |
|                              | Mr.  | on   |      |
| VOLTIGE                      | Miss |      |      |
|                              | Miss |      |      |
|                              | Mr.  | and  |      |
|                              | Mr.  |      |      |
| LE CARROUSEL LOUIS XV        | Mrs. | on   |      |
|                              | Mr.  | on   |      |
|                              | Miss | on   |      |
|                              | Mr.  | on   |      |
|                              | Mrs. | on   |      |
|                              | Mr.  | on   |      |
|                              | Miss | on   |      |
|                              | Mr.  | on   |      |
|                              | Mrs. | on   |      |
|                              | Mr.  | on   |      |
|                              | Miss | on   |      |
|                              | Mr.  | on   |      |
| CHANTILLY (g., 6 yrs.)       | Mr. XYZ |   |      |

— INTERMISSION —

Author's note: "Mr. ZYZ" represents you, the riding master, presenting a horse of your own schooling.

## SAINT GEORGE ACADEMY
Saturday and Sunday
May 1 and 2, 19....
SPRING CARROUSEL
second part

|                              |      |      |
| ---------------------------- | ---- | ---- |
| THE CHILDREN'S CARROUSEL     | Miss | on   |
|                              | Mr.  | on   |
|                              | Miss | on   |
|                              | Mr.  | on   |
|                              | Miss | on   |
|                              | Mr.  | on   |
|                              | Miss | on   |
|                              | Mr.  | on   |
| DRESSAGE SOLOS               | Mrs. | on   |
|                              | Mr.  | on   |
| LE CARROUSEL DES DAMES       | Mrs. | on   |
|                              | Miss | on   |
|                              | Mrs. | on   |
|                              | Miss | on   |
|                              | Mrs. | on   |
|                              | Miss | on   |
| GYMKHANA                     | Mrs. | on   |
|                              | Mr.  | on   |
|                              | Miss | on   |
|                              | Mr.  | on   |
|                              | Mrs. | on   |
|                              | Mr.  | on   |
| "1900"                       | Mrs. X presents MORNING GLORY (Sidesaddle) | |

— THE END —

Judges:                          Photography: Studio ABC
Steward:                                       22 Elm Street
Announcer:                                     Tel.:
Riders and horses are            Prizes courtesy of:
listed in the order                  Metropolitan Bootmakers
of their appearance                  Tally Ho Saddlery
                                     Jorrocks Book Store

The parade in which all horses take part, though spectacular, has also a
very practical purpose: it lets the horses see the exact décor, including spectators, where they are going to work. If despite all precautions, previous
rehearsals with music, flags, bleachers, spotlights, some do not take it calmly,
they will be less conspicuous here than in a solo or a carrousel.

For the first two solos give two calm horses to two accomplished riders.
Musical chairs where the carrousel horses are taking part limbers them up
and inures them to audience noise. The voltige gives the horses which have
participated in the Musical Chairs time for a breather and to be ready for
the carrousel. Since they will also serve the Children's Carrousel, you give
them time to rest during the Riding Master's presentation and the intermission.
The children's carrousel should be staged right after the intermission when
the horses are already limbered up, calm, though not yet tired. Besides it is
now growing late and some of the children might start getting fidgety.

The next two solos may be performed by two somewhat less experienced
riders than those of the first part. If of equal ability, this may be balanced
by giving the more difficult horses to those of the second part; if the difference, on the contrary, is rather stark, give them to those of the first. Thus,
as far as the spectators' impressions are concerned, the four solos will be
quite even. *Le carrousel des dames* is placed before the gymkhana, which is
reserved for the end because the nervous excitement it produces in the riders
is often communicated to the horses.

"1900" is a succession of simple maneuvers performed by a young lady in
the side saddle. It is the return to calm and presents a picture of elegance,
be it in period costume under the appellation of "1900," or in very formal
contemporary dress.

This question of dress and décor is not a matter  beneath the consideration
of true horsemen. Even in the most sophisticated carrousels and in haute-
école presentations, when presented in the framework of a show, staging,
costumes, lighting and music occupy an important place. Since we must carefully dose the difficulties of our carrousels and solos, prudently remain
slightly below the maximum capacities of horses and riders, we should make
maximum use of lighting, costume and musical effects; in one word, staging.

The carrousels and solos should be sparkling; avoid as far as possible the
walk where every fault is seen as through a magnifying glass. Use principally
the cadenced trot, interrupted here and there by a free extension. Keep the

canter for the end. Do not choose too solemn a musical accompaniment; the music of the 17th and 18th centuries offers abundant choice, and for the Children's Carrousel there are the military marches of all nations.

If you wish to lend a breath of the competitive spirit to your *fête,* the solo exhibitions may be judged and annotated. Prizes are usually offered by saddlers, bootmakers, bookstores specializing in equestrian literature; the School might offer one. . . . There also may be consolation prizes; for the unluckiest horseman, the most elegant horsewoman, etc.

Above all, your *fête* must be such that at the close spectators and performers alike will be saying, "over already?" Your numbers must follow one another swiftly and not last too long. Do not give your audience time to get accustomed to any one part. In a show, one hour of amusement cannot make up for one minute of boredom.

### SAINT GEORGE ACADEMY

Saturday and Sunday
May 1, and 2, 19....

EQUESTRIAN DAYS

May 1
in the school, 8 p.m.

| | | |
|---|---|---|
| PARADE | Mr. | on |
| | Mrs. | on |
| | Mr. | on |
| | Miss | on |
| | Mr. | on |
| | Mrs. | on |
| | Mr. | on |
| | Miss | on |
| | Mr. | on |
| | Mrs. | on |
| | Mr. | on |
| | Miss | on |
| | | |
| "EMPIRE" — Carrousel | Mrs. | on |
| | Mr. | on |
| | Miss | on |
| | Mr. | on |
| | Mrs. | on |
| | Mr. | on |
| | Miss | on |
| | Mr. | on |
| | Mrs. | on |
| | Mr. | on |
| | Miss | on |
| | Mr. | on |
| | | |
| VOLTIGE | Miss | |
| | Miss | |
| | Mr. | and |
| | Mr. | |
| | | |
| GOLDEN KNIGHT H., (5 yrs.) | Mr. XYZ | |

—INTERMISSION—

| THE CHILDREN'S CARROUSEL | Miss | on |
| | Mr. | on |
| | Miss | on |
| | Mr. | on |
| | Miss | on |
| | Mr. | on |
| | Miss | on |
| | Mr. | on |
| GYMKHANA — 1st Heat | Miss | on |
| | Mr. | on |
| | Mrs. | on |
| | Mr. | on |
| | Miss | on |
| | Mr. | on |
| DRESSAGE SOLOS | Mrs. | on |
| | Mr. | on |

## SAINT GEORGE ACADEMY

Saturday and Sunday
May 1, and 2, 19....

### EQUESTRIAN DAYS

May 2
in the arena, 10 a.m.

| GYMKHANA — 2nd Heat | Miss | on |
| | Mr. | on |
| | Mrs. | on |
| | Miss | on |
| | Mr. | on |
| | Miss | on |
| THE GAME OF THE ROSE | Miss | on |
| | Mr. | on |
| | Mr. | on |
| | Mr. | on |

—INTERMISSION—

## HORSE SHOW

| No. | Horse | Owner | Rider | Faults | Time |
| --- | --- | --- | --- | --- | --- |
| 1 | Halali | M. F. Jones | Owner | | |
| 2 | Iowa II | E. L. Doe | M. G. Smith | | |

Author's Note: The Game of the Rose is played in two heats, three if necessary. The Horse Show may be produced in two parts, or shortened, depending on the audience, and a carrousel be substituted for the second part.

The third suggested program presupposes either a large club or the participation of several. It should be extremely varied and well adapted to the type of outdoor ring you have. Games and jumping competitions should predominate over dressage tests and carrousels which are better suited to the riding hall. The level of those participating in carrousels and dressage tests in an open air show must, to obtain equivalent results, be superior to that in an indoor performance. On the other hand, horse shows inside the hall, be it ever so big, make the same kind of course more difficult to negotiate than if it were outdoors. If you are lucky enough to manage a large club and can count on other clubs to participate, you have the possibility of organizing two shows: a Winter Show (such as the first program) given in the School, and a Spring Show given in the Arena, the latter patterned on the second program, or else as follows.

**SAINT GEORGE ACADEMY**

Saturday and Sunday
May 1, and 2, 19....

SPRING FESTIVAL

Saturday
2 p.m.

CARROUSEL
GAME OF THE HOOP by teams
GAME OF THE ROSE

—INTERMISSION—

HORSE SHOW I

—THE END—

Sunday
2 p.m.

GAME OF THE HOOP finale
JUNIOR HORSE SHOW

—INTERMISSION—

RELAY RACE
HORSE SHOW II

—THE END—

The finale of the game of the hoop may be played by teams or individually. The definitive winners of the horse show are picked from the total of exhibitors of both days.

The jumping events may be diversified. For the first day's horse show, for example, set a time limit, though the time element, within this limit, does not enter into the scoring. Where there is a tie, there is a jump-off, and the stop watch does go into action. A program must be established which will interest the audience, *i.e.*, it must not drag its feet and have some elements of suspense. A greater number of short offerings is preferable to a lesser number of long ones. Where there is a question of eliminations, any number of exhibitors must be accepted; the event, only incidentally a spectacle, is principally a test for selecting horses and riders. Spectators, going there to see four or five horses they know, are interested exclusively in the technical aspect. But a *fête* is something else; there the audience is king and must be entertained.

In order to plan a horse show, you must have at least 500 by 300 feet of ground suitable for the horses' legs. The popular sand makes for good going, provided it is not too deep. The upkeep is easy (harrowing and sprinkling); and while turf is prettier it is harder to care for and obliges riders to calk their horses' shoes.

The paddock must be of a size to hold a score of riders at once. The trial bar is placed into its center so it may be jumped both ways.

From the judges' stand all obstacles must be visible. If your course comprises a water jump, a judge ought to be posted there; because from the judges' stand it is impossible to tell with absolute certainty whether or not a fault is committed there. The same goes for all obstacles which may be partially hidden from the judges' view. If the time is clocked by stop watch, the starting and finishing lines must, for maximum precision, be in front of the judges' stand.

A great part of the success or failure of your horse show depends on your course architect's ability to balance the course. If it is too difficult for the majority of exhibitors and horses, he disheartens everyone, including the horses; if it is too easy, there is no suspense and the event falls flat. Moreover, the course must be easily altered so as to avoid loss of time between two successive events.

I am giving you a few sample courses, some of which I used in a ring which had a great number of solid obstacles because it served principally as a training ring.

It is preferable to have but ten or twelve well-made and well-placed obstacles rather than fifteen sloppily made and haphazardly placed. Do not use exceedingly light but rather thick bars painted in two colors. Build your obstacles with a considerable front (4 to 6 yards). The number of spread jumps should equal the number of vertical jumps.

The solid fences are marked with capital letters on the figure which gives you a picture of the different obstacles.

A. Superposed boards over a ditch.

B. An oxer over a ditch.

C. A ditch with sloping sides. The bottom is filled with water. Three superposed bars are placed in the middle. The width of the ditch taken at ground level is too great for the horse to clear. He must go down and take off from the slope in order to clear the obstacle.

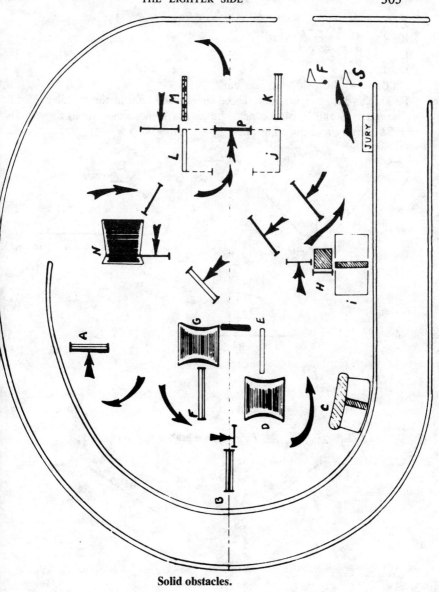

**Solid obstacles.**

D. Bank.

E. A thick brush jump with a bar so the horse cannot brush through it.

F. The same obstacle with a ditch preceding the hedge.

G. Bank

H. Water jump preceded by a hedge.

I. Ditch with very sloping sides. A rivulet at the bottom. At the top of each side there is a small bank with two bars.

J.  
K.  
L.  } Road crossings.  
M.  

N. Bank with brush jump and bar.

P. Ditch with straight sides. Three superposed bars in the middle.

The letters S and F, placed near the judges' stand beside small flags, indicate the starting and finishing lines.

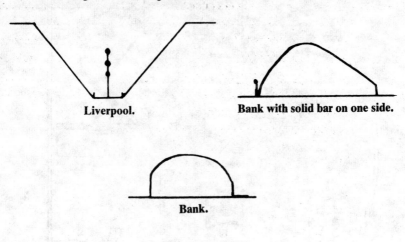

Liverpool.                    Bank with solid bar on one side.

Bank.

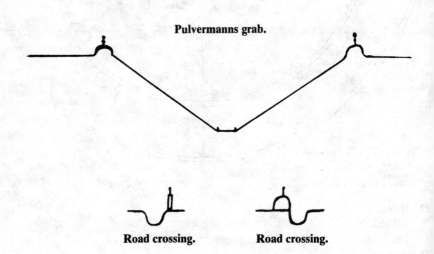

Pulvermanns grab.

Road crossing.            Road crossing.

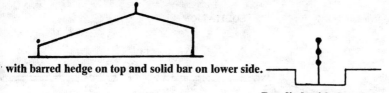

with barred hedge on top and solid bar on lower side.

**Dry ditch with three bars.**

My three examples are courses of different difficulties: The first is suitable for junior exhibitors with rather restricted experience. The second is comfortable for skilled riders. The third is more difficult, mainly as concerns conduct. The fourth and fifth comprise only mobile obstacles.

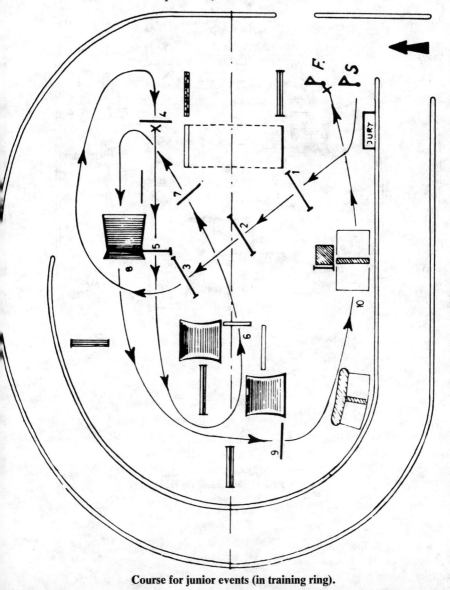

**Course for junior events (in training ring).**

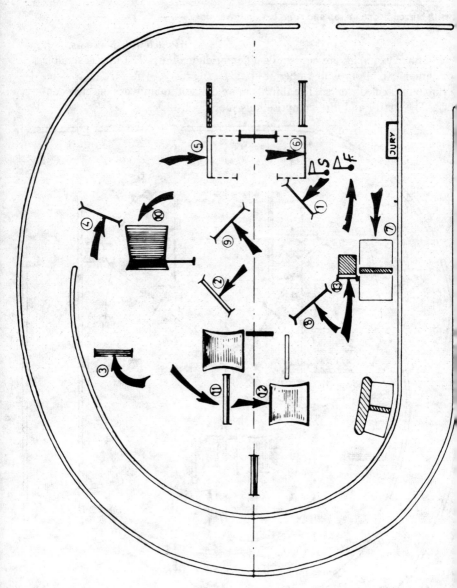

**Course for skilled riders (in training ring).**

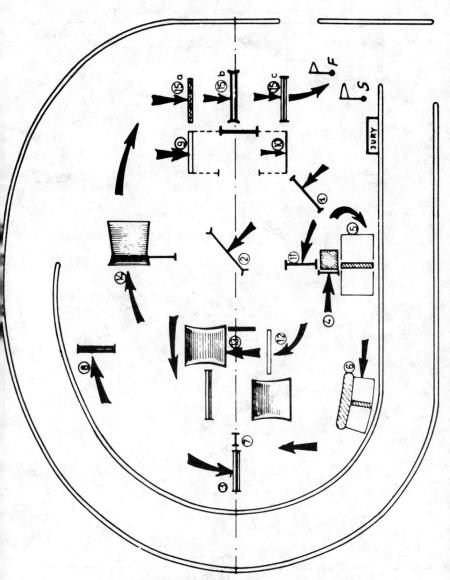

**Course for accomplished riders (in training ring).**

These courses comprise only mobile obstacles.

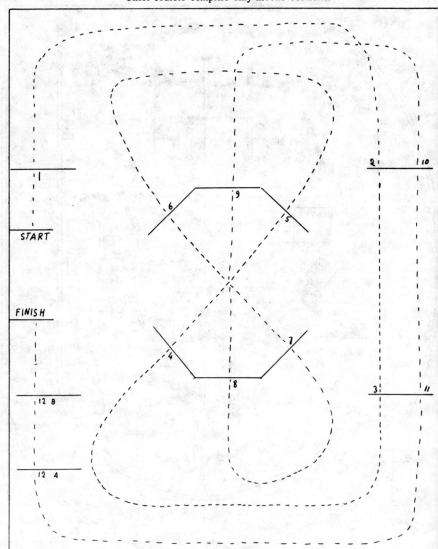

Course composed of mobile obstacles only.

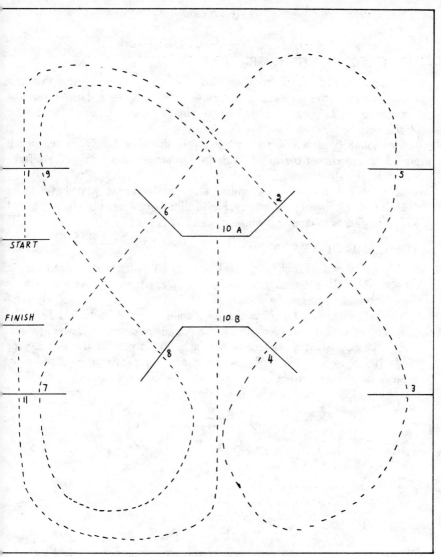

**Course composed of mobile obstacles only.**

## Games

## THE GAME OF THE ROSE

Three horsemen are bent on capturing, within a span of three minutes, a rose pinned to the shoulder of a horsewoman. If by then the rose has not been taken, the lady has won the heat; or else the winner is the gallant holder of the rose.

This game is played in two, if necessary three, heats. The riders, each placed at one end of the arena, wait for the start at the signal of a referee who also signals the end.

They should ride, without spurs, very handy horses who have never dreamed of kicking (polo ponies are ideal mounts for this game), bitted with a snaffle, noseband and running martingale.

## THE GAME OF THE HOOP

Five or six poles about 6 feet high are placed in the arena. Each carries a hoop which the rider must, in minimum time, seize with his crop or with a six-foot stick representing a lance.

The difficulty may be increased by placing a small obstacle where the hoop comes within the rider's reach. If a fault is committed over the obstacle, the contestant must return and jump it again; thus the penalty for the fault is automatically transformed into time, simplifying the judges' task.

Since the horse has to be controlled with one hand, management difficulties may be added between the hoop-bearing poles, such as a straight line of

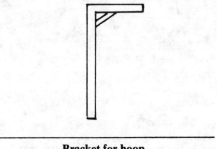

**Bracket for hoop.**

about ten upright sticks at distances of about three yards around which the horse must turn without knocking them down.

The game is easily made harder or simpler through the size of the hoops. Bracket-shaped poles simplify the attachment problem, since the hoops are simply hung over the horizontal bars.

## MUSICAL CHAIRS

Let us say, ten riders form a circle around nine chairs placed on an inner circle, chair-backs turned toward the center. At the start of the music, the riders strike off into a canter. As soon as it stops, all dismount and, without letting go of their horses, sit down on chairs. Whoever has failed to catch a seat is eliminated. After another chair has been lifted, the game continues and at every stop of the music one more rider is eliminated and one more chair withdrawn. When at long last there are but two riders and one chair left, they are placed at fifteen yards from it, awaiting, at the canter on a ten-yard circle, the stop of the music to dismount first and then to cover on foot, horses in hand, the distance separating them from the chair. The rider seated wins.

## RELAY RACES

are contested among several teams, no more than four at a time, or else a stop watch must indicate the winning team. They are composed of no less than three, no more than five riders lined up at opposite ends of the arena (lengthwise). Let us presuppose four teams formed by three riders each. Teams A, B, C, D.

At one end of the arena we have stationed behind each other the Nos. 1 and 3 of the four teams. At the opposite end the Nos. 2 of the four teams are stationed, facing them. One judge per team is posted at each end in addition to the referee (making 8 judges).

At the referee's signal, the four Nos. 1 start and each must hand, not

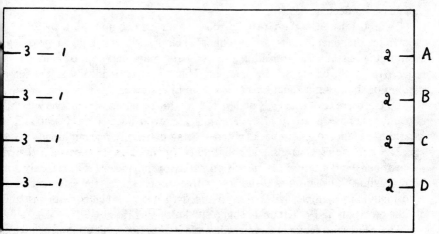

**Relay race for four teams of three horsemen each.**

throw, his crop to his team-mate No. 2. If it drops, the arriving rider must dismount, pick it up, mount again and hand it over. No. 2 in turn may not start unless he holds the crop. The same is true for No. 3. The team whose No. 3 gets in first is the winner. If there are more than four teams, each starting team must be clocked.

To give an extra twist to the game, only horses No. 1 need be saddled and their saddles then serve horses 2 and 3. In this case, riders 1 and 2 must await their team-mates' arrival on foot, the saddles being the tokens. As soon as rider No. 1 arrives alongside No. 2, he unsaddles his horse without anyone's help, gives the saddle to No. 2 who, in turn, must saddle his horse unaided.

## GYMKHANAS

There is no sense in enumerating the countless combinations one can find. Since these games are usually just right for those who are neither up to riding in a carrousel nor on an obstacle course, it is more than anything else a question of common sense in choosing the difficulties in accordance with the level of the participants.

### *Carrousels*

Let me give you one great model carrousel from which you may draw a great variety of simpler, shorter ones, or such as do not require quite as much space, plus three examples of how this may be accomplished. Each model represents an average of difficulty within its kind, which you may increase or decrease at will.

Take, for instance, the Great Carrousel. You may complicate it by turning down the diagonal in half-pass, by changing circles with a flying change of leg, rather than making the transition at a trot. You may simplify it by eliminating the Wind Mill, or the Spiral, or both. This carrousel is ideally suited for a group of six horsemen and six horsewomen in costume.

Le Carrousel des Dames is no less esthetic for being easier, and very useful where you have a group of decorative ladies who have a good seat and a certain elegance on horseback, without being extremely accomplished.

The Children's Carrousel although very simple, can be most effective if performed with the greatest precision. It is by no means suitable only for raw beginners; because, as is the case with every carrousel, the same exercise, no matter how simple, is far from being the same if executed with just the right precision and a certain brilliance of horse and rider.

The Merry-Go-Round, as you will notice, does not at any moment divide into two groups and is the kind you will be grateful to have when dealing with a half dozen or so of gifted smaller children. They sometimes are very well able to execute the maneuvers, while too young to memorize their sequence reliably, and you might want to recruit a mature adolescent to command it very discreetly on horseback.

Though, as I said before, two carrousels made up of the very same figures are worlds apart if one of them is performed by accomplished riders on perfectly and highly schooled horses, the other by medium riders on passable horses, you are lucky indeed if, rather than a few cracks, you have groups of reasonably efficient, disciplined horsemen and women; for the work of the ensemble overshadows that of the individual, and, let me repeat, it is better to have a simple carrousel well performed than one more complicated lacking cohesion and homogeneity. Effective, tasteful décors, costuming, *"son et lumière"* will enhance the purely technical excellence, as haphazard treatment of such accessories would seriously impair the general effect.

The carrousels I am giving you, or those you might yourself cut from the cloth of the Great Carrousel, must be adapted to the riders, horses and facilities available. You will notice that my examples are variously based on rings where the entrance faces the grandstands (ideal), where it is located on the same side as the grandstands (about the worst that could happen), on the long, and on the narrow, side. You will find sketches of an Olympic Arena (60 by 20 m), of a regulation ring for dressage tests of reduced size (40 by 20 m), and of a minimum size riding school ring (22 by 16 m).

Any kind of carrousel must be rehearsed for months on end, after a long period during which its component parts have been practiced isolatedly. Long before the day of the show, you and your riders must practically have ceased to be consciously aware of their sequence, hard put to recite it, but able to trace it in the sawdust with your toe at the drop of a derby.

The best and, indeed, most professional, way of memorizing a carrousel is walking and re-walking it in the ring on foot, although a young lady I know exclusively "rides it on paper," careful to turn the wrist with the different movements and conversions; but she is a writer. Though admittedly more of a writer than a rider, her system works remarkably well, and I have seldom if ever seen her during rehearsal of a critical movement strike out on her own in one of those abrupt and apparently willful changes of direction which leave the straying rider in sudden splendid isolation, the rest of the group aghast, the instructor in distraction.

### The Great Carrousel

TWELVE RIDERS

At A, enter at a walk, single file, on the center line. At X, No. 1, always

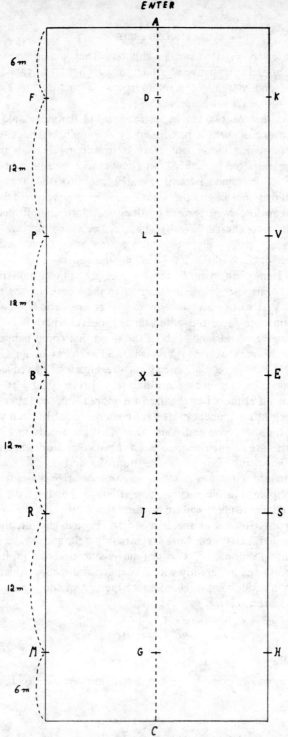

Olympic arena. Length = 60 m. Width = 20 m.

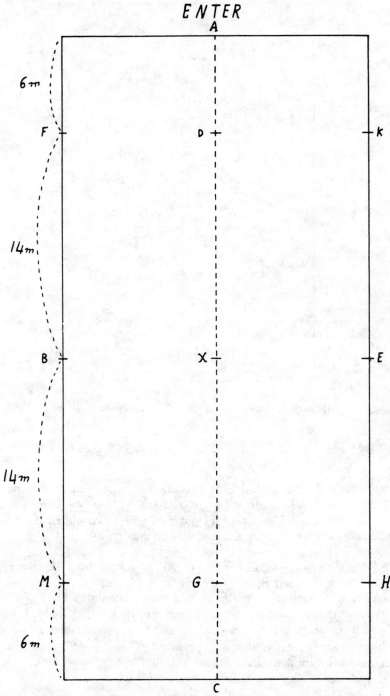

**Official arena of reduced dimensions.   Length = 40 m.   Width = 20 m.**

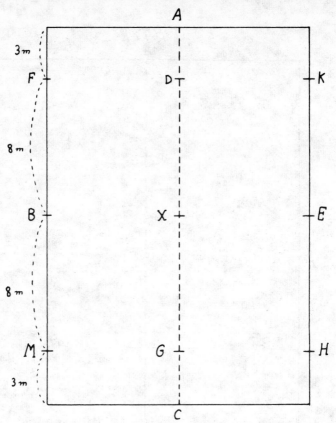

**Minimum-size arena.   Length = 22 m.   Width = 16 m.**

on the center line, advances up to I, going two horses' lengths beyond it, and halts. No. 2 follows the same line and halts behind No. 1 on the line R-S. At X Nos. 3-5-7-9-11 take the oblique to the right, while Nos. 4-6-8-10-12 take the oblique to the left, and stop on the line R-S.

Salute.

Advance at a walk on the center line. At C, odd numbers left rein, even numbers right rein. At H, odd numbers leave the track in the direction of X. At M, even numbers leave the track in the direction of X.

At X, trot, once more in single file, even numbers having inserted themselves between odd. At A, odd numbers left rein, even numbers right rein; each group keeps a horse's length between riders. At F, odd numbers, at K even numbers, turn down the diagonal, extended trot, crossing At X, Nos. 2

**Half-pass by threes. Cadre Noir, Saumur. (Courtesy Col. de Saint-Andre)**

assing between 1 and 3, etc. At H, odd numbers cadenced trot; at M, even numbers, cadenced trot. At C, turn down the school, riders retaking their respective places (1-2-3-4-, etc.). At D, half-volte, odd numbers left rein, even numbers right rein. At X, single file re-forms.

At G, half-volte, odd numbers left rein, even numbers right rein. At X, single file re-forms. At A, odd numbers left rein, even numbers right rein and each group distributes itself evenly on a long side. At C, turn down the school, keeping the distances taken on the long sides. When the entire group is on the center line, *i.e.*, No. 1 between A and D and No. 12 between G and C, volte individually, odd numbers left rein, even numbers right rein. Take and finish turn-down.

At A, odd numbers left rein, even numbers right rein. At M for No. 1, at H for No. 2, both groups execute a volte individually: odd numbers left rein, even numbers right rein. At C, turn down the school by twos; Nos. 1 and 2 boot to boot, Nos. 3 and 4 boot to boot, etc. At X, volte consecutively for each group; odd numbers left rein, even numbers right rein. At A, odd numbers left rein, even numbers right rein. At M, for No. 1, at H for No. 2 both groups execute a turn across the school individually, No. 1 crossing No 2 on the left. At H for No. 1, at M for No. 2, groups change rein.

At C, turn down the school in single file, both groups interlocking. At A all riders left rein. At B, Nos. 1-2-3-4 turn across the school individually At E, the first four riders change rein. At B, Nos. 5-6-7-8 same exercise. At B, Nos. 9-10-11-12 same exercise. At E, the groups of four change rein (right rein). All riders are now on the right rein.

At B, the first six riders turn across the school individually and change rein. The other six riders same exercise when No. 7 arrives at the point where No. 1 has turned. All riders are now on the left rein.

At B, all riders turn across the school individually and change rein. For the departure in the three last maneuvers (turn-across by 4, 6, and 12), the letter B must be the central point, i.e., for the turn-across by fours, two riders must have gone beyond B and the other two still be this side of it when the turn-across is started. The same goes for the turn-across by six's and by twelve's. Thus it is useful in a carrousel to set as many guidemarks as needed.

After the last turn-across all riders are on the right rein. At A, turn down the school. At C, odd numbers left rein; even numbers right rein. At A, turn down the school by twos, boot to boot (1 and 2, 3 and 4, etc.). At X, odd numbers turn left. At E, track to the left. At X, even numbers turn right. At B, track to the left. Both groups are on the left rein in closed formation.

At B for No. 1, at E, for No. 2, both groups turn across the school individually, up to the center line A-C. Nos. 1 and 2 are boot to boot in reverse. The riders are to the left of their respective head riders, Nos. 1 and 2, who serve as pivots, while Nos. 11 and 12 represent the wing tips. Both groups execute a 360 degree conversion to the right. For the necessary cohesion, the wings should bear to the right, so as to stay boot to boot. The turn across the school is completed after the conversion and the groups change rein; now being, after regaining the track, on the right rein. At C, for No. 1, at A for No. 2, the groups start into a canter. At A for No. 1, at C for No. 2, the groups execute a volte. Ahead after the volte. At S for No. 1, at P for No. 2, the groups form a circle of a 20 m diameter. At P for No. 2, the centers of these two circles are, respectively for the odd and even numbers, the letters I and L. Since the two circles have a radius of 10 m, the groups pass, each, at 2 m from point X which is at a distance of 12 m from the centers of circles I and L. The head riders must meet when they cut across line A-C. After

**The courbette on the circle. Cadre Noir, Saumur. (Courtesy Col. de Saint-André)**

two complete rounds on the circle, the riders change circles, passing by X and crossing on each other's left.

At X, check to a trot and request the left canter. The odd numbers are now on the circle the center of which is the letter L, on the left rein, while the even numbers are on the circle the center of which is the letter I, also on the left rein. After two complete rounds on the circle, ahead, odd numbers passing by P, even numbers passing by S.

At M for No. 1, at K for No. 2, the groups check to a trot. At C for the odd numbers, at A for the even numbers, turn down the school. At X, the odd numbers turn right. At E, they take the track to the left. At X, the even numbers turn right. At B, they take the track to the right. At A, turn down the school in single file, the even numbers inserting themselves among the odd. At C, all riders on the left rein.

At V form a SPIRAL of a 20 m diameter the center of which is the letter

L. It is progressively tightened to the maximum and then unrolled by the head riders by a half right turn. When the spiral has been completely unrolled, crossing over line A-C, change circles, passing by X; the figure is repeated on the left rein the center being the letter I. When it has been completely unrolled, the riders arriving at S, ahead, track to the right. At B, form a spiral of a 20 m diameter the center of which is the letter X, always at a trot. When No. 1 begins to unroll the spiral, he starts into the left canter and finishes to unroll it at this gait.

At E, ahead at a canter, track to the left. At A, at a canter, turn down the school consecutively. At X, No. 1 checks to a walk and advances to the point of the initial salute, the entire group following him in that same formation.   Salute.

### Le Carrousel des Dames

## EIGHT RIDERS

At A, enter track to the right; at a walk by the long side K-H. When rider No. 2 arrives at C, the first three riders turn down the school individually and halt on the line BXE. When rider No. 6 arrives at C, the last five riders turn down the school individually and halt at a horse's length behind the first three; rider No. 6 behind rider No. 2.   Salute.

Break at a walk. Upon arrival on the track of the narrow side(A) track to the left. At B, trot, once around. At H, turn down the diagonal, extending the trot. At F, cadenced trot. At K, turn down the diagonal, extending the trot. At M, cadenced trot. At C, turn down the school. At A, odd numbers track to the left, even numbers track to the right. At F for odd numbers, at K for even numbers, turn down the diagonal, extending the trot. Crossing at X, the odd numbers passing in front of the even numbers. At H for odd numbers, at M for even numbers, cadenced trot.

At C, turn down the school, the two groups interlocking (1-2-3-4-, etc.). At D, half-volte, left for odd numbers, right for even numbers.   Riders re-form a single group on the center line A-C (between X and G, point to be determined in accordance with the size of the ring and the number of riders).

At C, odd numbers track to the left, even numbers track to the right. At K for rider No. 1, at F for rider No. 2, the two groups perform a volte individually. At A turn down the school, the groups interlocking. At G for the rider No. 1, the riders perform a volte individually, left for odd numbers, right for even numbers. At C, odd numbers track to the left, even numbers track to the right. At A, turn down the school, at G half-volte left for odd numbers, right for even numbers. Riders re-form a single group on the center line A-C (between X and D, point to be determined).

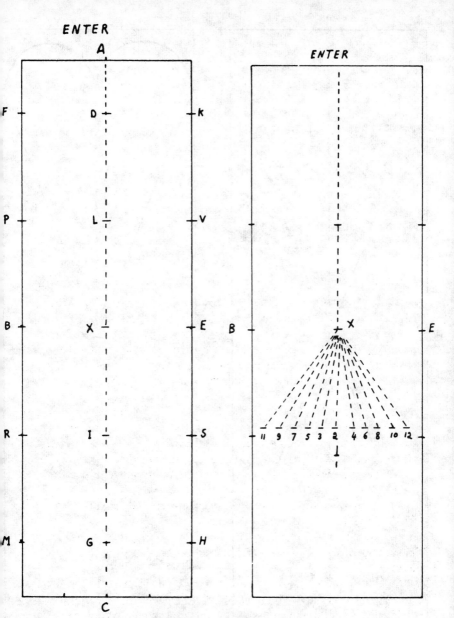

**Principal figures used in the great carrousel.**

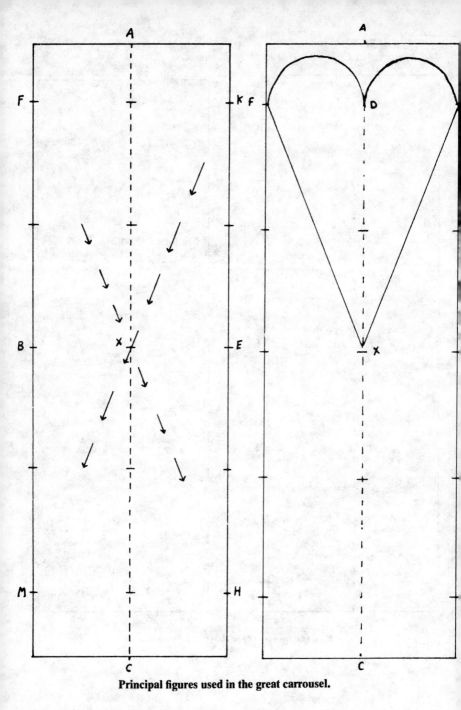

**Principal figures used in the great carrousel.**

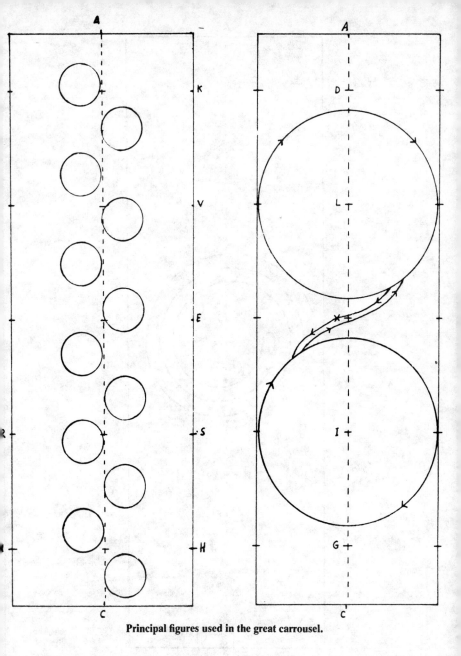

**Principal figures used in the great carrousel.**

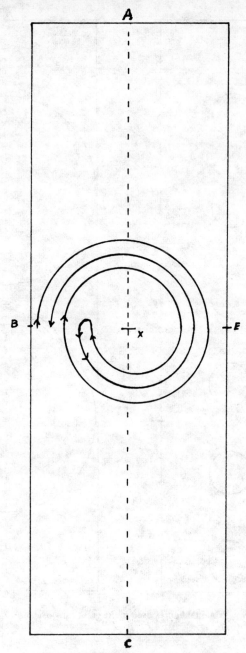

**Principal figures used in the great carrousel.**

At A, track to the left. At C, start into the left canter. At A, form a circle, described twice. Change circles, passing through X. At X, check to a trot, start into right canter. At C, form a circle, described twice. At C, check to a trot. Ahead, once around.

At E, check to a walk. At C for rider No. 2, the first three riders turn down the school individually and halt on the line BXE. At C for rider No. 6, the last five riders (Nos. 4-5-6-7-8) turn down the school individually and halt at a horse's length behind the first three; rider No. 6 behind rider No. 2 who halts at X. Salute, break, exit.

### The Children's Carrousel

## EIGHT RIDERS

At E, enter by twos. Group Y track to the left, Group Z track to the right. At B where the groups face each other, turn across the school individually, halt on center line A-C. Salute.

Break at a walk as follows: The head rider of Group Y starts into the turn across the school (X-E), followed by the head rider of Group Z. The two groups interlock during this maneuver, each rider passing through the letter X before starting into the turn across the school. During this maneuver, the riders are placed in the following order: head rider of Group Y, head rider of Group Z, rider No. 1 of Group Y, rider No. 1 of Group Z, rider No. 2 of Group Y, rider No. 2 of Group Z, etc.

At E, Group Y track to the left, Group Z track to the right. At A for Group Y, at C for Group Z, turn down the school. At X, Group Y turns left, Group Z turns left. At E for group Y, at B for Group Z, track to the left. At A for Group Y, at C for Group Z, trot, once around the track.

At M for Group Y, at K for Group Z, half-volte. At K for Group Y, at M for Group Z, half-volte in reverse. At A for Group Y, at C for Group Z, form a circle, make it twice. Change circles, the Groups crossing on their right, passing through X. Make a circle twice, ahead, both Groups track to the right, once around.

At C we have Head Rider Y, at A we have Head Rider Z. At F, upon arrival of head rider Y, and at H upon arrival of head rider Z, both Groups turn across the school individually and change hands. At M upon arrival of head rider Y, and at K upon arrival of head rider Z, both Groups turn across the school individually and change hands.

At A for Group Y, at C for Group Z, start into the right canter, twice around the track. At A for Group Y, at C for Group Z, check to a trot. At H for Group Y, at F for Group Z, half-volte. At A for Group Y, at C for Group Z, start into left canter, twice around the track. At A for Group Y, at C for Group Z, check to a trot, once around the track.

At B for Group Y, at E for Group Z, check to a walk. At C for Group Y, at A for Group Z, turn down the school. At X, Group Y turns right and Group Z turns left up to E.

The riders are placed by TWOS (one of Group Y, one of Group Z). At E, Group Y track to the right, Group Z track to the left. At B, both Groups turn acrooss the school individually and halt on the center line A-C. Salute, break, and at a walk, by twos exit, passing through the letter X.

### Merry-Go-Round

#### EIGHT RIDERS

At E, enter single file at a walk, turn right, track to the left. When head rider arrives at M (with the group spaced evenly so as to take up the length of wall), turn across the school individually and halt on center line C-A. Salute and break, track to the right. At A, head rider leads off at a trot, twice around. At K, turn down the diagonal to M. At H, turn down the diagonal to F. At A, turn down the school to C, track to the right, once around. At F, head rider leads the turn across the school individually. At K, he leads track to the left. At C, form circle and make it twice. Change circles. At A, another circle is formed and made twice. At K, ahead. At F, half-volte; ahead, once around. At F, Half-volte in reverse. At A, right canter, twice around. At A, check to a trot. At H, half-volte. At A, left canter, twice around. At A, check to a trot, once around. At A, check to a walk. At M, head rider leads the turn across the school individually. Halt on center line C-A. Salute. Exit single file.

### Solos

In the *dressage* solo, the performer is on his own, and while he does not have to fear the true or imagined faultiness of the mechanism of which he is a part in a carrousel, neither can he count on it to carry him and/or his horse along, or to blur, by its multiplicity, a blunder on his part. Here he cannot hope for the audience's eye to be, just at that moment, focused on another corner of the hall. The factor of group coordination—such a headache while he was riding in the carrousel—would at this moment seem to be a blessing. But here he is all by himself under the spotlight; and every gesture counts. He is carrying the entire burden of dexterity, precision, elegance, and consequently ease and self-assurance, on his straight, drawnback shoulders. Therefore you must, physically and psychologically, be very sure of those you select for dressage solos.

The final precision of the collective work in your carrousels lies very particularly in the give-and-take of a corner cut here or rounded there; while in a solo performance precision becomes totally objective and every movement must be perfect, not perfect in relation to something else. So you must be able to rely on your performer and his mount to execute the solo impeccably down to the smallest detail, which requires it to be custom-made for both.

Here, then, even more truly than in a carrousel, a simple combination of simple movements presented with the ease and brilliance which springs from at least a slight superiority of the two performers (horse and rider) to their act is greatly preferable to a cliff-hanging presentation of highly sophisticated maneuvers.

At E, enter at a walk.

At X turn right.

At A, track to the left.

At B, turn across the school.

At X, halt.

Salute.

Walk to

    E track to the left.

At A, volte.

At F, turn down the diagonal in half-pass.

At H, track to the right.

At C, volte.

At M, turn down the diagonal in half-pass.

At K, track to the left.

At B, trot.

At C, volte.

At H, turn down the diagonal, extending the trot.

At F, track to the right.

At A, volte.

At K, turn down the diagonal, extending the trot.

At M, track to the left.

At E, left canter, once around.

At E, check to a trot.

At K, half-volte.

At B, right canter, once around.

At B, check to a trot.

At E, check to a walk.

At B, turn across the school.

At X, halt.

**Salute.**

A *two-horse tandem* is a spectacular addition to your program. Contrary to what you might think, it does not require great skill, and it should not be hard to find a good leader among your horses. It should, nevertheless, like all other numbers of your show, be prepared well in advance.

The leader must be exercised to the long reins, and you must be able to obtain free starts, straight halts, taut long reins, voltes, half-voltes. This achieved, you may begin rehearsals in the saddle.

Your mount must be easy, calm at sight of the whip and unmoved by the long reins alongside his head. At the first rehearsal, be content to travel the track at a walk, to make several halts, to obtain free starts, in such a way that the long reins always remain taut, the capital point of the elementary work. The turns will then not present great difficulties, one of which, the most common, comes from the "floundering" of the leader who, if not "framed" by the long reins as if between the two shafts of a carriage, tends to swing to the inside of the curve to be followed.

Your equipment will be: a leather surcingle with a ring for the reins to pass through and two or three buckles for a very precise adjustment of the side reins at the top of each side; a Pelham, to the upper rings of which (at mouthpiece level) the side reins are attached, while the long reins are buckled onto the lower rings; two reins with several D's at their ends by which they are buckled to the surcingle; a whip which may be used moderately and lightly during the first rehearsals but which, the day you present your tandem, shall be but an ornament.

### Dressing Up for the Show

The horse's toilet is an art, particularly as concerns the mane. By clipping it, leaving it thick, or thinning it out, keeping it long, or trimming it down, an artist can change the looks of a horse. Here we shall discuss only the special care the well-groomed horse receives before a show.

## THE MANE

If your horse's mane is clipped, pass the clippers over it a day or two before, go over the crest with the whisk to make the dandruff fall and finish up with a damp sponge.

Otherwise, you may or may not plait the mane. If you do not, you might have to shorten and thin it. Do this by pulling out the longest hairs with a comb, taking the ones below, just a few hairs per strand.

For plaiting, it must be medium short; too short, it would not plait. Wet it down with the water brush and divide the mane into seven or eight even parts. Divide the hair of each into three even strands and plait them. Stop each braid with cotton thread or, better, rubber bands. Tuck in the end of each braid by turning it under at about its middle; end down, of course.

For "ribbons" use white, black or red cotton thread (whichever matches best your horse's coat). Twist it around and around, thread against thread without overlapping for about half an inch. Do not forget the forelock which is entitled to a braid of its own.

## THE TAIL

Its length is a matter of fashion; but it is usually cut off at two fingers' breadth beneath the point of the hock. Before you cut, look how your horse is carrying it in action; it does not fall the same at a halt, and its length should be right in action. Snip away easily, upward and from the outside in. At the root it must also be depilated on the sides and underneath. The few fine hairs remaining after depilation are cut with rounded scissors. Smooth the hair by wetting it with a sponge and then bandaging the tail, though not too tight; a few hours later, you simply slide the bandage down the tail.

## THE CHECKER PATTERN*

You can draw a checkerboard on the croup by wetting the hair with a sponge moistened with sugarwater (the sugar takes the place of brilliantine) and then, facing one side of the croup and beginning at its middle line, drawing toward you a fine-tooth comb about two inches long. Stop after two inches, so as to form a square. Start again at the middle line, leaving a two-inch space between the first and second square; and so forth. When you get to the end of one row, start another, the squares lined up quincunx fashion; and so to the end. Do not forget the other side of the croup.

## TACK

You may use breast-plates and white bandages, the latter tight enough not to come unwound during the carrousel, but not so tight as to stop circulation.

If a dressage solo is performed by a grey horse, black bandages stand out better than white, as with a very dark horse the lambskin pad enhances the tack, and the lambskin noseband, provided it is not too thick and its size in harmony with the horse's head.

Solid-colored rather dark pads do a great deal for a carrousel. If they

*See hack champion "Blue Link," Hippology.

have at the front of each side a small leather thong ending in a buckle through which you pass the front billets, you can be sure that everything will stay in place.

Generally, identical rules of good taste apply to horse and rider: the most classic accoutrement is the most effective. I shall not dwell on the truly universal "uniform" for horse shows, white or cream-colored breeches, black coat and boots, hunt cap or, at the most, a black derby or top hat, white piqué tie or stock; for anything else would be unthinkable.

But even in numbers requiring period costume, admit no fantasy and use for a model the most sober, rather than the flashiest, of the ladies on the canvas of the Queen's Carrousel. If ever you have a yen for dressing your horsemen "*à la mode de 1900,*" do so only if all can either afford a good tailor and hatter or can persuade them to let their carrousel model as publicity for the house. I shudder at the memory of my own young, thoughtless years, when a friend and I rode in a flower corso on the beach where Proust met Albertine. We were attired, for its turn-of-the-century motto, in, I hate to say it, rented redingotes and top hats; I looked like Svengali, my shorter friend like the Mad Hatter, and whenever the picture comes to hand or mind . . . no, I am sorry, but this book's illustrations end here.

# Bibliography

G. Steinbrecht. *Le Gymnase du Cheval.*

Gen. Decarpentry. *Equitation Académique.*

Gen. L'Hotte. *Questions Equestres.*

Prof. Lecoq. *L'Extérieur du Cheval.*

J. Jacoulet et C. Chomel. *Hippologie.*

Lt. Col. R. Froissard. *Traité de Thérapeutique Vétérinaire.*

R. S. Summerhays. *Encyclopaedia for Horsemen.*

# Index

*(The letters in parentheses — E, H, I, LS, S, T — indicate headings in the text: Equitation; Hippology; Instruction; The Lighter Side; Schooling; Training.)*

## A PERSONAL WORD FROM MELVIN POWERS
## PUBLISHER, WILSHIRE BOOK COMPANY

Dear Friend:

My goal is to publish interesting, informative, and inspirational books. You can help me accomplish this by answering the following questions, either by phone or by mail. Or, if convenient for you, I would welcome the opportunity to visit with you in my office and hear your comments in person.

Did you enjoy reading this book? Why?

Would you enjoy reading another similar book?

What idea in the book impressed you the most?

If applicable to your situation, have you incorporated this idea in your daily life?

Is there a chapter that could serve as a theme for an entire book? Please explain.

If you have an idea for a book, I would welcome discussing it with you. If you already have one in progress, write or call me concerning possible publication. I can be reached at (213) 875-1711 or (818) 983-1105.

Sincerely yours,
MELVIN POWERS

*12015 Sherman Road*
*North Hollywood, California 91605*

# MELVIN POWERS SELF-IMPROVEMENT LIBRARY

## ASTROLOGY

_____ ASTROLOGY: HOW TO CHART YOUR HOROSCOPE *Max Heindel* 5.00
_____ ASTROLOGY AND SEXUAL ANALYSIS *Morris C. Goodman* 5.00
_____ ASTROLOGY MADE EASY *Astarte* 5.00
_____ ASTROLOGY, ROMANCE, YOU AND THE STARS *Anthony Norvell* 5.00
_____ MY WORLD OF ASTROLOGY *Sydney Omarr* 7.00
_____ THOUGHT DIAL *Sydney Omarr* 4.00
_____ WHAT THE STARS REVEAL ABOUT THE MEN IN YOUR LIFE *Thelma White* 3.00

## BRIDGE

_____ BRIDGE BIDDING MADE EASY *Edwin B. Kantar* 10.00
_____ BRIDGE CONVENTIONS *Edwin B. Kantar* 7.00
_____ BRIDGE HUMOR *Edwin B. Kantar* 5.00
_____ COMPETITIVE BIDDING IN MODERN BRIDGE *Edgar Kaplan* 7.00
_____ DEFENSIVE BRIDGE PLAY COMPLETE *Edwin B. Kantar* 15.00
_____ GAMESMAN BRIDGE—Play Better with Kantar *Edwin B. Kantar* 5.00
_____ HOW TO IMPROVE YOUR BRIDGE *Alfred Sheinwold* 5.00
_____ IMPROVING YOUR BIDDING SKILLS *Edwin B. Kantar* 4.00
_____ INTRODUCTION TO DECLARER'S PLAY *Edwin B. Kantar* 5.00
_____ INTRODUCTION TO DEFENDER'S PLAY *Edwin B. Kantar* 5.00
_____ KANTAR FOR THE DEFENSE *Edwin B. Kantar* 7.00
_____ KANTAR FOR THE DEFENSE VOLUME 2 *Edwin B. Kantar* 7.00
_____ SHORT CUT TO WINNING BRIDGE *Alfred Sheinwold* 3.00
_____ TEST YOUR BRIDGE PLAY *Edwin B. Kantar* 5.00
_____ VOLUME 2—TEST YOUR BRIDGE PLAY *Edwin B. Kantar* 5.00
_____ WINNING DECLARER PLAY *Dorothy Hayden Truscott* 7.00

## BUSINESS, STUDY & REFERENCE

_____ CONVERSATION MADE EASY *Elliot Russell* 4.00
_____ EXAM SECRET *Dennis B. Jackson* 3.00
_____ FIX-IT BOOK *Arthur Symons* 2.00
_____ HOW TO DEVELOP A BETTER SPEAKING VOICE *M. Hellier* 4.00
_____ HOW TO SELF-PUBLISH YOUR BOOK & MAKE IT A BEST SELLER *Melvin Powers* 10.00
_____ INCREASE YOUR LEARNING POWER *Geoffrey A. Dudley* 3.00
_____ PRACTICAL GUIDE TO BETTER CONCENTRATION *Melvin Powers* 3.00
_____ PRACTICAL GUIDE TO PUBLIC SPEAKING *Maurice Forley* 5.00
_____ 7 DAYS TO FASTER READING *William S. Schaill* 5.00
_____ SONGWRITERS' RHYMING DICTIONARY *Jane Shaw Whitfield* 7.00
_____ SPELLING MADE EASY *Lester D. Basch & Dr. Milton Finkelstein* 3.00
_____ STUDENT'S GUIDE TO BETTER GRADES *J. A. Rickard* 3.00
_____ TEST YOURSELF—Find Your Hidden Talent *Jack Shafer* 3.00
_____ YOUR WILL & WHAT TO DO ABOUT IT *Attorney Samuel G. Kling* 5.00

## CALLIGRAPHY

_____ ADVANCED CALLIGRAPHY *Katherine Jeffares* 7.00
_____ CALLIGRAPHER'S REFERENCE BOOK *Anne Leptich & Jacque Evans* 7.00
_____ CALLIGRAPHY—The Art of Beautiful Writing *Katherine Jeffares* 7.00
_____ CALLIGRAPHY FOR FUN & PROFIT *Anne Leptich & Jacque Evans* 7.00
_____ CALLIGRAPHY MADE EASY *Tina Serafini* 7.00

## CHESS & CHECKERS

_____ BEGINNER'S GUIDE TO WINNING CHESS *Fred Reinfeld* 5.00
_____ CHESS IN TEN EASY LESSONS *Larry Evans* 5.00
_____ CHESS MADE EASY *Milton L. Hanauer* 3.00
_____ CHESS PROBLEMS FOR BEGINNERS *edited by Fred Reinfeld* 5.00
_____ CHESS SECRETS REVEALED *Fred Reinfeld* 2.00
_____ CHESS TACTICS FOR BEGINNERS *edited by Fred Reinfeld* 5.00
_____ CHESS THEORY & PRACTICE *Morry & Mitchell* 2.00
_____ HOW TO WIN AT CHECKERS *Fred Reinfeld* 3.00
_____ 1001 BRILLIANT WAYS TO CHECKMATE *Fred Reinfeld* 5.00
_____ 1001 WINNING CHESS SACRIFICES & COMBINATIONS *Fred Reinfeld* 5.00

_____ SOVIET CHESS *Edited by R. G. Wade*   3.00

## COOKERY & HERBS

_____ CULPEPER'S HERBAL REMEDIES *Dr. Nicholas Culpeper*   3.00
_____ FAST GOURMET COOKBOOK *Poppy Cannon*   2.50
_____ GINSENG The Myth & The Truth *Joseph P. Hou*   3.00
_____ HEALING POWER OF HERBS *May Bethel*   4.00
_____ HEALING POWER OF NATURAL FOODS *May Bethel*   5.00
_____ HERB HANDBOOK *Dawn MacLeod*   3.00
_____ HERBS FOR HEALTH—How to Grow & Use Them *Louise Evans Doole*   4.00
_____ HOME GARDEN COOKBOOK—Delicious Natural Food Recipes *Ken Kraft*   3.00
_____ MEDICAL HERBALIST *edited by Dr. J. R. Yemm*   3.00
_____ VEGETABLE GARDENING FOR BEGINNERS *Hugh Wiberg*   2.00
_____ VEGETABLES FOR TODAY'S GARDENS *R. Milton Carleton*   2.00
_____ VEGETARIAN COOKERY *Janet Walker*   4.00
_____ VEGETARIAN COOKING MADE EASY & DELECTABLE *Veronica Vezza*   3.00
_____ VEGETARIAN DELIGHTS—A Happy Cookbook for Health *K. R. Mehta*   2.00
_____ VEGETARIAN GOURMET COOKBOOK *Joyce McKinnel*   3.00

## GAMBLING & POKER

_____ ADVANCED POKER STRATEGY & WINNING PLAY *A. D. Livingston*   5.00
_____ HOW TO WIN AT DICE GAMES *Skip Frey*   3.00
_____ HOW TO WIN AT POKER *Terence Reese & Anthony T. Watkins*   5.00
_____ WINNING AT CRAPS *Dr. Lloyd T. Commins*   4.00
_____ WINNING AT GIN *Chester Wander & Cy Rice*   3.00
_____ WINNING AT POKER—An Expert's Guide *John Archer*   5.00
_____ WINNING AT 21—An Expert's Guide *John Archer*   5.00
_____ WINNING POKER SYSTEMS *Norman Zadeh*   3.00

## HEALTH

_____ BEE POLLEN *Lynda Lyngheim & Jack Scagnetti*   3.00
_____ DR. LINDNER'S SPECIAL WEIGHT CONTROL METHOD *P. G. Lindner, M.D.*   2.00
_____ HELP YOURSELF TO BETTER SIGHT *Margaret Darst Corbett*   3.00
_____ HOW YOU CAN STOP SMOKING PERMANENTLY *Ernest Caldwell*   3.00
_____ MIND OVER PLATTER *Peter G. Lindner, M.D.*   3.00
_____ NATURE'S WAY TO NUTRITION & VIBRANT HEALTH *Robert J. Scrutton*   3.00
_____ NEW CARBOHYDRATE DIET COUNTER *Patti Lopez-Pereira*   2.00
_____ REFLEXOLOGY *Dr. Maybelle Segal*   4.00
_____ REFLEXOLOGY FOR GOOD HEALTH *Anna Kaye & Don C. Matchan*   5.00
_____ 30 DAYS TO BEAUTIFUL LEGS *Dr. Marc Selner*   3.00
_____ YOU CAN LEARN TO RELAX *Dr. Samuel Gutwirth*   3.00
_____ YOUR ALLERGY—What To Do About It *Allan Knight, M.D.*   3.00

## HOBBIES

_____ BEACHCOMBING FOR BEGINNERS *Norman Hickin*   2.00
_____ BLACKSTONE'S MODERN CARD TRICKS *Harry Blackstone*   5.00
_____ BLACKSTONE'S SECRETS OF MAGIC *Harry Blackstone*   5.00
_____ COIN COLLECTING FOR BEGINNERS *Burton Hobson & Fred Reinfeld*   5.00
_____ ENTERTAINING WITH ESP *Tony 'Doc' Shiels*   2.00
_____ 400 FASCINATING MAGIC TRICKS YOU CAN DO *Howard Thurston*   5.00
_____ HOW I TURN JUNK INTO FUN AND PROFIT *Sari*   3.00
_____ HOW TO WRITE A HIT SONG & SELL IT *Tommy Boyce*   7.00
_____ JUGGLING MADE EASY *Rudolf Dittrich*   3.00
_____ MAGIC FOR ALL AGES *Walter Gibson*   4.00
_____ MAGIC MADE EASY *Byron Wels*   2.00
_____ STAMP COLLECTING FOR BEGINNERS *Burton Hobson*   3.00

## HORSE PLAYERS' WINNING GUIDES

_____ BETTING HORSES TO WIN *Les Conklin*   5.00
_____ ELIMINATE THE LOSERS *Bob McKnight*   5.00
_____ HOW TO PICK WINNING HORSES *Bob McKnight*   5.00
_____ HOW TO WIN AT THE RACES *Sam (The Genius) Lewin*   5.00
_____ HOW YOU CAN BEAT THE RACES *Jack Kavanagh*   5.00

| | | |
|---|---|---|
| \_\_\_\_ MAKING MONEY AT THE RACES *David Barr* | | 5.00 |
| \_\_\_\_ PAYDAY AT THE RACES *Les Conklin* | | 5.00 |
| \_\_\_\_ SMART HANDICAPPING MADE EASY *William Bauman* | | 5.00 |
| \_\_\_\_ SUCCESS AT THE HARNESS RACES *Barry Meadow* | | 5.00 |
| \_\_\_\_ WINNING AT THE HARNESS RACES—An Expert's Guide *Nick Cammarano* | | 5.00 |

### HUMOR

| | |
|---|---|
| \_\_\_\_ HOW TO FLATTEN YOUR TUSH *Coach Marge Reardon* | 2.00 |
| \_\_\_\_ HOW TO MAKE LOVE TO YOURSELF *Ron Stevens & Joy Grdnic* | 3.00 |
| \_\_\_\_ JOKE TELLER'S HANDBOOK *Bob Orben* | 5.00 |
| \_\_\_\_ JOKES FOR ALL OCCASIONS *Al Schock* | 5.00 |
| \_\_\_\_ 2000 NEW LAUGHS FOR SPEAKERS *Bob Orben* | 5.00 |
| \_\_\_\_ 2,500 JOKES TO START 'EM LAUGHING *Bob Orben* | 5.00 |

### HYPNOTISM

| | |
|---|---|
| \_\_\_\_ ADVANCED TECHNIQUES OF HYPNOSIS *Melvin Powers* | 3.00 |
| \_\_\_\_ BRAINWASHING AND THE CULTS *Paul A. Verdier, Ph.D.* | 3.00 |
| \_\_\_\_ CHILDBIRTH WITH HYPNOSIS *William S. Kroger, M.D.* | 5.00 |
| \_\_\_\_ HOW TO SOLVE Your Sex Problems with Self-Hypnosis *Frank S. Caprio, M.D.* | 5.00 |
| \_\_\_\_ HOW TO STOP SMOKING THRU SELF-HYPNOSIS *Leslie M. LeCron* | 3.00 |
| \_\_\_\_ HOW TO USE AUTO-SUGGESTION EFFECTIVELY *John Duckworth* | 3.00 |
| \_\_\_\_ HOW YOU CAN BOWL BETTER USING SELF-HYPNOSIS *Jack Heise* | 4.00 |
| \_\_\_\_ HOW YOU CAN PLAY BETTER GOLF USING SELF-HYPNOSIS *Jack Heise* | 3.00 |
| \_\_\_\_ HYPNOSIS AND SELF-HYPNOSIS *Bernard Hollander, M.D.* | 5.00 |
| \_\_\_\_ HYPNOTISM *(Originally published in 1893) Carl Sextus* | 5.00 |
| \_\_\_\_ HYPNOTISM & PSYCHIC PHENOMENA *Simeon Edmunds* | 4.00 |
| \_\_\_\_ HYPNOTISM MADE EASY *Dr. Ralph Winn* | 5.00 |
| \_\_\_\_ HYPNOTISM MADE PRACTICAL *Louis Orton* | 5.00 |
| \_\_\_\_ HYPNOTISM REVEALED *Melvin Powers* | 3.00 |
| \_\_\_\_ HYPNOTISM TODAY *Leslie LeCron and Jean Bordeaux, Ph.D.* | 5.00 |
| \_\_\_\_ MODERN HYPNOSIS *Lesley Kuhn & Salvatore Russo, Ph.D.* | 5.00 |
| \_\_\_\_ NEW CONCEPTS OF HYPNOSIS *Bernard C. Gindes, M.D.* | 7.00 |
| \_\_\_\_ NEW SELF-HYPNOSIS *Paul Adams* | 7.00 |
| \_\_\_\_ POST-HYPNOTIC INSTRUCTIONS—Suggestions for Therapy *Arnold Furst* | 5.00 |
| \_\_\_\_ PRACTICAL GUIDE TO SELF-HYPNOSIS *Melvin Powers* | 3.00 |
| \_\_\_\_ PRACTICAL HYPNOTISM *Philip Magonet, M.D.* | 3.00 |
| \_\_\_\_ SECRETS OF HYPNOTISM *S. J. Van Pelt, M.D.* | 5.00 |
| \_\_\_\_ SELF-HYPNOSIS A Conditioned-Response Technique *Laurence Sparks* | 7.00 |
| \_\_\_\_ SELF-HYPNOSIS Its Theory, Technique & Application *Melvin Powers* | 3.00 |
| \_\_\_\_ THERAPY THROUGH HYPNOSIS *edited by Raphael H. Rhodes* | 5.00 |

### JUDAICA

| | |
|---|---|
| \_\_\_\_ SERVICE OF THE HEART *Evelyn Garfiel, Ph.D.* | 7.00 |
| \_\_\_\_ STORY OF ISRAEL IN COINS *Jean & Maurice Gould* | 2.00 |
| \_\_\_\_ STORY OF ISRAEL IN STAMPS *Maxim & Gabriel Shamir* | 1.00 |
| \_\_\_\_ TONGUE OF THE PROPHETS *Robert St. John* | 7.00 |

### JUST FOR WOMEN

| | |
|---|---|
| \_\_\_\_ COSMOPOLITAN'S GUIDE TO MARVELOUS MEN Fwd. by *Helen Gurley Brown* | 3.00 |
| \_\_\_\_ COSMOPOLITAN'S HANG-UP HANDBOOK Foreword by *Helen Gurley Brown* | 4.00 |
| \_\_\_\_ COSMOPOLITAN'S LOVE BOOK—A Guide to Ecstasy in Bed | 7.00 |
| \_\_\_\_ COSMOPOLITAN'S NEW ETIQUETTE GUIDE Fwd. by *Helen Gurley Brown* | 4.00 |
| \_\_\_\_ I AM A COMPLEAT WOMAN *Doris Hagopian & Karen O'Connor Sweeney* | 3.00 |
| \_\_\_\_ JUST FOR WOMEN—A Guide to the Female Body *Richard E. Sand, M.D.* | 5.00 |
| \_\_\_\_ NEW APPROACHES TO SEX IN MARRIAGE *John E. Eichenlaub, M.D.* | 3.00 |
| \_\_\_\_ SEXUALLY ADEQUATE FEMALE *Frank S. Caprio, M.D.* | 3.00 |
| \_\_\_\_ SEXUALLY FULFILLED WOMAN *Dr. Rachel Copelan* | 5.00 |
| \_\_\_\_ YOUR FIRST YEAR OF MARRIAGE *Dr. Tom McGinnis* | 3.00 |

### MARRIAGE, SEX & PARENTHOOD

| | |
|---|---|
| \_\_\_\_ ABILITY TO LOVE *Dr. Allan Fromme* | 7.00 |
| \_\_\_\_ GUIDE TO SUCCESSFUL MARRIAGE *Drs. Albert Ellis & Robert Harper* | 7.00 |
| \_\_\_\_ HOW TO RAISE AN EMOTIONALLY HEALTHY, HAPPY CHILD *A. Ellis* | 5.00 |

| | | |
|---|---|---|
| ____ | MAGIC OF THINKING BIG *Dr. David J. Schwartz* | 3.00 |
| ____ | MAGIC OF THINKING SUCCESS *Dr. David J. Schwartz* | 7.00 |
| ____ | MAGIC POWER OF YOUR MIND *Walter M. Germain* | 7.00 |
| ____ | MENTAL POWER THROUGH SLEEP SUGGESTION *Melvin Powers* | 3.00 |
| ____ | NEVER UNDERESTIMATE THE SELLING POWER OF A WOMAN *Dottie Walters* | 7.00 |
| ____ | NEW GUIDE TO RATIONAL LIVING *Albert Ellis, Ph.D. & R. Harper, Ph.D.* | 7.00 |
| ____ | PROJECT YOU *A Manual of Rational Assertiveness Training Paris & Casey* | 6.00 |
| ____ | PSYCHO-CYBERNETICS *Maxwell Maltz, M.D.* | 5.00 |
| ____ | PSYCHOLOGY OF HANDWRITING *Nadya Olyanova* | 7.00 |
| ____ | SALES CYBERNETICS *Brian Adams* | 7.00 |
| ____ | SCIENCE OF MIND IN DAILY LIVING *Dr. Donald Curtis* | 7.00 |
| ____ | SECRET OF SECRETS *U. S. Andersen* | 7.00 |
| ____ | SECRET POWER OF THE PYRAMIDS *U. S. Andersen* | 7.00 |
| ____ | SELF-THERAPY FOR THE STUTTERER *Malcolm Frazer* | 3.00 |
| ____ | SUCCESS-CYBERNETICS *U. S. Andersen* | 6.00 |
| ____ | 10 DAYS TO A GREAT NEW LIFE *William E. Edwards* | 3.00 |
| ____ | THINK AND GROW RICH *Napoleon Hill* | 7.00 |
| ____ | THINK YOUR WAY TO SUCCESS *Dr. Lew Losoncy* | 5.00 |
| ____ | THREE MAGIC WORDS *U. S. Andersen* | 7.00 |
| ____ | TREASURY OF COMFORT *edited by Rabbi Sidney Greenberg* | 5.00 |
| ____ | TREASURY OF THE ART OF LIVING *Sidney S. Greenberg* | 5.00 |
| ____ | WHAT YOUR HANDWRITING REVEALS *Albert E. Hughes* | 3.00 |
| ____ | YOUR SUBCONSCIOUS POWER *Charles M. Simmons* | 7.00 |
| ____ | YOUR THOUGHTS CAN CHANGE YOUR LIFE *Dr. Donald Curtis* | 7.00 |

## SPORTS

| | | |
|---|---|---|
| ____ | BICYCLING FOR FUN AND GOOD HEALTH *Kenneth E. Luther* | 2.00 |
| ____ | BILLIARDS—Pocket • Carom • Three Cushion *Clive Cottingham, Jr.* | 5.00 |
| ____ | CAMPING-OUT 101 Ideas & Activities *Bruno Knobel* | 2.00 |
| ____ | COMPLETE GUIDE TO FISHING *Vlad Evanoff* | 2.00 |
| ____ | HOW TO IMPROVE YOUR RACQUETBALL *Lubarsky Kaufman & Scagnetti* | 5.00 |
| ____ | HOW TO WIN AT POCKET BILLIARDS *Edward D. Knuchell* | 5.00 |
| ____ | JOY OF WALKING *Jack Scagnetti* | 3.00 |
| ____ | LEARNING & TEACHING SOCCER SKILLS *Eric Worthington* | 3.00 |
| ____ | MOTORCYCLING FOR BEGINNERS *I. G. Edmonds* | 3.00 |
| ____ | RACQUETBALL FOR WOMEN *Toni Hudson, Jack Scagnetti & Vince Rondone* | 3.00 |
| ____ | RACQUETBALL MADE EASY *Steve Lubarsky, Rod Delson & Jack Scagnetti* | 5.00 |
| ____ | SECRET OF BOWLING STRIKES *Dawson Taylor* | 5.00 |
| ____ | SECRET OF PERFECT PUTTING *Horton Smith & Dawson Taylor* | 5.00 |
| ____ | SOCCER—The Game & How to Play It *Gary Rosenthal* | 5.00 |
| ____ | STARTING SOCCER *Edward F. Dolan, Jr.* | 5.00 |

## TENNIS LOVERS' LIBRARY

| | | |
|---|---|---|
| ____ | BEGINNER'S GUIDE TO WINNING TENNIS *Helen Hull Jacobs* | 2.00 |
| ____ | HOW TO IMPROVE YOUR TENNIS—Style, Strategy & Analysis *C. Wilson* | 2.00 |
| ____ | PSYCH YOURSELF TO BETTER TENNIS *Dr. Walter A. Luszki* | 2.00 |
| ____ | TENNIS FOR BEGINNERS, *Dr. H. A. Murray* | 2.00 |
| ____ | TENNIS MADE EASY *Joel Brecheen* | 4.00 |
| ____ | WEEKEND TENNIS—How to Have Fun & Win at the Same Time *Bill Talbert* | 3.00 |
| ____ | WINNING WITH PERCENTAGE TENNIS—Smart Strategy *Jack Lowe* | 2.00 |

## WILSHIRE PET LIBRARY

| | | |
|---|---|---|
| ____ | DOG OBEDIENCE TRAINING *Gust Kessopulos* | 5.00 |
| ____ | DOG TRAINING MADE EASY & FUN *John W. Kellogg* | 3.00 |
| ____ | HOW TO BRING UP YOUR PET DOG *Kurt Unkelbach* | 2.00 |
| ____ | HOW TO RAISE & TRAIN YOUR PUPPY *Jeff Griffen* | 5.00 |

*The books listed above can be obtained from your book dealer or directly from
Melvin Powers. When ordering, please remit $1.00 postage for the first book
and 50¢ for each additional book.*

# Melvin Powers

12015 Sherman Road, No. Hollywood, California 91605

# HOW TO GET RICH IN MAIL ORDER
*by Melvin Powers*

Contents:
1. How to Develop Your Mail Order Expertise 2. How to Find a Unique Product or Service to Sell 3. How to Make Money with Classified Ads 4. How to Make Money with Display Ads 5. The Unlimited Potential for Making Money with Direct Mail 6. How to Copycat Successful Mail Order Operations 7. How I Created A Best Seller Using the Copycat Technique 8. How to Start and Run a Profitable Mail Order, Special Interest Book or Record Business 9. I Enjoy Selling Books by Mail—Some of My Successful and Not-So-Successful Ads and Direct Mail Circulars 10. Five of My Most Successful Direct Mail Pieces That Sold and Are Still Selling Millions of Dollars Worth of Books 11. Melvin Powers' Mail Order Success Strategy—Follow It and You'll Become a Millionaire 12. How to Sell Your Products to Mail Order Companies, Retail Outlets, Jobbers, and Fund Raisers for Maximum Distribution and Profits 13. How to Get Free Display Ads and Publicity That Can Put You on the Road to Riches 14. How to Make Your Advertising Copy Sizzle to Make You Wealthy 15. Questions and Answers to Help You Get Started Making Money in Your Own Mail Order Business 16. A Personal Word from Melvin Powers     **8½″ x 11″ — 352 Pages . . . $21 postpaid**

# HOW TO SELF-PUBLISH YOUR BOOK AND HAVE THE FUN AND EXCITEMENT OF BEING A BEST-SELLING AUTHOR
*by Melvin Powers*

An expert's step-by-step guide to marketing your book successfully

**176 Pages . . . $11.00 postpaid**

## A NEW GUIDE TO RATIONAL LIVING
*by Albert Ellis, Ph.D. & Robert A. Harper, Ph.D.*

Contents:
1. How Far Can You Go With Self-Analysis? 2. You Feel the Way You Think 3. Feeling Well by Thinking Straight 4. How You Create Your Feelings 5. Thinking Yourself Out of Emotional Disturbances 6. Recognizing and Attacking Neurotic Behavior 7. Overcoming the Influences of the Past 8. Does Reason Always Prove Reasonable? 9. Refusing to Feel Desperately Unhappy 10. Tackling Dire Needs for Approval 11. Eradicating Dire Fears of Failure 12. How to Stop Blaming and Start Living 13. How to Feel Undepressed though Frustrated 14. Controlling Your Own Destiny 15. Conquering Anxiety

**256 Pages . . . $7.50 postpaid**

## PSYCHO-CYBERNETICS
A New Technique for Using Your Subconscious Power
*by Maxwell Maltz, M.D., F.I.C.S.*

Contents:
1. The Self Image: Your Key to a Better Life 2. Discovering the Success Mechanism Within You 3. Imagination—The First Key to Your Success Mechanism 4. Dehypnotize Yourself from False Beliefs 5. How to Utilize the Power of Rational Thinking 6. Relax and Let Your Success Mechanism Work for You 7. You Can Acquire the Habit of Happiness 8. Ingredients of the Success-Type Personality and How to Acquire Them 9. The Failure Mechanism: How to Make It Work For You Instead of Against You 10. How to Remove Emotional Scars, or How to Give Yourself an Emotional Face Lift 11. How to Unlock Your Real Personality 12. Do-It-Yourself Tranquilizers     **288 Pages . . . $5.50 postpaid**

## A PRACTICAL GUIDE TO SELF-HYPNOSIS
*by Melvin Powers*

Contents:
1. What You Should Know About Self-Hypnosis 2. What About the Dangers of Hypnosis? 3. Is Hypnosis the Answer? 4. How Does Self-Hypnosis Work? 5. How to Arouse Yourself from the Self-Hypnotic State 6. How to Attain Self-Hypnosis 7. Deepening the Self-Hypnotic State 8. What You Should Know About Becoming an Excellent Subject 9. Techniques for Reaching the Somnambulistic State 10. A New Approach to Self-Hypnosis When All Else Fails 11. Psychological Aids and Their Function 12. The Nature of Hypnosis 13. Practical Applications of Self-Hypnosis     **128 Pages . . . $3.50 postpaid**

*The books listed above can be obtained from your book dealer or directly from Melvin Powers.*

## Melvin Powers
12015 Sherman Road, No. Hollywood, California 91605